What people are

No Bosses

A prime goal of Albert's work is to help to reinvigorate that common understanding and to revive the commitment to mutual aid and solidarity, and most important, to spell out in some detail how the goals can be realized.
Noam Chomsky

"No bosses" means that no one tells anyone what to do from above, not owners or commissars. "But, how do things get done?" comes the inevitable question. To answer it, Michael begins analytically, methodically, by first answering the question, "How should things not get done?"
Yanis Varoufakis

Michael Albert's *No Bosses* is easy reading, thanks to his unique folksy style, but heavy thinking. Be ready to challenge your own narrow view of "the possible." I recommend that after every sentence, paragraph or chapter that has you saying, "Nice idea but it just won't work," remind yourself that the present system doesn't work (unless, of course, you think Jeff Bezos deserves to make $10 million an hour and the climate crisis is not an existential threat). So read it with delight at the creative ways we can organize—asap—to sweep Mr. Moneybags into the dustbin of history and create the new equitable, participatory, empowering and sustainable world that we want to live in.
Medea Benjamin, author and co-founder of CODEPINK.

Tired of working for a boss but don't want just to trade your boss for a new boss? Tired of living in a system run by bosses but don't want to swap it for a system run by other bosses? Take

a look at Michael Albert's *No Bosses: A New Economy for a Better World*. You'll have a hard time finding a better guide to moving from capitalism to a genuinely free, equal, and participatory economy.
Jeremy Brecher

Michael Albert has the courage and the background to propose solutions to the multitude of our social problems in his new book. Also, he has the life experience to suggest: "Don't just cling and curse. Swim." For this he uses one of the most important words in our social vocabulary: "Resist"! Resistance in essence is a moral act. Also, we do not resist alone. We resist together with our neighbour, or as he puts it, "all people share responsibilities".
Nikos Raptis, civil engineer (retired) and writer

The collapse of socialist and Soviet-type experiments became a heavy burden for post-capitalist perspectives precisely at a time when they are most needed. Michael Albert has devoted his life to re-creating visions and a strategy towards a better future. *No Bosses: A New Economy for a Better World* offers a refined, compelling argument in favor of a non-capitalist, participatory economics. His vision is of utmost importance for people and social movements struggling for a better world.
Ezequiel Adamovsky

Michael Albert firmly rejects capitalism, often through bluntly questioning its basic tenets. Why should people who already have so much be entitled to get more? Why not admire and pursue excellence and expertise without rewarding it with undue material wealth or social power? The arguments in *No Bosses* go well beyond iconoclasm. Seriously and carefully, Albert aims to create a framework, a "scaffold," for a worthy economic plan. Building on three decades of research, he

describes participatory economics with enjoyable candor, raising as many questions as he answers and inviting readers to set cynicism aside. My advice: equip yourself with a big "Why not?" and give this vision plenty of attention.
Kathy Kelly, activist and author of *Other Lands Have Dreams, from Baghdad to Pekin Prison*

After Sanders and Black Lives Matter, amidst COVID and Global Warming, many ask what's next? Michael Albert's new book, *No Bosses*, proposes an answer for economics from self-managed decision making to balanced work and from equitable incomes to ending class division. *No Bosses* should be widely read as we assess the way forward in this unprecedented moment in the history of this nation.
Dr Ron Daniels, social and political activist, President of the Institute of the Black World 21st Century

No Bosses

A New Economy for a Better World

No Bosses

A New Economy for a Better World

Michael Albert

zer0 books

Winchester, UK
Washington, USA

JOHN HUNT PUBLISHING

First published by Zero Books, 2022
Zero Books is an imprint of John Hunt Publishing Ltd., No. 3 East St., Alresford, Hampshire SO24 9EE, UK
office@jhpbooks.com
www.johnhuntpublishing.com
www.zero-books.net

For distributor details and how to order please visit the 'Ordering' section on our website.

ISBN: 978 1 78279 946 7
978 1 78279 958 0 (ebook)
Library of Congress Control Number: 2021942237

A CIP catalogue record for this book is available from the British Library.

Design: Stuart Davies

UK: Printed and bound by CPI Group (UK) Ltd, Croydon, CR0 4YY
Printed in North America by CPI GPS partners

Contents

Acknowledgments

Participatory economics has been around for 30 years. Way too many people have contributed directly, much less indirectly, to properly acknowledge them all here. I can only mention those who have literally interacted with drafts of this book, who have contributed to particular formulations that it includes, or who provided a foundation on which it grew.

And with that constraint, I thank Lydia Sargent, who was there every step of the way—until now. Robin Hahnel, together with whom I first set out participatory economics and who has worked ever since incredibly productively and insightfully, advocating and refining it, particularly addressing the economics profession. Stephen Shalom, who has been a constant source of insight from the outset and who first developed the ideas that have become known as participatory polity. Cynthia Peters, who has also always been available for advice and correction and who with Lydia Sargent first developed the ideas that have become known as participatory kinship. Justin Podur, another confidant and critic and the initial author of what he liked to call polyculturalism, sometimes called Intercommunalism, sometimes participatory communalism. Peter Bohmer, a powerful ally from the beginning, always wise, always involved in the grassroots, always refining participatory economics as but one part of his multitudinous educational and activist pursuits. And Noam Chomsky. I have no way to tell just how much of participatory economics wouldn't exist without Chomsky's example and his impact on myself, on Robin Hahnel, and really on everyone who has played a role in the participatory project. But likely, a whole lot of it.

And, lest these acknowledgments grow too long and my emotional unraveling at writing them grows too intense, my heartfelt thanks collectively goes as well to: Ezequiel

Adamovsky, Lonnie Ray Atkinson, Jessica Azulay, Fintan Bradshaw, Jeremy Brecher, Paul Burrows, Leslie Cagan, Sandy Carter, Savvina Chowdhury, Jason Chrysostomou, John Cronan, Ron Daniels, Brian Dominick, Barbara Ehrenreich, Vince Emanuele, Mark Evans, Bill Fletcher Jr., Jerry Fresia, Andrej Grubacic, Todd Jailer, Antti Jauhiainen, Brian Kelly, Kathy Kelly, Mel King, Pat Korte, Joris Leverink, Meaghan Linick Loughly, Mandisi Majavu, David Marty, Daniel Marty, Bridget Meehan, Eugene Nulman, Harpreet Paul, Milan Rai, Nikos Raptis, Paulo Rodriguez, Eric Sargent, Anders Sandstrom, John Schall, Alexandria Shaner, Uruj Sheik, Juliet Shor, Chris Spannos, Nicholas Stylopoulos, Mitchell Szczepanczyk, Brian Tokar, Taylan Tosun, Tom Vouloumanos, Pat Walker, Tom Wetzel, Sean Michael Wilson, Florian Zollmann, and whoever I have managed to unintentionally not name, I hope with no ill effects.

There is another kind of contributor, people who preceded and otherwise never knew the participatory project but whose thoughts played a role in generating the values and commitments at the root of the project. Again the list is too long to present in full, but to not mention the following would feel too wrong to be party to. Mikhail Bakunin, Alexander Berkman, Murray Bookchin, Maurice Brinton, Cornelius Castoriadis, Shulamith Firestone, Emma Goldman, Andre Gorz, Peter Kropotkin, Alexandra Kollantai, Rosa Luxemburg, Anton Pannekoek, Rudolf Rocker, Sheila Rowbotham, Arundhati Roy, and Bertrand Russell.

I am getting older. It happens. So is Robin Hahnel getting older. That happens too. And I would like to thank my younger self and the younger Robin Hahnel and to apologize to each. There are some places in this book that I am pretty sure recirculate only modestly altered prior formulations whose origin I no longer even know. Was it me? Was it Robin? Was it both of us writing together? Was it someone else? Does it matter?

I don't think so. I think what matters is whether the proposed economic vision has merit. Can it inform current pursuits? Can it contribute to ultimate aims? I hope it can.

Preface To No Bosses

by Noam Chomsky

I am very pleased to be able to say a few words about the most recent of Michael Albert's very important contributions, which I have been following with great interest and appreciation since we met in the mid-1960s.

As for myself, when asked to summarize my general stance on the socio-economic and political order, I express my sympathy for libertarian socialist (anarcho-syndicalist) goals, and for the core anarchist principle: relations of hierarchy and domination carry a heavy burden of proof; they must demonstrate their legitimacy, and when they cannot do so—which is the norm—they should be dismantled in favor of more just human relations and institutions.

One of the relations of domination that can't pass the test is bosses: subordination to a master is an illegitimate attack on fundamental human rights. Hence a core principle is "No Bosses," Albert's theme in the present work

This is hardly a novel thought. For millennia, the principle was taken for granted—for free men, that is, not women or slaves. In the early days of the industrial revolution, working people—by then men and women, the eloquent and militant "factory girls"—fought bitterly against the imposition of what was commonly called "wage slavery," subordination to a master. The illegitimacy of wage slavery was so much a part of common understanding that it was a slogan of Lincoln's Republican party. Working men and women created a lively and independent press, written and produced by those driven by need into the brutal industrial system. In their journals they condemned "the blasting influence of monarchical principles on democratic soil." They recognized that this assault on elementary human rights will not be overcome until "they who work in the mills [will] own them," and sovereignty will return to free producers. Then working people will no longer be "menials or the humble subjects of a foreign despot, [the absentee owners], slaves in the strictest sense of the word [who] toil…for their masters." Rather, they will regain their status as "free American citizens."

The basic ideas articulated in the labor press were shared by independent farmers in what was then a mostly agrarian society. Radical farmers in Texas and throughout the Midwest joined together to free themselves from the domination of Northeast capital and finance and to run their own affairs in the "cooperative commonwealth" to which they aspired. Their Populist movement—remote from today's "populism"—began to construct links with the Knights of Labor, the rising labor movement. That could have expanded to a new era of radical democracy, but it was beaten down by state and private force.

The US has an unusually violent labor history. Labor historian David Montgomery writes that "Modern America had been created over its workers protests, even though every step in its formation had been influenced by the activities, organizations, and proposals that had sprung from working class life," not to speak of the hands and brains of those who did the work.

Nineteenth century workers, repeating the common view that a daily wage is a form of slavery, feared that a day might come when wage slaves "will so far forget what is due to manhood as to glory in a system forced on them by their necessity and in opposition to their feelings of independence and self-respect" and hoped that that day would be "far distant."

A prime goal of Albert's work is to help to reinvigorate that common understanding and to revive the commitment to mutual aid and solidarity, and most important, to spell out in some detail how the goals can be realized.

I met Michael in 1966, shortly after he arrived as a Freshman at MIT, where I spent almost all of my professional life. Within a few years, he and his friends had radicalized the MIT student body, with large effects on Cambridge and Boston as well. It was inspiring and edifying. Since then, Michael and I have been close friends. We have, however, travelled somewhat different paths.

Michael has spent some of his time addressing the kinds of social and political issues that have been my own priorities, problems of domestic society, international affairs, activist opportunities and possibilities. But he has moved on in several different directions. He has been engaged, very successfully, in creating alternative institutions based on our generally shared principles, often working together with his late, great, personal partner Lydia Sargent; and he continues actively to do so, with constant new initiatives. At the same time, along with a number of others, including in particular Robin Hahnel, Michael has elaborated the kinds of anarchist principles we both favor, mainly, but not exclusively, regarding economic vision. I once wrote that, "The task for a modern industrial society is to achieve what is now technically realizable, namely, a society that is really based on free, voluntary participation of people who produce and create, live their lives freely within institutions they control , and with limited hierarchical structures, possibly none at all." Michael has impressively refined, elaborated, and carried forward that task.

I have watched these pursuits with enthusiastic support for the first, creation of new alternative institutions, and with more modulated support for the second, elaboration and advocacy of economic vision. Modulated, because I have some concerns. Do we know enough about humans and society to construct detailed plans, or should more space be left for experimentation and learning? Should we take our vision further than general guidelines, perhaps those of the anarcho-syndicalist principles to which we are both sympathetic? How does the pursuit of more specific goals affect the actual work of activists under current circumstances?

So while I have continually admired Michael's and others' steadfast drive for their visionary agenda, I have sometimes wondered if they had taken it too far.

These questions are considerably sharpened by Michael's new book, *No Bosses: A New Economy for a Better World*.

In inaugurating the neoliberal assault that the global population has endured for 40 years, along with her partner Ronald Reagan, British Prime Minister Margaret Thatcher gave the world the acronym TINA: "There Is No Alternative."

Not an innovation. The claim that what is being imposed by power is the only possible world has been a prominent bulwark of oppressive systems for as long as they have existed. The hope is that the claim will become what Gramsci called "hegemonic common sense," unchallengeable, a condition of life, like the air we breathe. Or like the conception that the highest goal is to find a way to spend most of one's waking life subordinated to a master, who controls every detail of your existence; to have a job.

Michael has always felt that to break free from these fetters people should have a strong shared view of how their general aspirations can be manifested in actual social structures. He has sought to determine the essential conditions we must attain if we are to eliminate oppressive hierarchy and institute authentic self-management.

In the chapters that follow, Michael examines closely a wide range of such issues, developing modalities of self-management, equity, solidarity, diversity, sustainability, internationalism, and participation as guides for proposing better ways of organizing society while freeing ourselves from ingrained habits and assumptions.

The chapters do not provide a complete blueprint, but rather the essentials, or what Albert calls a "scaffold," for future experience to fill out. The scaffold describes and advocates a natural and built Commons, workers' and consumers' self-managing councils, a division of labor that balances empowering tasks among all workers, a norm that apportions income for duration, intensity, and onerousness of socially valued labor, and finally not markets or central planning, but instead participatory planning by workers and consumers of what is produced, by what means, to what ends. It makes a compelling case that these features can be brought together in a spirit of solidarity to establish a self-managing, equitable, sustainable, participatory, new economy, with a rich artistic and intellectual culture as well.

The book then discusses the relation of the economic vision that is its core concern to aims for polity based on work by Stephen Shalom, aims for kinship based on work by Lydia Sargent and Cynthia Peters, and also aims for culture, ecology, and international relations, as well as some implications of the participatory economic vision for activist practice in our present cruel and potentially even suicidal world.

In a final chapter, Albert responds to questions that might cross the mind of various readers on completing the book. What is the lineage of the viewpoint developed here? What are the disagreements among its advocates? What are its prospects? What difference does it make for activism today? These are questions that Albert has encountered repeatedly, and has thought through carefully.

Does *No Bosses* produce what it claims to deliver? That of course is a question that readers will have to decide for themselves after what should be an engaging and thought-provoking journey.

Preface to No Bosses

by Yanis Varoufakis

Markets may have spread everywhere like a boisterous virus, from the realm of genes to space, but there are still oases out there not yet wholly infected. One is the family. Imagine that after an extended family dinner that has taken the parents enormous time and effort to organise, cook, and serve, their teenage daughter Jill responds to a request to help with the dishes with the question: "Mum, dad, because I can't be bothered, how much do you want to take the task off my hands?" No price could ever compensate for the moral outrage that Jill's question will, one hopes, engender.

But it is not just within family life where marketisation and exchange value are a jarring dissonance. Imagine a bunch of passengers whose airplane crash-landed in a desert. Shaken but thirsty, they fan out in search of water. One of them, Jack, discovers an oasis, complete with a water spring. What if he claims ownership rights over the spring and demands of his fellow survivors labour services in return for water, or even money and property transfers upon their return to civilisation? Surely, they have the right, indeed the duty, to ignore Jack and share the water.

These common-sense reactions to the logic of commodification are, today, exceptions to—and thus a sad reminder of—the stupendous triumph of the extractive powers of private property and their abstract form: money. Capitalism has succeeded in alienating us from our natural tendency, as a species, to do things cooperatively. This is why Michael Albert's new book, *No Bosses: A New Economy for a Better World,* is such a breath of fresh air: It helps us retrieve from within ourselves the suppressed conviction, shared by every human being, that it is not alright to live under the tyranny of market forces weaponised by cunning bosses.

Bossing people around, of course, predates capitalism by millennia. However, capitalism has achieved something quite remarkable: It has managed to disguise the most authoritarian variety of bullying—i.e., the power of capital—into something that passes credibly as the exercise of freedom in a setting of equals. It has taken Jill's and Jack's outrageous behaviours and made them the norm, the mindset, the ideology of an ironclad global system that only 'extremists' like us question.

The problem with us 'extremists', i.e., those of us critical of capitalism and other exploitative economic systems, is that we have concentrated too much on criticism of what *is* and avoided talking about what a post-capitalist future worth fighting for ought to *be* like.

Karl Marx notoriously refused to talk about communism, except in one-liners or vague terms, defending his silence by stating that it was his duty to demonstrate how capitalism's internal contradictions guarantee its transcendence while it is the duty of the working class to decide what mode of production and distribution follows capitalism. This excuse for not coming up with a post-capitalist blueprint was one that I also hid behind for decades, until in 2020 I ran out of excuses and came up with my own blueprint. [Editor's addition: See *Another Now*: a novel, New York: Melville House and London: Penguin]

However, unlike us cowards who came late to the party, if at all, Michael Albert has been at it since the 1960s. Together with various fellow travelers, Robin Hahnel in particular, Michael has valiantly tried to answer the pivotal question: How can we scale up a cooperative, collective approach that emerges as both common sense and justice-in-action in the two examples above—where Jill's and Jack's behaviour exposed the lunacy of commodification? This is a hard nut to crack.

After the family dinner, what to do is obvious: Those who

did little of the shopping, food preparation, decorating, serving etc., should do the washing up and cleaning. As for the desert, anyone who disagrees with the right of the thirsty to share the water spring in the oasis should have their heads examined. But, what happens when division of labour is necessary at a large scale? Or, to paraphrase Lenin, by which decision-making process do we decide who tells whom what to do?

Michael's book partly answers the question with its title. 'No bosses' means that no one tells anyone what to do from above, not owners or commissars. "But, how do things get done?", comes the inevitable question. To answer it, Michael begins analytically, methodically, by first answering the question "How should things *not* get done?" The first thing that we must never do, he says, is to accept Jack's sick idea that a minority with asymmetric private property rights (like the ones Jack demanded in the oasis he 'discovered'), or even asymmetric work circumstances, get the right to boss the rest around.

It is fine to own your toaster, and to use it as you please, but it is not fine to own the industrial oven to which human labourers must be attached to produce others' daily bread. It is fine to have insights, knowledge, skills, and experience able to inform wise decision-making, but it is not fine for a fraction of the population to monopolise empowering conditions, while the rest of the population simply obeys their commands. Michael calls this empowered group, who by circumstance, not by ownership, control outcomes, a coordinator class and it is but one of the main themes of the book that to attain classlessness we must not only remove the owner's ownership, but we must also disperse fairly the coordinator class's empowering tasks and roles by way of a new division of labor.

This is not a book for readers wedded to the idea of privately owned factories, offices, and digital platforms. *No Bosses: A New Economy for a Better World* is a book for those of us who take for granted the need to end private property over the means of production but who crave an answer to the question: "How do we manage commonly owned resources and means of production?" Before beginning to answer it, we need to dissect this question into two separate ones: First, how do we run a collectively operated firm or company to produce specific quantities and qualities of products and services? Secondly, who decides, and how, the quantity and quality of products and services to be produced by different firms?

If a firm is to have no boss, capitalist or what Michael calls coordinator, then all its workers must self-manage within a democratic framework. One way to do this is for a workers' assembly to elect decision-makers and to approve by majority voting the business plan these coordinators put to them. Michael rightly, I think, dismisses this because elected bosses are still bosses and will quickly amass the capacity, circumstances, and mindset to repress those they coordinate and to reproduce themselves as a class. His alternative is to propose self-organising units that fulfill obligations to the rest of the society as specified in an overarching plan arrived at by workers and consumers councils—with, to the extent possible, each worker having influence on matters that affect them in proportion to how they are affected, and with wages that reflect the relative unpleasantness of the work they do, the number of hours they wish to dedicate to the firm, and their intensity of effort.

Keen to keep markets at bay, Michael extends what he calls his 'self-managing approach' (which seems to me a form of radical contractarianism) to beyond the firm. So, he answers the broader question of who decides which goods and services different firms must produce in the same manner that he answers the question of how a firm produces given outputs. This, he proposes, should be accomplished via a cooperative negotiation among workplace and consumer councils who arrive at a plan that specifies how many bicycles, electric cars etc. the firms capable of producing these things should supply to the citizen-consumers in light of proposals for what the population wishes to consume.

In short, Michael proposes cooperatively negotiated plans wherein firms and consumers settle on what must be produced and then self-managed choices by members of each firm, in context of the firm's overarching responsibilities, decide how these products will be manufactured. The bulk of *No Bosses* thus comprises Michael's discussion of the features of this participatory economic process, its implications for daily life more broadly and, additionally, his responses to anticipated criticisms.

If one is adamant, like Michael, that markets should be driven to extinction, this version of anarcho-syndicalism is an attractive alternative—possibly the only one. In *No Bosses* Michael gives a brilliant account of the best thinking along these lines making it a must-read for anyone who is open not only to the eradication of private property of productive means but also to the replacement of central planning and markets with a new form of allocation—one based on self-management, equity, and solidarity. Additionally, Michael argues that, in addition to addressing consumers' needs and desires, his proposals point to an efficient management of society's commons, including the ecological ones.

As a reader who does not think that markets should be eradicated once means of production are socialised, I nonetheless found *No Bosses: A New Economy for a Better World* an invaluable guide to the possibilities and limits of an economic system which leaves no room to markets for the purposes of allocating scarce resources. As such, I feel we all have a debt of gratitude to Michael for taking to its logical limits the ambition to end all reliance on the price mechanism.

Having said that, I remain skeptical regarding some of Michael's specific proposals. For example, the replacement of bosses with sequential bargaining negotiations. Or the new type of division of labour he proposes. And especially the replacement of markets as means of connecting firms and consumers by worker and consumer decentralized planning that takes place within and between his proposed worker and consumer councils and federations of councils.

While I see how Michael's proposed organisation would rid workers of individual bosses and market pressures, I fear they may end up being bossed around by tyrannical majorities. Having, for instance, to seek the approval of a council before you are allowed to try out new things, either as a firm or as a worker within a firm, appears to me also as a form of oppression and an impediment to genuine innovation.

Michael's book is, however, deliciously open-ended. He calls what he has offered not a blueprint but a scaffold on which future people, in light of future experiences, will add the details, to arrive at a fully functioning economy. His aim is not so much that his vision becomes reality, as that a post capitalist vision emerges that is sufficient to attract wide and deep support, to inform planting the seeds of the future in the present, and to guide efforts at change which are undeniably now a matter of life and death for everyone.

In this context, Michael's scaffold seeks to provide the institutional features essential for classlessness, collective self-management, and equity. Michael wants future people to take his scaffold and add to it what is missing to create a functioning economy without, however, compromising its fundamental principles. But it is at this point that my questions and qualms return: Can this be done by relying exclusively on negotiated plans and without adding a price mechanism somewhere along the scaffold? Who decides how resources in fixed supply are to be distributed (e.g., the current housing stock, agricultural land between different cooperatives)? How is international trade to be conducted? Can this be done by relying exclusively on negotiated plans and without adding a price mechanism? If there is a role for money, what is it and who issues it?

The seeds of answers to these questions are in *No Bosses* and I shall, therefore, leave it to you, dear reader, to assess and to develop them—as Michael wants you to do. So, I conclude with the remark that, like Michael, I too yearn for a world in which we can live free of the tyranny of bosses and market competition—a world in which Jill's and Jack's mindsets are confined to the Museum of Human Miseries. Michael's new book is a remarkable study of the economic arrangements necessary to achieve this today, even if I retain a hunch that, while we have a duty to eradicate bosses and private property immediately, markets will still have a role to play for quite some time.

Introduction: Beyond Depravity, A New Economy

Tell no lies. Claim no easy victories.
Amilcar Cabral

It's been a long A long time coming But I know a change gonna come Oh, yes it will.
Sam Cooke

Behind closed doors I write. Outside people die. Outside the wealthy get richer. Outside the poor get poorer. This is America. This is the world. March, 2021.

Fifty eight years ago Sam Cooke sang "a change gonna come." Yesterday Arundhati Roy asked, will we walk through "a gateway between one world and the next...dragging the carcasses of our prejudice and hatred, our avarice, our data banks and dead ideas, our dead rivers and smokey skies behind us? Or [will] we walk through lightly, with little luggage, ready to imagine a new world? And ready to fight for it?"

Winter, spring, summer, fall, 2021, 2022, 2023...Will we mobilize vociferously but nonetheless slip-slide toward downbeat normality? Will we organize deeply and thereby dance toward upbeat liberation? Will we suffer miserably in a gasping old world? Will we flourish gloriously in a better new world?

To transcend disease, depravity, sadism, catastrophe, and firestorm, Big Change will have to come. But Big Change will require steadfast, informed collectivity. Big Change will require unified motion. Big Change will require no lies.

But Big Change to what?

Don't deny the obvious. Humans can be cruel.

Israeli virus-infected settler gangs spit on Palestinians to sicken them. American youths gleefully call the virus a "Boomer Remover." Teenage parties invite guests with Covid, charge admission, and offer prizes for whoever first gets virus-ed. Kids kill classmates to rule school corridors. Corporate vermin impose misery to enlarge profits. Nations pour hard rain onto other nations. Militarized police crush bare necks dead. Pharmacies impose murderous vaccine apartheid. Landlords produce raging homelessness. Employers endlessly impoverish. Media lies. Cruelty.

Don't deny the obvious. Humans can be kind.

Mutual aid proliferates street to street, home to home. Blacks revolt. Whites join. Neighbors share. Organizers block evictions. People deploy selflessness. Change rears up. Desire grows. Material resources appear. Optimism rises. Trillions for the already rich? Why not trillions for the unnecessarily poor? Bailouts for the unceasingly elevated? Why not health care, housing, education, and empowerment for the tediously trampled? Pragmatism pivots left. I've got your back. You've got mine. Produce integrity not pollution. Distribute dignity not submission. Save the planet. Kindness.

As desperation surges we cling to hospitals, druggists, and police. As mortification multiplies we beseech banks, corporations, courts, and legislatures. As outrage explodes we curse them all. As insurgency rises we assault them all.

Society's institutions spit floods. Society's institutions deploy leaky life rafts. North, south, east, and west. High water everywhere. High water rising higher. What to do? What's the lesson? Reject internalized docility. Reject habitual obedience. Replace leaky life rafts.

Don't just cling and curse. Swim. Don't just hunker down. Reach out. Don't just mobilize. Organize. We have no choice. Nine to five heart attack machines are everywhere. There will be no easy victories. We overcome or we die. Apocalyptic rhetoric? No. This is the coming of the third decade of the twenty-first century.

Suffer the verities of virus? Resist. Suffer the ravages of racism? Resist. Suffer global climate dissolution? Resist. Suffer gender deprivation? Resist. Suffer economic impoverishment? Resist. But not so fast. Prior decades teach that needing Big Change will not alone win Big Change. Desiring Big Change will not alone win Big Change. Even believing Big Change is gonna come—will not alone win Big Change. Resist to what end?

We hate how contemporary life constricts and kills. We are courageous, committed, and confident. We resist. But without shared vision of what we seek, our courageous, committed, and confident resistance will ultimately deposit us back where we began. Without capacity and consciousness to persist, we will travel from outsized Covid, resurgent racism, and flaming fascism back to normal-sized business as usual. We will cling to leaky life rafts—but not replace them. We will polish the old nasty normal—but not end it. And the old nasty normal will end us.

To attain a better world we must replace today's institutions like a transplant replaces a dying heart. Keep society breathing while we operate. Scorched earth would burn us too.

Our actions must mitigate present-day injustice. To do less would be callous.

Our actions must win changes in the present. To do less would forego the experience of struggle that arouses people to seek more.

Our actions must envision, advocate, seek, and finally win a succession of new presents that accelerate into a better future. To do less would forego hope and produce despair.

But into what future?

When we suffer losses our experiences must inform later wins. When we enjoy victories our experiences must ensure that we fight on to a new world. Our losses and our victories must together accumulate awareness, connections, and organization. We must win a trajectory of synchronized gains. We must bury the old and birth the new. To do less would lose. We must win.

Win what?

Do I sound naive? Does this sound pie eyed? Here is the harsh truth. We have no other choice. Alone on foot in the desert, we must walk until we reach water. To curse the sun's heat and bemoan the sand's seeming endlessness while standing still guarantees death. We must walk, march, prance, dance, run.

But where to?

First, what values can inform a long march to a new world?

- That all people share responsibilities and benefits fairly.
- That all people collectively self-manage their own situations.
- That social options and outcomes express the full diversity of human potentials.
- That all people feel solidarity and even empathy toward all other people.
- That across the world, what's good for one is warranted for all.
- That the planet enjoys sustainability and stewardship.

Second, what changes can ensure that a better future fulfills such guiding values? What arrangements can ensure that we always wisely and ceaselessly invest in the day after tomorrow's tomorrow? What attitudes and practices can ensure that we continually re-harmonize with each other and with our ever-changing planet?

A new world should always be busy being born. A new world should never be busy dying. But what new norms and structures can meet that high standard?

To seek what we want, we must envision it and describe it. Okay, already, let's get on with it. But wait, there is an important caveat. To build a bridge over troubled waters we have to pre-conceive fine details. But to build a bridge to a better future is different. We have no capacity to pre-conceive fine details. More, it is not our place to determine the detailed preferences of everyone in a better future.

We cannot know finely detailed future choices even if we had a right to do so. It is beyond our experience. More, a worthy future will reveal many good choices that will differ from one time to another, from one society to another, and even within a single society from one region to another. There is no one worthy future.

For our new future we should not propose, share, and pursue a detailed blueprint. We should envision only what we can now show to be necessary for future citizens to be prepared, able, and institutionally propelled to determine their own finely detailed fates. We should propose a scaffold of a new world. A scaffold can provide hope, guidance, and means. A scaffold can accept details when experience yields them. A scaffold doesn't go too far. A scaffold can go far enough.

Different people typically hear an advisory like the above differently. Many people's books, essays, and other works claim to address a vision for a better future but first analyze past and present relations. When the dust settles the resultant works are typically 90 percent, 95 percent, or even 99 percent about what we endure and barely at all about what we want. The 90 percent, 95 percent, or even 99 percent about what we endure provides sound arguments that prove our present is perverse. But the 1 percent, 5 percent, or even 10 percent about what we want falls horribly short of providing worthy, workable, vision. *No Bosses: A New Economy for a Better World* is not going to fit on the same shelf as those works. *No Bosses* may be less eloquent. Some of *No Bosses'* arguments may prove less sound. As a proposal *No Bosses* will propose, not declare. It will need improvement from ideas still to be thought and from experiences still to be had.

No Bosses mainly addresses economics. Its every page knows, however, that we don't live by economy alone. We also need vision for racial and community, gender and sexual, political, international, and ecological relations to overcome cynicism, provide hope, inspire efforts, and orient strategy. Does *No Bosses* present a sufficiently useful, workable, and evidenced scaffold for experience to fill out?

Chapter one offers a short list of key vision-orienting values.

Chapters two through seven respectively address economic Commons, decision-making, classless division of labor, equitable income, rejected markets and central planning, and finally new participatory planning.

Chapter eight considers how our proposed economic vision might intersect new community, kinship, political, and ecological vision.

Suppose our economic vision would be classless, equitable, self-managing, and consistent with equally visionary new cultural, kinship, political, international, and ecological relations. Nonetheless, a question would remain. Would our vision be just a thought dream or could we navigate from where we are today to where we hope to arrive tomorrow? Chapter nine offers a bit of strategy, a bit of tactics, and a bit of mindset.

A final more personal chapter assesses and situates the whole discussion. A short bibliography then points to some selected sources and references.

Some books entertain and edify. Some books inspire, engage, and instigate. *No Bosses* would love to do all that but mainly seeks to prod and provoke. Will you find its economic vision sufficiently worthy to elaborate, advocate, and use as you see fit?

Finally, what might we call our proposed economic vision?

Originally it was called participatory economics, or parecon for short. Some have taken to calling it participatory socialism as a part of participatory society. But a rose by any other name would smell as sweet—and a thorn by any other name would hurt as deep. Rose or thorn? You decide.

1

Values for A Better World

If we don't stand for something, we may fall for anything.
Malcolm X

Do not go where the path may lead, go instead where there is no path and leave a trail.
Ralph Waldo Emerson

All around apocalyptic novels portray pathology. Blockbuster movies display depravity. Disease ravages. Ecological nightmares rampage. Inexorable inequality, raging racism, surging sexism, and advancing authoritarianism all assassinate dignity.

Billboards reborn as cyber screams pummel our nerves and butcher truth. "Hunker down," they order. "Serve self," they holler. Despair goes viral. Virus goes normal.

Pundits pontificate that it is easier to think about apocalypse than to envision a new world. The end, is it really our only friend? But pundits be damned. Desires visibly rise. What new world might our new desires seek?

How can living, breathing, suffering, struggling souls on fire envision a better future? Three ways suggest themselves:

- Reject current reality's debilitating racism, sexism, authoritarianism, and classism. Preserve what remains.
- Reject past visions' debilitating authoritarianism and narrowness. Extend what remains.
- Proclaim positive values we want a better world to actualize. Describe new institutions to implement those values. Celebrate what emerges.

- The first two approaches reject existing evil to seek future good. Nice idea. The third approach establishes positive aims to seek future good. Nice idea. Luckily we don't have to choose. We can pro-actively embrace positive future features and firmly dismiss past ills we reject.

Finding Worthy Values

Start with positive social values. How?

Perhaps we should divide society into a few fundamental functions and propose a value for each. That's a plan. Plans are worth trying.

But what functions should we highlight? Why not follow activist wisdom?

Every society makes decisions. Decisions dramatically affect life prospects. What role do I play? What role do you play? What role do we all play in the decisions that impact me, you, and all of us? What degree of influence do we each wield? What do we value for better decision-making?

Every society delivers burdens and benefits that dramatically affect life prospects. Do we become poor, rich, or something in between? Do we endure too many burdens? Do we enjoy too few benefits? What do we value for a better distribution of burdens and benefits?

Every society has people who delightedly, neutrally, or antagonistically engage with one another. These engagements dramatically impact how we feel and what we can achieve. Do we aid or fleece one another? Do we respect or denigrate one another? What do we value for how people might better relate to one another?

Every society offers people a range of options and outcomes. The breadth of these options and outcomes impacts the enrichment, suffering, or boredom in our lives. Do limited options homogenize us? Do diverse options fulfill us? What do we value for a better range of options?

Every society inhabits an environmental context. Can we breathe the air around us? Does available food and water make us sick or well? Do we reside in natural beauty or endure unnatural ugliness? Do we face high waters rising, garbage proliferating, and extinction encroaching, or do we harmonize supportively with our surroundings? What do we value for better relations with ecology?

Every society exists among other societies. Do societies fear or celebrate one another? Do societies attack or support one another? Does each society exploit the rest and vice versa, or does each society elevate the conditions of the rest to be as good as its own conditions and vice versa? What do we value for international relations among better societies?

Finally, every society contains a population with diverse characteristics. Do some citizens become beneficiaries of enlightened values while other citizens remain regulated and repressed? Or do all citizens participate and benefit comparably? What do we value for the applicability of our values?

In a philosophical treatise a chosen value to answer any of the above questions might receive a whole book or even a whole library of books for its exposition and defense. In this first chapter, we give only two of the areas more than a paragraph. Is that enough, too much, or too little? You judge. If it is enough, continue. If it is too much, pick and choose, and then continue. If it is too little, add, and then continue. That is how conceiving a better world gets started.

A Value for Decision-Making

Decision-making and being subject to decisions occurs all over social life. In homes, parents and children do it. In workplaces, owners, managers, and workers do it. It happens in churches and ball parks. It happens in malls and on farms. It happens in courtrooms and concert halls. Decision-making is at the heart of society's political system and is comparably central to economy, culture, and kinship. Outcomes involve choices. Choices require decisions. Who makes them?

Typically, people decide. A parent, a boss, a pastor, a consumer, a community, a population decides. Less obviously, social relations decide. Markets, media, and structures of diverse kinds decide.

So what is a worthy value for decision-making?

An obvious candidate is one person one vote majority rule. But democracy is far from universally applicable. At work, while one person one vote majority rule may make sense for many decisions, it certainly would not make sense for many others. Suppose I have a desk, I am arranging items on it. Should the whole workforce vote? Suppose you and ten others work together as a team in a workplace where 190 others also work. You propose something new for your nine workmates and you. Should 200 vote? But what if you propose for your team that you have really loud rock music in your area? What if that music would be heard by all 190 in the surrounding workplace? Should you ten decide that alone?

Decisions differently affect people. A potential norm arises. Everyone should have a say in decisions in proportion to how much they are affected by them. Decisions that affect only me, I should make unilaterally. Decisions that affect all members of a group and not others, the group should make unilaterally. In a group making decisions, if you are more or less affected, you should have more or less say. This we call participatory self-management. People should have a say in decisions to the extent they are affected by those decisions. This proposed decision-making value treats everyone alike. But is it workable? Is it achievable? Is it compatible with other values we favor?

To accomplish perfect participatory self-management will often be impossible or at any rate unduly time consuming. Luckily, to achieve participatory self-management to everyone's broad satisfaction and so that deviations are at most modest should be quite sufficient. It is still a demanding standard but, if attained, it would treat everyone fairly and consistently. But would it lead to good outcomes?

The hardest part would be the broadest part. For example, when I decide to consume some item from the social product something goes to me that could have gone to others elsewhere. Others elsewhere should have some say. But how can new institutions give me a say and give you a say across town? How can they give me much more say about what I consume and you much less but still some say about that? And what kind of say?

My consumption also likely impacts the environment. That affects everyone everywhere, slightly for each, but a lot in total. Again, people beyond me need to have a say. Can we achieve that? In what manner?

The same holds for what a workplace produces. It directly affects those doing the work. It indirectly affects those consuming the result and those afflicted with harmful by-products, and even those who might have wanted to use the inputs for something else. How do we involve all the impacted people yet simultaneously ensure wise choices?

Our new institutions will have to take all these various issues very seriously, particularly when we consider how to combine tasks into jobs and how to accomplish allocation. Self-managements becomes our first guiding value.

A Value for Benefits and Burdens

Societies affect the benefits and burdens we each receive. This is most obviously a matter of income and expenses, but it also arises in families, schools, courtrooms, elections, churches, and hospitals.

To hone in on a possible value for apportioning benefits and burdens, perhaps considering income is the most direct route. We work. We receive income. What should determine its amount?

Should we get for our income:

- An amount in proportion to what our property adds to the social product?
- An amount in proportion to what we, by our own labor, add to the social product?
- An amount we can take due to our bargaining power?
- An amount we say we need?
- An amount in proportion to our effort and sacrifice doing socially useful work?

Of course we shouldn't get back the specific things that our machines and employees or that we ourselves specifically produce. If I produce bicycles my income should not be just bicycles. I should get back a claim on the social product (after some goes to investment, and some to provide free goods as well to provide income for those who cannot work). So we each get food, housing, clothes, and whatever. But should the size of our overall share of the social product depend on the value of our property's output, on the value of our own personal output, on what we can take, on what we say we need, or on our socially-valued effort and sacrifice?

Our task is to settle a norm for remuneration in a new economy. Let's call what we seek equity. How then can we equitably apportion responsibilities and benefits? What is fair? What will function well? Which norm should be our norm?

Regarding the economy, you likely wouldn't read these pages if you thought that Jeff Bezos should get tens or even hundreds of billions of dollars for owning Amazon. So let's reject income for property without further ado, though we will return to details in due course. (A caveat: some may think owning is okay, because maybe they can become an owner. I have to wonder if any slaves thought people owning other people was okay because maybe they would own someone, someday.)

Similarly you likely agree that our value for income ought not be that if you have more bargaining power you get to take more income and if you have less bargaining power you get to take less. That would establish a thug's economy. We aren't thugs. So let's also summarily reject rewarding income for bargaining power.

Now comes something more substantial and at first glance more just. We should get back in proportion to what we by our efforts add to the social product. If we add more, we should get more. If we add less, we should get less. This norm (as well as the two above) will get more attention in chapter five but for now suffice it to say that we reject this third norm albeit for less obvious reasons than we have for rejecting income for property or for power. In essence, we reject rewarding income for luck in the genetic, tools, jobs, and workmates lottery. You are born with a quick brain, fine eye, emotive voice, outstanding strength, lightning speed, or exceptional vision—or you are lucky enough to have better tools, you produce something more essential, or you have better workmates. Chapter five will argue that in each of these cases, there is no reason to pile excess income on top of your good luck.

As to getting what you say you need/want, that would be undeniably wonderful, and it is of course essential for anyone who cannot work, but as we will also address in chapter five it would be unviable as an overall norm for producing outputs that match what is sought. It would also provide no guidance for investment or even for wise apportionment of limited resources, labor, and tools. The problem is that with people getting whatever they ask for, the economy hears that people want x, and that people want y, but not how greatly they want x, y, or anything else.

So we come to what we do favor, which is that we get income for our effort and sacrifice in producing socially desired outputs. We get income, that is, for the duration, intensity, and onerousness of our socially-valued work. If we usefully work longer, harder, or in worse conditions than the social average, we earn more than the social average. If we usefully work less long, less hard, or in better conditions than the social average, we earn less than the social average. Can we implement that norm for remuneration? Would attaining that norm be viable and worthy? For now, like self-management, equitable remuneration is a proposed value we can aspire to. We will see if an economy can embody it and how doing so would improve on rewarding output (much less property or power) as we proceed. Equity becomes our second guiding value.

A Value for Human Interrelations

Our third area of concern is simpler than decision-making and remuneration and also less controversial. As much as possible economic interactions should not be antagonistic. They should not be a rat race. They should not be a zero-sum game. I should not benefit more only if you benefit less. People should not see one another as opponents, as means to an end, or as obstacles to avoid or overcome. Instead, my well being should depend on everyone else's well-being and vice versa. Social institutions should cause us to employ our capacities for empathy. Social institutions should cause us to feel and enjoy solidarity toward one another. Solidarity becomes our third guiding value.

A Value for Range of Life Options

Like solidarity, a value for range of life options is uncontroversial. We cannot do all things at once. We cannot even do all things ever. Partly we don't have the time. Partly we don't have the capacity. Partly we don't have the means. As a result we can benefit from enjoying the achievements of others. Other things being equal, the more our relations and outcomes are homogenized, the more our life options are impoverished. The more our relations and outcomes are multifold, the more our life options are enriched. Valuing diversity negates any inclination to remove conflict or hierarchy by removing differences. Valuing diversity avoids a mindset that would put all our eggs in one basket. Valuing diversity establishes a mindset that preserves multiple options lest any single option proves unwise. Among other virtues it promotes personal and collective flexibility. Diversity becomes our fourth guiding value.

A Value for Environmental Relations

Do we favor exploiting and despoiling our environment at the expense of future generations? Or do we favor accounting for the impact of our actions on our surroundings taking into account our own well-being but also the well-being of our children, our children's children, and thereafter? Even more aggressively, but equivalently, are we sentient or stupid? Far-seeing or myopic? Relations to our environment evidence civility, sanity, and even humanity—or evidence the opposite. Should we value sustainability? Does that set too low a bar? If we carefully clarify its meaning as we proceed, sustainability can be our fifth guiding value.

A Value for International Relations

This is another straightforward issue. What we value for our society we should value for all societies. Peace, mutual aid, and respect are watchwords for relations among societies. Each society should have relations with all societies that permit and even facilitate all preferred values being met by each and all. Diversity with solidarity. Equity with self-management. Sustainability for all. Internationalism is our other values writ large. To keep us alert to it, internationalism becomes our sixth guiding value.

A Value for the Applicability of Our Values

Finally, what good would it be to choose fine values but then apply them to a limited selection of people or have them be unviable? Viable self-management, equity, solidarity, diversity, sustainability, and internationalism are not for only some people. Society's benefits and burdens, its rights and responsibilities, should be for everyone. Participation for all who can participate is our seventh guiding value for envisioning new institutions for a new society.

What's Next?

The above values may morph a little depending on which part of society we think about. Think about politics and equity might usefully become justice. Think about culture/community or gender and we may highlight race and ethnicity or highlight gender and sexuality. Our hope is that when we think about how an economy ought to meet needs, develop potentials, and not waste things we value, our shared values will give us an agreed standard to organize our thoughts. Our shared values will orient us to ask, "how will what we propose for production, consumption, and allocation fulfill our preferred values," rather than to ask "how will what we propose for production, consumption, and allocation implement some old ideological scripture."

2

Who Owns What?

Imagine no possessions. I wonder if you can.
John Lennon

There is only one party in the United States: the Property party... and it has two right wings: Republican and Democrat.
Gore Vidal

Economies include ownership relations, modes of making decisions, ways of organizing tasks into jobs, norms for determining incomes, and relations that mediate who produces and who consumes what.

So, to start, the values that we put forward last chapter should guide us. So what should we think about owning things and especially owning places where people work? Do we need some new approach, or can we maintain the ownership relations we have?

That's Mine, Dammit

You own your shirt and your cell phone. You decide what to do with them. You decide how to display them. You decide when and how to use them. I don't make such decisions about your shirt or cellphone. You do not make such decisions about my shoes or TV. That seems right. Owning items we receive from the overall social product makes ethical and economic sense. It has no particular downside vis a vis our values.

In contrast, Mr. Moneybags owns a company. It produces some important good. It mines some important resource. It provides some important service. Mr. Moneybags decides what to do with his company. He oversees the products of his company. He oversees the employees he hires to make his company productive. I can't decide those things, nor can you, nor can any of Mr. Moneybags' employees. Mr. Moneybags has dominion over his company like you have dominion over your shirt and cellphone. Does that make ethical and economic sense?

Ownership conveys dominion over that which is owned. It's true for you and your shirt and cellphone. It's the same for Mr. Moneybags and his company. Mr. Moneybags wonders, "If you can own your shirt and cellphone, why can't I own my shirt and cellphone factories?"

Personal dominion over a shirt and a cellphone doesn't subvert self-management, eviscerate equity, smash solidarity, deny diversity, and submerge sustainability. Personal dominion over a shirt and a cellphone doesn't subvert the participation, dignity, and freedom of others.

But dominion by Mr. Moneybags—and roughly 2 percent of the population—over the resources, venues, tools, and technologies necessary to produce shirts, cellphones, and everything else, and over the work lives of those Mr. Moneybags hires to do his bidding, does subvert self-management, equity, solidarity, diversity, and ecological sustainability. It does subvert participation, dignity, and freedom.

I believe it is highly likely that people choosing to read this book already agree that the 2 percent who own what we can call "means of production" or "productive assets" accrue vastly more income and exert vastly more say over outcomes than warranted. They severely lack empathy for those below. They aggressively narrow options. They rapaciously violate ecology. They diminish participation, dignity, and freedom.

The property problem is therefore that sensible rules for owning personal possessions become horrific rules when extended to owning resources, tools, and workplaces because resources, tools, and workplaces affect the lives of countless people beyond their owners.

The personal rules for owners of shirts and cellphones benefit everyone. The same rules for owners of society's productive assets munificently serve those owners, but impoverish and degrade everyone subject to the owners' decisions.

It turns out that to abide by our values we should preserve personal ownership of clothes, swing sets, books, and furniture, but not personal ownership of resources, machinery, and workplaces. This is the underlying reason why critics of capitalism have always proposed eliminating private ownership of productive assets.

Such ownership elevates owners, called capitalists, above all others. It conveys incredible wealth and power to the owners and consigns the rest to various levels of enforced obedience and imposed impoverishment all the way down to total subordination and abject poverty, called wage slavery.

But if Amazon's owner, Jeff Bezos, shouldn't own and thereby have dominion over Amazon, what's the alternative? That is the property problem for which anyone who wants a better economy needs to have an answer.

If a bunch of Moneybags can't own and thereby accrue a very large part of the contribution to society's social product of Amazon or any other company, who should get such wealth?

We will soon make a case that workers should get income for the duration, intensity, and onerousness of the socially valued work they do, while people who cannot work should get an average share. Additionally, of course, some of society's product should go to meeting collective needs for health care, safety, public roads, and schooling. Some should also go to new construction and research for the future. The property point is only that none should go to anyone on the grounds they own productive assets. However, that is only half the issue. It is only half because the dominion that ownership currently conveys is not only about income. It is also about control.

That's Our's In Common, Dammit

Owners in our current economy make decisions about what to produce, how to produce it, who does the work, what they are paid, and much else. If there are no longer owners of companies, mines, and workplaces, who should make such decisions and by what calculus and methods?

We will soon propose that such decisions should not be the purview of some individual or group simply because they have a document that says they own the companies, mines, or workplaces in question. We should all be able to agree on that.

Some say the alternative to private ownership should be that the state should own the companies. Others say the alternative should be that workers in the unit in question should own it. Still others say that nearby communities should own it. Or that the entire population should own it.

A conceptual problem is that all these proposals fixate on ownership as if owning is somehow essential so we have to allot ownership somewhere. But why?

Imagine being shipwrecked with a bunch of others on some unreachable island. You all know you will be there for many years. You have to arrange yourselves to produce, distribute, and consume goods and services.

You have a big meeting of the new residents of the lost island. Some confident gray suited fellow stands and says, "In the real world, I owned a big company. I should own a big chunk of this island's land and resources. Then, I can run those, hire many of you, and help everyone thrive. I see 20 others like me among you, and 980 folks who worked for people like me, before. So let's establish ourselves here as we were before. Twenty owners and nine hundred and eighty workers for owners. My land, my resources, my workplaces (once you build them), and your wages—received from me. Twenty owner deciders and 980 beneficiaries of owner's decisions."

I hope you will agree that this wannabe owner should be

given a shovel and the patience due a person suffering a severe mental malady.

On our imagined island it is easy to see that if we say people's income should have nothing to do with something called ownership, and if we also say people's influence over outcomes should have nothing to do with something called ownership, then there is nothing left for ownership of productive assets to convey.

The immediate conclusion is that no one and no thing should own society's productive assets just like no one should own the sky or the oceans. The concept of owning makes no sense when applied to the island's land or resources, and it also makes no sense applied to its mines and workplaces. Such ownership should not exist.

The issue at stake isn't some abstract notion of deeds to mines and workplaces. It is, instead, the very tangible issue, who should get the wealth created by mines and workplaces and who should decide what mines and workplaces do and how they do it? If not owners—and surely we can agree it ought not be owners—then who?

Our equity value will guide us toward a proposal for income. Our self-management value will guide us toward a proposal for decision-making.

But before those steps, if no one is to own them, how do we view resources, workplaces, tools, and even knowledge and skills? A useful concept to apply is the Commons. All these productive assets are either gifts of nature, like warmth from the sun and resources from beneath the ground, or they are products of a long history of human creative activity, like technology, knowledge, and skills. They are parts of a natural and a built Commons which should together be respected and used responsibly for the benefit of all society. To misuse or waste them is a sin against nature and our own history that diminishes our future.

The property problem is thus partly eliminating the usual arrangement in which some few people own and oversee productive assets. But it is also partly replacing those few owners as beneficiaries and rulers of these gifts of nature and these products of human history with, instead, a new and different approach. And it is also a matter of having the rest of a new economy interface compatibly with that new approach to our natural and built Commons. Which approach is in turn a matter for coming chapters.

What this chapter has already set forth, however, is that we propose no private ownership of productive assets, which means we propose no capitalists, which means we propose no more capitalism. What we don't yet know is what we propose to take capitalism's place.

3

Who Decides What?

The most common way people give up their power is by thinking they don't have any.
Alice Walker

Most everybody I see knows the truth but they just don't know that they know it.
Woody Guthrie

We have proposed collective self-management as a value for "who decides what" in a new economy and in any other realm of life as well. We can easily see that to fulfill that ethical aim, even if not to the third decimal place of precise accuracy, at least to everyone's broad satisfaction, is a quite demanding standard. It would treat everyone fairly. It would respect equity, solidarity, and diversity. It would be ethically admirable. But can we do it? And if we can do it, how can we do it? And finally, if we can do it, will the way we do it introduce any offsetting debits?

Whys and Hows of Self-Management

To see why it is hard to attain self-management, consider that when I decide to consume some item from the overall social product, something goes to me that could have gone elsewhere. This means the choice affects others elsewhere. To have collective self-management requires that those others elsewhere have some say, and all together, have quite a lot of say.

Similarly, a decision to consume some particular item often impacts the environment. An item's production, use, or disposal might entail pollution that affects people elsewhere, perhaps slightly for each, but a lot in total. Again, to have self-management everyone has to have some say, and all together have to have a whole lot of say.

Another example: If I decide to wear my black socks tomorrow and not my blue ones, overwhelmingly that choice affects only me so I should decide dictatorially with no one else getting much or even any say. But suppose I decide to consume some of my audio equipment ferociously loudly. It dramatically affects all in hearing range. In that case, shouldn't they have some and perhaps a lot of say, maybe even veto power? Finally, if a workplace is spewing fumes that contribute to global warming and thus threaten human existence, somehow all those who will suffer the effects need their preferences to count.

These are all manageable complexities, albeit they will entail institutions beyond the relatively simple ones focused in this chapter—but, for now, let's start simple.

Consider inside a workplace. Suppose we assume, for the moment, that influence from people outside the workplace is well addressed by structures still to be discussed—which is admittedly a large assumption. In that case, what implication does advocating collective self-management have for decisions inside the workplace—a question one can of course ask for families, communities, religious institutions, and political institutions.

First, all the workers in the workplace will be affected by many workplace decisions so they will all together need a venue and methods by which to have their say. Let's call this, as have others before us, the workers council. We propose that the workers council is the whole workforce empowered to meet, deliberate, and tally votes to arrive at decisions when need be. What else could it be? If we call a collective vehicle of workers to make decisions in a workplace by any other name it would still be a workers council.

Some decisions will affect all workers essentially equally. The length and timing of the workday, when the lights are on or off, duration and time of breaks, use of air conditioning, and the total output and therefore total work level. Also norms, if needed, about clothing, noise levels, or what holidays to observe. So a first thought is that perhaps the workers council, a time-honored structure that has long been considered central to any kind of workers' self-management, can operate totally according to one person one vote majority rule.

But wait a minute. Do all these decisions in fact actually affect everyone equally? What if those with families and those without have markedly different dependency on the timing of arrival and departure from work? What if some people have conditions that make air conditioning far more important for them? What if different workers of different nationalities or religions are differently impacted by holiday choices?

The answer for how to handle such variations within workforces is ultimately up to each workplace to determine. After all, we have in mind that they collectively self-manage themselves. As one approach, sessions of workers councils in each workplace might first arrive at various procedures deemed sufficient—or, when possible, ideal—for giving affected parties appropriate say in particular types of decisions. This menu of mutually ratified procedures might include one person one vote majority rule for some situations, but two thirds needed, or consensus needed, and so on, for other situations. Likewise different workplaces might settle on different methods of conveying information and on different durations and procedures for deliberation in different cases. Perhaps the list of available options for deliberations and tallies would be revisited yearly or bi-yearly and it certainly could be different in different workplaces due to their different features and the different preferences of their workers. However, once such agreed procedures exist in a workplace, one could be quickly chosen, as appropriate, for each new issue or for categories of issues and deliberations could proceed. It would be in everyone's interest to handle such matters without undue time-wasting while attending to the needs of all involved.

Complicating deliberations and votes within a workers council, many workplace decisions reverberate outward. What technology we employ affects what we produce and therefore what others get to consume. What energy we use and what we do with our waste affects neighbors, and perhaps far more widely. To implement collective self-management, such decisions would have to be made in ways that give appropriate influence to affected workers in the specific workplace, but also to affected folks outside that workplace. This trajectory of thoughts about how to make decisions is the purpose of settling on guiding values. The guiding values provide standards for generating and also for assessing proposals for new institutions.

Problems and Virtues of Self-Management

Some would reply, phooey on self-management. Let's just let one person decide. It's much less messy. Let's strive to have the best decider be that person. It's more efficient. Our contrary claim for democracy, and beyond democracy for self-management, is that imposed order is not, in fact, less messy. Instead imposed order merely obscures messiness. Imposed order hides/ignores people being alienated and even suffering inferior outcomes. It appears less messy only if we don't value the input that is excluded and don't count the accruing damages.

Within the guideline of seeking collective self-management, one workplace could lean toward using more streamlined methods of decision-making. Another workplace could lean toward more careful methods that allot more time for hearing and exploring minority views. Indeed, people might very sensibly choose where they want to work in part due to their taste for more or less detailed workplace decision-making procedures. Over time and with experience, we would expect various approaches would presumably prove better at arriving smoothly and rapidly at desirable and collectively respected decisions. Those approaches would presumably be used more often. However, within each firm it would be up to the firm's workers council. The workers council would, in this view, become the main repository of decision-making power within each workplace. Not an owner, not a boss. Collective self-management.

The above brief discussion applies as well to the consumption side of economics. Individuals consume individual goods and services from the overall social product. But so do neighborhoods, counties, and states consume collective goods and services from the overall social product. And, like for workers, consumers' choices affect themselves, whether individually or in groups, but also others. So, by analogy, for collective consumption of neighborhood pools, county parks, state utilities, or national security, we propose consumer councils as the venue of consumer decision-making, with the same kinds of reasoning and flexibility regarding their methods noted above for workers councils.

Various day-to-day implications of all this will become more concrete when we eventually address how workers and consumers can arrive at actual choices of what and how much to produce and consume via new allocation institutions. But, even for this brief introduction to economic decision-making, we have to raise two additional concerns. One is a complaint that turns out to be rather simple to resolve. The other is a derivative need that is far more complex and consequential for a future new economy and society, and even for how we might win such a future economy.

First, some complain that extensive participation in decision-making would diminish the quality of decisions made. Whether in a workplace or a neighborhood, why shouldn't Joe get more or less say depending on how good a decision-maker he is? By preventing that, doesn't the participatory approach undercut the benefits of expertise? Won't we suffer bad decisions?

The answer to this complaint is that the opinions of experts are of course incredibly valuable. But should the fact that Joe is an expert in engineering or chemistry or whatever else consequential to some decision, convey to Joe more say even in a decision that quite strongly involves engineering or chemistry? We should certainly consult Joe's expertise. But for a choice affecting Joe's work team or Joe's workplace, after he is consulted why shouldn't Joe have a say like all others, rather than an elevated say? The point is, Joe is not an expert in how much a decision matters to you or I, or in how you or I feel about it. We are the world's foremost experts in our own preferences. And to honor our special and unparalleled expertise regarding our own preferences, collective self-management says we should have a say in the decision even while we should also of course pay close attention to Joe's expert insights.

Consider an intimately connected concern. Susan has proved over time to have an incredible facility for always advocating decisions that experience later shows to be exceptionally wise. She is a very good decision-maker. She is simply the best decision-maker in the workplace. She is best by a large margin. Okay, why not simplify everyone's time commitments by having Susan make all decisions? Even if we ignore that these assumptions are highly unreal in virtually any context, and are certainly highly unreal once we have fully participating and highly prepared workers who each bring to deliberations and votes different experiences, and even if we ignore the corrupting impact Susan's lordly influence would likely have on Susan's consciousness, this logic ignores the value of each person feeling that decisions respect his or her input and say.

To think experts shouldn't just offer their wisdom for others to evaluate and even learn from, but should themselves decide outcomes would not only rule out collective self-management, it would also rule out even limited democracy. The reason we shouldn't rule out either is both that no such general and universal expertise as Susan's exists, and, even more important, people's exclusion from decisions that affect them creates problems far worse than a somewhat worse choice being made even if that did happen now and then. Participation matters.

That sounds compelling, but a related more complex issue that collective self-management in workplace and consumer councils raises, in addition to raising the question of finding actual institutions able to provide appropriate say relative to those outside the councils, is how to ensure that all workers (and consumers) are prepared to contribute positively to decision-making. For even after agreeing that we are each the world's foremost expert in our own preferences, we cannot deny that if we have lots of workers who lack the confidence, skills, and knowledge to make important decisions well—then even if we apportion voting rights appropriately and provide relevant time for deliberation, their uninformed and unskilled involvement will give us seriously flawed results. In a good economy, what prevents that?

More specifically, we will soon argue that in most current workplaces the number of people in the whole workforce in a position to have informed opinions is roughly one out of every five. Why is that, and how do we raise it to five out of five as a precondition for having effective, optimal, self-managed, decision-making? We consider universal preparedness for decision-making next chapter, and there we also consider related issues of class relations and class rule. Our answer for the economy, as we will see, turns out to raise the issue of how to better apportion tasks into jobs via a new non-corporate division of labor.

But, for now, inside a workplace, we can already propose that how a work team allocates its time and arranges and conducts its activities is largely or even completely the team's choice, assuming, that is, that the team operates in accord with broader agreed decisions taken by the whole workplace or the whole society for the timing of holidays, the length of the work day, the level and character of workplace product and output, and so on.

Within a team, what affects only the team is their's to decide. Within a team, if someone is dramatically affected by some aspect, then according to our self-management ethic, he or she would get more say about that aspect. And within a team, if folks outside are affected, then by some means they too would impact the decisions that affect them.This approach to decisions in context of overarching other decisions will recur at many points in thinking through economic but also other social structures.

For now, however, to achieve collective self-management, it follows that some decisions may best be taken by one person one vote majority rule because everyone is comparably affected, but other decisions may best require two thirds to pass, or even a variant of consensus in cases where anyone might be horrendously adversely affected so that everyone should have a veto. Likewise, some decisions will presumably have more time set aside for deliberation, especially of dissenting views—and some less. Maybe hiring a new member requires in one workplace, for example, two-thirds to pass though anyone can veto, but perhaps not in another workplace which opts for a different approach.

It turns out that with a self-management view, diverse ways of tallying preferences become methods that we judiciously choose so as to best approximate self-management. Self-management is the overarching principle, not one person one vote, or consensus, or any other approach chosen in a particular case to serve self-management in that case. We propose that councils choose among deliberation and voting procedures to attain self-management as best they can without spending more time or resources than they wish to allot to the process.

In other words, we choose to not always favor one person

one vote majority rule. One person one vote majority rule is not an absolute to always respect. We instead propose to have one person one vote majority rule only when it is the best way to attain or to at least best approximate self-management for all who are affected by a particular decision. One person one vote majority rule of everyone on my work team about my choice of socks would be idiotic. One person one vote with three quarters support required for adding a new hire to a work team—but anyone on the team who feels strongly that the proposed addition would make his or her life miserable, can veto—might make excellent sense.

Using different methods in different situations may seem strange, but it turns out that when we are free to do so it is how caring friends or workmates most often relate to one another even now. It is not as unfamiliar as an abstract description might make it appear. You are with a group deciding on a movie to go to. If a movie is proposed that someone has seen, he or she likely gets a veto. Otherwise, perhaps majority rule, or maybe consensus. Different strokes for different folks and for different situations.

We All Decide

So the answer to the question who decides what, is that we propose that everyone participates in deciding issues that affect them with each person having a level of influence in proportion to the degree they will be affected. This is not mere rhetoric. It is not for academic sessions, and then back to humdrum reality. It is a serious goal to attain. As such, even if councils agree with this goal, the "who decides what" problem for an economy still has two critical issues to address: First, how do we ensure that everyone has experiences and circumstances that convey sufficient skills, confidence, and information to make good decisions? And second, how do we incorporate the desires of people who are affected at a distance so they can appropriately influence decisions enacted locally?

Societies are socially entwined systems of institutions and people. Each new feature we propose for a new economy puts limits on and establishes requirements for other new features that will need to work along with it. That is an unfolding characteristic of thinking about vision, whether economic or any other. And so, we proceed to consider the character of work in a new economy.

4

Who Does What?

They say sing while you slave and I just get bored.
Bob Dylan

I put my heart and my soul into my work, and have lost my mind in the process.
Vincent Van Gogh

Why do some people dominate in an economy and others endure being dominated? Is the only important factor generating that horrible outcome ownership relations? Having discussed eliminating ownership relations, have we fully found the source and rejected the cause of one class dominating another? This chapter, titled "Who Does What," takes up the task of ensuring that five out of five workers are well equipped to participate in decision-making. It focuses on how we ought to apportion tasks to form jobs in each workplace to ensure a self-managing economy. It claims that this focus adds a new dimension to the pursuit of classlessness.

Out with the Old Boss, In with the New Boss

While rarely acknowledged, in capitalism among all the multitude of jobs that people do, around 20 percent include a mix of tasks that convey information, skills, confidence, and social ties that facilitate participation in decision making. The other 80 percent include a mix of primarily rote and repetitive tasks that exhaust, deaden, deskill, isolate, and un-inform to the point where they neither prepare nor incline people to participate in decision-making. This difference is built into the skewed distribution of empowering tasks. Moreover, this difference is great enough to define a class division and engender class rule. Indeed, this difference is so great that unaddressed it will subvert even the otherwise best laid plans to institute self-management.

To keep this difference in workplace circumstances in our thinking, we give it a name. We call those who monopolize empowering tasks the "coordinator class." We call those who do overwhelmingly disempowering tasks the "working class." Naming things facilitates paying attention to them. A different and actually prior label for the coordinator class is "the professional managerial class" which was Barbara and John Ehrenreich's name for it. But whatever name you prefer, the claim is that this set of people has a markedly different position in the economy than do other workers and that this difference has profound implications for their lives and their relations to one another. More, we claim this difference is so substantial that it defines a class division rooted in economic relations. It gives coordinators markedly better conditions of work, greater influence over work, and higher income than it gives workers.

More, we claim this division—coordinators above and workers beneath—is intrinsic to the way we typically structure jobs so that some employees monopolize empowering tasks while other employees do only disempowering tasks. In other words, just as having some people own productive assets turns them into a class with different influence and income than others have, so too having some people monopolize empowering work turns them into a class with different influence and income than others have.

Finally, we claim that even if a workplace wants to be democratic, if it retains a corporate division of labor wherein some people do overwhelmingly empowering work while others do overwhelmingly disempowering work, then the class division between the empowered and the disempowered employees will inevitably subvert everyone's initially democratic or even self-managing desires. That is, even without owners present, and regardless of contrary hopes, the 20 percent coordinator class will dominate the 80 percent working class. Even with self-managing intentions, the trajectory of change will become out with the old boss, in with the new boss.

Consider a case where even short of establishing a whole new economy, a particular workplace is doing poorly. The capitalist owners jump ship to pursue larger profits elsewhere. The coordinator class engineers, designers, managers, and accountants all decide the workplace will sink without the owners so they too seek positions elsewhere. The workers, however, have nowhere to run. They stay to make a go of it. What happens?

We don't need to guess. Two decades ago in Argentina the above happened with a great many workplaces winding up in the hands of their working class employees. I had the opportunity to speak to an assembly of representatives from a few dozen such firms.

At first, milling about, the attendees were jovial. They talked animatedly with one another. They were from many Argentine workplaces and were in many cases meeting each other for the first time. To begin, we went around the room for introductions and a brief report on each attendee's workplace experience. The reports from respective workplaces began. The mood shifted. By the seventh report, the room was subdued, even mournful. Excitement over achievements was silenced by reports of decline. These workers took over their firms. They created councils and instituted democratic and even self-managed decision-making. They established largely equal wages. They got their failing firms working effectively. But they reported that after a time, even with all those changes, all the old crap was returning. One said, "I never could imagine myself saying it, but maybe Margaret Thatcher was right when she said 'there is no alternative.' We took over excitedly. We transformed joyously. And now it is unraveling."

At that point, I interrupted to ask if people felt this was due to human nature and the complexities of economic necessity. Most nodded. They had denied it when taking over, but they now feared or even believed it. My take, offered then, was different. I suggested that perhaps it wasn't human nature or some necessity of complex production that was bringing back all the old crap. I asked, "when you took over your firms did you keep the jobs pretty much as they had been before?" Of course they did. They said it wasn't an issue. My question sounded to them like I was asking whether they still had lunch breaks. Of course they did, it wasn't an issue.

Then we talked about the corporate division of labor and its implications. We together realized that to put some workers into coordinator positions and others into working class positions was what had caused all the old crap to start coming back. They were all working class before, but some began to become coordinator class by doing the empowering jobs. Those doing empowering jobs began to dominate council meetings. They had the needed information. They had the confidence to develop agendas. Attendance of others began to fall because others didn't want to attend meetings which ran according to agendas set by the coordinators and dominated by coordinator speeches and proposals. Others did not want to sit in such meetings, relegated to watching and obeying. And then the wages paid to the coordinator class, as decided by the coordinator class, started to rise. And their conditions steadily improved. The coordinators, initially at one with everyone else, were then separated from others by their newly undertaken empowering work. The coordinators had come to feel they were smarter, more responsible, and more essential. They deserved more. They paid themselves more. And the wages paid the others, the workers, as decided by the coordinator class, started to deteriorate. The upshot was that the old crap didn't return due to an inexorable outcome of human nature or of the intrinsic requirements of complicated work. The old crap returned due to a social choice that wasn't even consciously made. The workers had routinely, reflexively, maintained the corporate division of labor. And that corporate division of labor had in turn routinely, reflexively subverted sought results.

It is easy to see similar dynamics in many workers' co-ops and nonprofits and left projects that have no owner. To their credit, they have less accumulated power and wealth at the top than were there an owner. But when they keep a corporate division of labor, coordinators become enshrined as the new rulers. Indeed, once we know what to look for—a corporate division of labor subverting self-management and equity—we can see that the history of what is now called twentieth century socialism, as well as of capitalism's nonprofit and publicly owned firms, all demonstrate the pattern. In each case it is out with the old 2 percent top dogs, Goodbye owner capitalist class. Elation. But then it is in with the new 20 percent top dogs. Hello empowered coordinator class. Depression.

This simple but incredibly important pattern is that even after private ownership of a workplace is eliminated and even with workers councils wanting to create new relations, if we keep a corporate division of labor, empowered employees will become a dominant coordinator class and will keep disempowered employees down as a subordinate working class. The former coordinators will rationalize that the workers need coordinator leadership. They need coordinator guidance. Not long after, the coordinators will look in their respective mirrors and tell themselves that they are better able to utilize and appreciate higher income and better conditions.

Removing the old owner-boss but retaining the old division of labor elevates empowered employees to make virtually all decisions. Before long, they enlarge their own incomes in the distorted belief that they deserve more than the workers they rule over. The coordinators see themselves as aiding workers below. The workers resent the coordinators—at the same time as they want their kids to become one.

More, this division between coordinators and workers is structural. The opposed situations and interests are blatant and built in. So too are the contrasting behaviors and broad personal beliefs. The hierarchical results are undeniable. That nearly everyone accepts that the corporate division of labor is an unavoidable necessity is also evident and highly advantageous to those who benefit from the arrangement. The class antagonisms are intense. Often, in capitalism, coordinator/worker antagonisms are more intense day to day than owner/worker antagonisms for the obvious reason that workers rarely directly personally encounter owner dismissiveness, arrogance, paternalism, and cruel hostility head on—but workers do directly personally encounter all that from coordinator class members nearly all the time. But is this arrangement natural? Is it unavoidable?

To have managers, doctors, lawyers, accountants, and public officials empowered by their work, while assembly workers, short order cooks, and cleaners do only disempowering rote and routine tasks, leaves the empowered employees to set agendas, dominate outcomes, accrue excessive income, and feel that they deserve their greater power and wealth on account of their superior (socially monopolized) knowledge, skills, and capacities, and that the disempowered workers deserve their subservience on account of their (socially imposed) lesser knowledge, skills, and capacities. In other words, it demolishes prospects for equity, self-management, and solidarity.

It follows that to maintain a corporate division of labor in a new economy will subvert prospects for it being a desirable economy. In other words, as evidenced by the earlier description of the experience of Argentine workers, if workers take over, even if they have wonderful values and desires, if they preserve a corporate division of labor their wonderful values and desires will fade away. Institutions matter. Bad ones can trump good desires and even good intentions. Some changes take more time, more transition, but transition we must. But if it is essential to reject the corporate division of labor, what can take its place?

Out with the Old Boss, in with No Bosses

Once we ask for an alternative, a solution becomes evident. If we must reject defining jobs so that 20 percent of the workforce has means and desires to rule over 80 percent who lack means and expect to be ruled, then the solution must be to steadily redefine jobs so that daily tasks comparably prepare all employees to contribute to collective self-management.

Imagine we visit a world where we see that the workforce has two parts. One part rules. The other part obeys. The ruling members all eat good food. The ruled members all eat horrible food. Suppose it is also obvious that the good food strengthens, enlightens, and inspires people and the bad food weakens, stunts, and depresses people.

We would easily determine that to eliminate this hypothetical world's food-generated class division we would have to let everyone share the good food. We would need to balance good food apportionment. We should even, of course, increase the amount of good food. If we failed to do all that, it wouldn't matter what else we wanted or even what else we did. The monopolization of good food by some while relegating others to bad food would overcome desires for self-management and even for meaningful democracy.

Okay, in our world isn't it just as evident that to eliminate the worker/coordinator class division based on a skewed distribution of empowering tasks, we would ultimately have to share among all workers not good food but empowering tasks?

Isn't it just as clear that to eliminate the unwanted division of labor we need to balance jobs so that we all do a fair share of empowering and disempowering tasks precisely so that we are all well-equipped and inclined by our circumstances to participate in decision-making? Precisely so that one group, the coordinator class, is not dominantly empowered and inclined, while another group, the working class, is subordinately disempowered and disinclined?

If we want self-management, no matter how hard it might be or how long it may require to accomplish, won't we need to guarantee that no group monopolizes empowering tasks and dominates another group that is denied empowering tasks? It turns out that to attain self-management by eliminating class rule, not only would we have to remove the property relations that entitle capitalists to profits and dominion, but we would also have to remove the division of labor that makes coordinators a separate class above workers. We would have to ensure that all employees have shared interests in and ample capacity for decision-making. We would have to replace the corporate division of labor with a balanced distribution of empowering tasks.

If we retain a corporate division of labor we will preserve inequity, prevent solidarity, and destroy self-management. If we establish what we call balanced job complexes wherein everyone's work is comparably empowering, we will propel equity, solidarity, and self-management. This is the logic of institutions. They carry with them implications they impose on people who fill their roles, who interrelate by their rules. Pick bad institutions, impoverish life prospects. Pick good institutions, enrich life prospects.

Consider any workplace. Balanced job complexes, once attained, would mean no one would just do surgery or just clean up after surgeons. No one would only teach or only sweep. No one would only dig resources from a mine or only schedule the mine's operations. Balanced job complexes would mean all workers would do a mix of tasks such that each job's overall empowerment effect is broadly like that of all other jobs.

I apply to some workplace for a job I like. Unlike now, all available jobs are balanced for empowerment effects so that everyone's work prepares them to make informed, confident decisions. If we can balance job complexes without incurring some dire offsetting damage, then balanced job complexes will answer our question who does what by eliminating the coordinator/worker class hierarchy. It will fulfill the need that five out of five employees of workplaces, once all citizens are also earlier well educated, would be able to participate successfully in workplace decision-making.

But can we balance jobs without incurring dire offsetting damage? Can we get rid of the coordinator/worker class division that is based on empowerment differences? Can we make self-management viable and effective without crippling output or oppressing people? Ultimately, can we have classlessness by not only getting rid of the cause of capitalist class power, but by also getting rid of the cause of coordinator class power?

First, we should clarify that to do so, those who assemble cars today need not assemble computers tomorrow, much less would each person have to assemble every imaginable product. Nor would everyone who works in a hospital perform brain surgery as well as every other hospital function. Balanced jobs wouldn't eliminate different people doing different things as part of a sensible whole job. That is essential. But balanced jobs would ensure that over some reasonable time frame all able to work would have responsibility for some sensible sequence of tasks for which they would be well trained, but also such that no one would enjoy excessive elevation by the empowerment effects of their work.

Eliminating the source of consistent differences in empowerment effects would not mean that we have doctors who occasionally clean bed pans, or secretaries who every so often attend a seminar. Parading through the ghetto would not yield solidarity, nor would slinking through a country club confer status. Short-term stints in alternative circumstances—whether slumming or admiring—would not rectify long-term inequities in basic responsibilities.

Eliminating the source of consistent advantages in the empowerment effects of their work would mean, instead, that everyone would have a set of tasks that composed his or her job such that the overall implications for empowerment of that whole set of tasks would be broadly like the overall implications for empowerment of all other jobs for all other workers. Further, and this is even controversial for some advocates of the new economy we are aiming for, balancing must also occur across workplaces. The idea is that for an entire workforce to do only elite work in one workplace to have balance there, or for another workforce that does only rote work in one workplace to have balance there, would not challenge the hierarchical arrangement of the two relative to each other. We would need to balance job complexes for empowerment in each and every workplace, yes, but we would also need to ensure that workers have a combination of tasks that balance across workplaces. This would provide a new division of labor that would give all workers an equal chance of participating in and benefiting from workplace decision-making. This would establish a division of labor which does not produce a class division between permanent order-givers and permanent order-takers.

Since disparate empowerment at work inexorably destroys participatory potentials and creates class differences, and since as we will shortly see differences in quality of life at work could be justly offset by appropriate remuneration, we can here focus on only empowerment. In practice, though, there probably is not much difference. Balancing empowerment likely takes us a long way toward balancing quality of life.

Almost everyone is aware that typical jobs in familiar corporate contexts combine tasks with roughly the same empowerment characteristics so that each worker has a homogenous job complex and most people do one level of task. In contrast, to establish appropriate empowerment for all, a participatory economy will offer balanced jobs where everyone typically does a few levels of tasks. In that case, each worker has a particular bundle of diverse responsibilities, and each person's whole bundle—his or her whole job—prepares him or her to participate as an equal with everyone else in a self-managed workplace and also in societal decision-making.

Have I repeated myself? Yes. Why? Because these observations often fail to register as intended. I repeat, but even so I worry whether I have been clear. Let's try another version, unrealistically mechanical, and thus not quite real, but perhaps clearer for that reason.

Consider an idealized and simplified hypothetical capitalist approach to defining jobs where someone lists all possible tasks to be done in a workplace. Someone gives each task a rank of 1 to 20, with higher being more empowering and lower being more deadening and stultifying. We have hundreds or perhaps thousands of stripped-down tasks which our chosen workplace combines into actual jobs. No single task is enough to constitute a whole job. Some jobs may take only a few tasks, some may take many. When the corporate approach is adopted, each defined job is a bundle of tasks, but each task in that bundle has very nearly the same rating as all the others. As a result, in the hypothetical case, the corporate job bundle may come up with a 1, a 7, a 15, or a 20 as its average empowerment rating. The average could be any number on the scale, but the job itself will be a fairly homogenized bundle of tasks all rated about the same. In other words the job will be pegged to a position in a 1 to 20 hierarchy and all its component tasks will be at that rank or just a bit above or below. Rose gets mostly 5s, some 4s and 6s. Robert gets mostly 17s, some 16s and 18s. Of course in reality nothing remotely this mechanical occurs, but the result is attained nonetheless.

Now suppose we switch to an idealized and simplified hypothetical participatory economic workplace. There are quite a few differences in tasks due to the transition to a new type of economy for reasons to be discovered as we proceed, but still it is a long list. The tasks are still differentiated in terms of their empowerment effects, just as in the capitalist economy. Imagine, unrealistically, that we again rank each one of them from 1 to 20 (though there are fewer at the low end than before due to new investment priorities). However, tasks combined into jobs change dramatically. Instead of combining a bunch of 6s into a 6 job, and a bunch of 18s into an 18 job, every job is now a combination of tasks of varied levels such that each job in the workplace has essentially the same average grade.

Maybe the workplace is a coal mine and the overall average is 4 or maybe it is a factory and the average is 7 or it is a school and the average is 11 or it is a research center and the average is 14. Whatever the average for the unit is, everyone who works there has a job whose combination of tasks yields the same average. In the coal mine, where the average is 4, jobs may have tasks that are all rated near 4, or maybe a job has some 7s, 4s, and 2s but it averages to 4. Mechanical, yes. Fictitious, yes. It is a simplified image. In the research plant someone may have all 14s, or maybe a 4 and 5, a bunch of 13s, 14, and 15s, and a 19 or 20. The point is that every worker has a job. Every job has many tasks. The tasks are suited to the worker and vice versa. The tasks combine into a sensible agenda of responsibilities.

The average empowerment impact of the sum of tasks in any job in any workplace is roughly the same as the average empowerment for all other jobs in that workplace. When the workers come together in their workers councils, whether for work-teams, units, divisions, or the whole workplace, there is no subset of workers whose conditions have prepared them significantly better and left them significantly more energetic, or provided them with significantly greater relevant information or skills relative to everyone else, such that they will predictably dominate debate and outcomes. The preparation for participation owing to involvement in the daily life of the workplace is roughly equalized.

Of course, in real circumstances the procedures of job balancing are not precisely or likely even remotely such a precise numeric accounting. Actual procedures would instead likely involve a steady social exchange meshing and merging tasks into jobs, with workers broadly assessing the overall combinations and bringing them into accord with each other by tweaking the combinations far more fluidly than parceling out all tasks as if from some gigantic menu. But the graded menu image conveys the rough reality.

What should be clear already is, if it turns out to be preferred and desirable, there is no law of nature or of "job definitions" that precludes doing as we have suggested to a reasonably high degree of attainment of the sought end. Of course it cannot be perfect. There is no perfect grading of tasks, no perfect meshing of graded tasks into balanced jobs, and thus no perfect "numeric" balancing. In practice this occurs as a social dynamic enacted by human beings in complex circumstances. Of course it cannot occur at the flip of a switch, or the casting of a law. Full implementation requires transformation, transition, materially and socially. But short of perfection, workers councils in an established new economy, in an established new society could certainly balance jobs in each workplace quite well, tweaking the results over time to get an ever more just pattern of work. Still, even recognizing that we could achieve this, and even assuming compatibility with the rest of the economy, there remains a problem.

Empowerment Equity

Before addressing that problem, however, we should add a clarification to avoid a possible confusion. Balancing empowerment across jobs is not the same as balancing the amount or the type of intellect required for that job. That is, if you do some highly abstract theoretical physics that only a few other people on Earth can understand, your activity is not necessarily immensely more empowering than it is for me to help decide how we can best build automobiles, or for a chef at a restaurant to decide how to best cook a meal. If it were simply a question of intellect, then arguably no amount of balancing is going to get me and a new Stephen Hawking equalized. Thinking about unified fields requires too much intellect to balance. But when we are talking about empowerment, there are empowering tasks in all kinds of workplaces, including those that involve figuring out how to best do other jobs, how to best satisfy consumers, how to plan for the future, discussing such matters, making proposals about such matters, and in any case, thinking about elementary particles or cosmic black holes may not turn out to be all that socially empowering.

In balancing job complexes within each workplace for equal empowerment, the goal is to prevent the assignment of tasks from preparing some workers significantly better than others to participate in decision-making at that workplace. But balancing job complexes within workplaces does not guarantee that work life will be equally empowering across workplaces. To return to our simplified characterization, one workplace could average out at 7, another at 14, or even at 3 and 18. In such cases, those in the more empowering industries would be far better able to manifest their preferences throughout the broader economy. Indeed, over time, they could further polarize workplaces in the economy, with a subset of workplaces housing all the most empowering jobs and with the least empowering work ghettoized off into disempowering and menial workplaces—where the former oversee and rule the latter. Since this is obviously not our aim, we deduce that establishing conditions for a truly participatory and equitable economy will likely require cross workplace balancing in addition to balancing within each workplace.

The only way I can see to balance for empowerment across workplaces is to have people spend some time outside their primary workplace offsetting advantages or disadvantages that its average may have compared to the overall societal average. Using the simple model again, if you work in a coal mine that is a 4, and society is a 7, so to speak, you get to work considerable time outside the mine in another venue, raising your average to 7. If you work in a research facility that is a 13 in a society whose average is a 7, you would have to work outside that facility a considerable chunk of each week at rather onerous tasks to get down to the overall average of 7.

How might a participatory economy actually calibrate these balances? For that matter, how might people wind up in a particular workplace in the first place? Though any full answer requires a more developed picture of a participatory economy, including its means of allocation, and though no more complete answer would be unique in any event as we can't know all the approaches that might emerge from future experiences, and though in any event it is for future experimentation and preferences to decide between worthy options, likely differently in different situations, we cannot reasonably go further regarding job complexes without providing at least some clarification.

In a participatory economy, everyone will presumably have the right to apply for work wherever they choose (and presumably have education and home-life suitable for work they choose), and every workers council will presumably have the right to add any members they wish (using appropriate decision-making methods, of course). We have no choice but to wait until after describing participatory allocation to consider when and why workers councils would wish to add or release members, but for now it is sufficient to know that once the economy has a work plan for a coming period, each workers council may have a list of openings for which anyone can freely apply. So any worker could apply for any opening and move to a new workers council that wants them should they prefer it to their present council. In this respect, participatory job changing will presumably be superficially like changing jobs in a typical capitalist economy. But while the situation looks somewhat like a traditional labor market, it would be different.

First, in a traditional labor market, people generally change employment to win higher pay or to enjoy working conditions generally considered more desirable, not solely conditions they themselves prefer. But since the economy we propose would balance jobs across as well as within workplaces, and since it would remunerate effort and sacrifice but not output much less bargaining power (as we will soon describe), people will be unable to attain these traditional goals by changing workplaces. Instead, everyone will always have typical job and typical income conditions, and thus also an instance of the best available income and job conditions. On the other hand, if a person would prefer a different group of workmates, or working at a different combination of tasks due to his or her personal priorities and interests, of course she or he might have a very good reason to apply for a new job, perhaps even at a new workplace. In fact, to the extent that job complexes are balanced and pay is for effort and sacrifice, such personal reasons will be the only motives to move. Conversely, people's freedom to move to other workplaces will provide a check on the effectiveness of balancing job complexes across workplaces. Higher pay will not be available by changing jobs, nor will objectively better work conditions.

Just as workers must balance jobs internally in each workplace through a flexible discussion process (whose exact character could vary from workplace to workplace), so might delegates of workers from different councils and industries develop a flexible rating process to balance across workplaces. As one plausible solution, there could be "job complex committees" both within each workplace and for the economy as a whole. These committees might be responsible for proposing ways to combine tasks to achieve and when necessary update balanced work complexes within workplaces. The economy-wide committees would presumably arrange for those who work in less desirable and less empowering primary workplaces some time in more desirable and more empowering environments, and vice versa. Within a workplace, it would become clear that more fine-tuning of job assignments was required when more and more or fewer and fewer members of a workers council apply for one job or another. Similarly, the need for better balancing of conditions and job complexes across workplaces becomes evident the same way; that is, through excessive (or minimal) applications to switch to one workplace or another.

It should be clear that creating perfectly balanced job complexes is theoretically abstractly conceivable. But can it be done in real-life situations? Of course not. We are not talking about pure geometry nor even the engineering of bridges. We are talking about actual people and real social arrangements. But the point is, in an established new economy it could be done quite well and with deviations and errors being only deviations and errors, not systematic biases. Over time such errors would not multiply or snowball, but would instead invite correction. More, the entire process would be collectively self-managed. There would be no elite eager or even able to bend everyone else to their will. Each person would have circumstances collectively agreed upon by procedures respecting each person's appropriate input. If people combine their informed efforts at creating balanced jobs with participation in well-designed self-managing councils, there is every reason to expect them to attain a venue favorable to non-hierarchical production relations, and able to promote equity and participation and facilitate appropriate voting patterns. Still, you might reasonably wonder, in practical real world situations, could workers really combine tasks to define balanced job complexes within and across workplaces even reasonably well, much less as well as we suggest?

Provided we understand that we are talking about a social process that never attains perfection, and that it need only fulfill workers' own sense of balance, the answer is surely yes. The idea is that workers within each workplace could engage in a collective evaluation of their own circumstances. As a participatory economy emerged from a capitalist or from a market or centrally planned socialist past, there would no doubt be extensive discussion and debate about the characteristics of different tasks. It would take time, called transition, not only to define new jobs, but to train for them. Indeed it would be a matter of demands, victories, and sometimes setbacks. But once the first approximation of balanced complexes within a transformed workplace in a transformed economy had been established, thereafter regular adjustments would be relatively simple. For example, if the introduction of a new technology dramatically changed the human impact of some tasks, thereby throwing old jobs out of balance, workers might simply move some responsibilities within and across affected complexes to re-establish a desirable balance, or they might change the time spent at different tasks in affected complexes to attain a new balance.

A new balance need not and could not ever be perfect, just as prior old balances weren't perfect, nor would adjustments be instantaneous, nor would everyone be likely to agree completely with every result of a council-based determination of job composition, even in a well-established new economy, much less early on the road toward it. Individual preferences that deviate from one's workmates' preferences would presumably determine who would choose to apply for which balanced job. Most obvious, if I am less bothered by noise but more bothered by dust, I would no doubt prefer a job whose rote component required dealing with noisy machinery rather than a job with a responsibility to sweep. You might have opposite inclinations.

In practice, balancing between workplaces would be more complicated. How would arrangements be made for workers to have responsibilities in more than one workplace? Over time, balancing across workplaces might be determined partly through a growing familiarity with the social relations of production, partly as a result of evaluations by specific committees whose job includes rating job complexes in different plants and industries, and partly as a result of the pattern of movement of workers. That all this would be possible within some acceptable range of error and dissent ought to be pretty obvious once we realize that we aren't talking about instant corrections, or, for that matter, complete initial implementation all in one quick leap, or ever attaining some perfect result.

Basically, presumably, participatory economic job complexes would be organized so that every individual would be regularly involved in both conception and execution tasks, with comparable empowerment circumstances for all. The precision of the balance would depend on many factors, and would likely improve over time. The mechanical notion of numeric ratings of tasks would, I suspect, virtually never occur. Instead workers would discuss the characteristics of different tasks, different jobs, and come up with compromises and mixtures seeking a balance sufficiently accurate to fulfill the overarching aim. And that aim, at the heart of the proposal, would be the advisory that no set of individuals should permanently occupy positions that present them with unusual opportunities to accumulate excessive decision-making say. Every individual should instead occupy a position that guarantees him or her an appropriate amount of empowering tasks. In essence, by being careful about what tasks are grouped together into jobs, the empowerment costs and benefits of work would be equitably distributed. Corporate organization would disappear. Council organization plus balanced job complexes would prevail. The potential questions that would remain are whether—in concert with other essential innovations of a new participatory economy—balanced job complexes would have as much positive impact for solidarity, equity, diversity, and self-management as we seek, whether they would permit effective utilization of talents and resources to produce desired output, and also whether they would have undesirable effects that would outweigh their benefits.

Is This for Real?

If Margaret Thatcher, British Prime Minister of neoliberal pain, was still around at this point she would bellow: "Get serious! Of course this idiot proposal would have horrible effects. Doctors should clean bed pans? Managers should assemble products? Engineers should tote dirt? Are you insane? You have made your proposal clear alright. Clear that its losses would be enormous. Your alternative would be no alternative at all. It would so drastically diminish output as to negate any other modest gains. This is nonsense onstilts."

Mr. Moneybags would gleefully, aggressively shout agreement. Many doctors, lawyers, and other coordinator class members would concur, though one hopes less gleefully and aggressively. Even some and perhaps many workers, at least nowadays, would echo the sentiment.

Are our resurrected Thatcher and her various comrades correct? The first thing to note is that ending class hierarchy would be no modest gain. It would be enormous. But let's set that aside for a minute. If we balance jobs, will we suffer serious losses at all, much less losses greater than the gains?

Consider a hospital. If we compare one that has corporate organization to the same one that would have balanced job complexes (even if we ignore having eliminated in the latter the conflicts, tensions, and waste that ensues from class hierarchy) what do we see? Thatcher sees the people who were surgeons doing some rote tasks. She calculates the loss of their life-saving efforts and deduces, "We have lost 30 percent or maybe 40 percent, whatever, of their creative contributions to health. That is abysmal." And she asks a new economy advocate, "What are you saying about this obvious truth? You seriously want me to believe that from among people who before were cleaning rooms we will enjoy enough newly emerging quality surgery to make up for that decline? That is lunacy."

Thatcher has pinpointed the underlying issue. In a corporate arrangement 20 percent do empowered tasks, 80 percent do not. Thatcher's claim is that losing some part of the undeniably life saving contributions of the 20 percent is an unacceptable price to pay. My contrary claim is that among the 80 percent there resides more than enough untapped capacity to do much more than what the 20 percent, after job balancing, would no longer do. Their new contributions would more than make up the loss due to balancing all jobs. Who is right?

Consider 50 years ago. Overwhelmingly only white men were surgeons. Women, Blacks, Latinx, and so on were not. Of course, most who were not surgeons among women, Blacks, and Latinx (and also for that matter among white men) would under no circumstances become surgeons in a new economy. They would lack relevant capacities or inclinations. But history has already shown, for those too racist or sexist to have earlier seen what was always obvious, that what we might call the surgeon-potential among Blacks, Latinx, and women was earlier depressed by social subjugation, not by innate deficiency. Similarly, the participatory claim isn't that the 80 percent under capitalism will, with balanced jobs, all do brain surgery. It is that among the 80 percent, with full training, enriching life circumstances, and full empowerment and freedom, over time there will emerge enough surgical talent and inclination to make up for the 20 percent from earlier who already had those talents and inclinations newly having to do balanced jobs—and also enough talent and inclination to simultaneously make up all other coordinator tasks as well. Just as women, Blacks, and Latinx constituencies now generate ample talent and inclination for empowered jobs, so too for the 80 percent working class. The claim is that the 80 percent don't now lack innate capacity for doing a balanced job with some doing some surgery and some doing some other empowering work, but that their on-the-job circumstances in corporate jobs as well as in (also class-defined) prior home and school circumstances and training literally suppresses and even obliterates those innate capacities and inclinations.

Thatcher is resilient. She rallies. "But even if that's true," she urges, "think how much more of society's capacity would have to go to training more doctors, more lawyers, more scientists, and all the rest. It is a grotesque waste. Inefficient. Inefficient."

If I was answering in person, I have to admit that at this point I would have to struggle hard to not exude outrage and disdain, but to instead merely answer—"Yes, you are right, exactly so. [Oh, okay, so I would partly lose my self-control battle and inject a bit of sarcasm.] Just think of it. Society would have to spend considerable time and resources to develop the full capacities and inclinations of 80 percent who would otherwise be relegated to subordination. What a horrible pursuit. What a gross outrage. Instead of home life, education, and on-the-job circumstances preparing four-fifths of the population to only endure boredom and take orders, their capacities having been stifled, their inclinations crushed—in this new abominable situation that you label 'inefficient,' home-life, education, and on-the-job circumstances would liberate all."

To Thatcher's eyes and sadly not only to her eyes, in a last ditch attempt to reject balanced jobs, increased education, and improved circumstances for 80 percent of the population, she deems such a change a damnable cost and not a magnificent benefit. It is quite like a racist or a sexist claiming that liberating women, Blacks, and Latinx sectors of the population to nurture their potentials is a damnable cost, not a wonderful benefit. What is depressing and infuriating is that nowadays so many so reflexively accept these kinds of assumptions and the ensuing subjugation for working people, just as 50 years ago (and, sadly, sometimes still) so many accepted similarly antisocial claims about women, Blacks, and Latinx people.

Liberating 80 percent will not sacrifice output for an abstract aim. It will instead finally overcome an abstract imposition that has for so long curbed potentials in most and corrupted potentials in the rest. To institute job balancing for empowerment would not only remove the basis of coordinator domination of workers but would also hugely expand productive and creative potentials. It would advance conditions of equity, solidarity, and self-management for all.

We All Do Balanced Jobs

Who does what is no small matter. Want class rule? Maintain the corporate division of labor. Want classlessness? Balance jobs for empowerment. Which do we choose?

Since we want classlessness and not coordinator rule, we propose balancing jobs for empowerment as our third essential feature of a worthy new economy. This provides future citizens a context in which they can freely discover and implement their own desires.

But choice raises a question. How do we link workers here and there to consumers here and there, and vice versa, without un-doing balanced jobs, without subverting self-management, and without reimposing class division? A first step to that end, leading toward considering allocation writ large, is to next consider what we should do about income.

5

Who Earns What?

Everybody knows the dice are loaded…Everybody knows the fight was fixed The poor stay poor, the rich get rich
Leonard Cohen

Will the people in the cheap seats clap? And the rest of you, if you'll just rattle your jewelry
John Lennon

Imagine you are a student at a university. Custodians strike for higher wages. You support the strike. Or imagine you are a parent at a grade school. The teachers strike for better wages. You support the strike. Either way, a friend asks you, "Okay, me too, but how much should they earn? How much should anyone earn, whether a custodian, a teacher, or whatever?"

If the strike's aim is to win an immediate gain but also to prepare to win more gains so each limited gain paves a road toward winning a better economy and society, your friend's question moves beyond curiosity to priority.

Equitable Income

Suppose we call the total goods and services that any society produces society's pie. We feel that society's pie ought to be fairly divided among society's members. But what's fair? One way to distribute income in a new economy would say people ought to get more of the pie if they own property that contributes to the worth of the pie. If a deed stipulates that I own Amazon, then, I should get profits back as part of my income. Even if Jeff Bezos of Amazon just sits in a chair waving his deed, he should get as much income each workday as someone packing and moving boxes for him earns in 1000 years.

Yes, you read that right. If Bezos receives $12 billion in profits next year—which is not impossible and is only a fraction of what he accumulated in 2020—then he will earn about $50 million per workday. If Samantha, working for Jeff Bezos at a mid-level Amazon job, earns $50,000 a year, it will take her 1000 years to earn what Bezos earns in one day. As I calculate that and write it down, like you, I have trouble believing it but that doesn't deny the obvious. It is true.

If there is one thing nearly all anti-capitalists agree on, it is that property-based income propels property owners to lordlike dominion over workplaces and over virtually all of social life. Property-based income causes ceaseless class conflict over property-induced differences in wealth and power. It demolishes diversity by homogenizing each contending class. It subverts sustainability by giving centralized power an interest in exploiting nature to ceaselessly accumulate profits.

Property-based income also conveys to the rich power to direct national policies to favor their further enrichment, which in turn increases their power to further enlarge a perpetually expanding gap between themselves and the rest. Having passed the tipping point of insane inequality that leads to even more insane inequality, we now graphically see the doom that property-based income imposes. Particularly in the US, it is an accelerating slip-slide to hell.

For all those reasons, to eliminate property-based income a second income option we might opt for in a new economy is that people ought to get more income if they are strong enough to take more. They ought to get less income if they are sufficiently weak to be given less. If I can take more, great, I will. If you can't take more, too bad, you won't.

Now it may seem like this thuggish approach to distributing income is too ethically and socially odious for anyone to advocate. In fact, however, this is how markets largely operate.

And it happens day in and day out all around us.

With markets, if you have bargaining power based on property, based on a monopoly over information or skills, based on a bought-off government agency, based on a powerful professional organization, based on being male in a male dominated society, based on being white in a white dominated society, or, for that matter, based on having a good union, then you can take more than those lacking your source of power.

In contrast, if you have less bargaining power than others because, for example, your society is racist and you are in a racially subordinated constituency, or your society is misogynist and you are female, or because you are isolated and easily replaceable at work, then you get less income.

An interviewer once asked Al Capone, the famous American criminal, what do you think about America. Capone answered, "I love America, in America you get what you can take." Getting income for power was Al Capone's vision of bliss. The thuggish norm validates the aphorism that "nice guys finish last"—except for nice gals who likely finish last-er. No doubt Capone, not known for being nice, had good reason to like the idea of a thug's economy, but presumably you agree that a power-based option to distributing income would obliterate our favored values and that we should therefore keep looking for something appropriate for what we want for a better economy.

Next comes an option that many who say they are socialist support. People should receive back from society's pie a bundle of preferred items whose total value reflects the total value of what they contributed by their labor to society's pie.

If you and I pick cotton and you pick more each day, you should get that much more income than I get each day. And likewise if we tend patients, play music, wash dishes, play basketball, or whatever else—if you contribute more to society's pie, you should get more income in that same proportion.

After all, says the advocate of remuneration for personal

output, if you get less than what your work generated, someone else will get some of the value that you generated and that will be unfair. Likewise, if you get more than your work generated, you will get some value that someone else generated and that too will be unfair. To be fair, we should each get back for our labors income equal in value to the amount that we, by our labors, contributed to the total social product, and not more or less than that. Okay, the advocate acknowledges that there is a caveat. Some of society's pie should go to investment. Some should go to support free medical care. But after those and other similar allocations, what we get back should be proportionate to our personal contribution. It seems valid, but is it really? Would remunerating personal output yield the fair distribution of burdens and benefits that we want in a good economy? To answer that, we have to ask what might enable you to produce more worth than I produce over the same period of time?

You may be better equipped for the work. Maybe you are stronger, quicker, or better able to reason. Or you may have a plow and I only have a hoe. Or you may have a computer and I only have pencil and paper. Or maybe you have workmates who better enhance your ability to produce because they are more capable than my workmates are. Or, finally, maybe you surgically produce brain repairs whereas I manually produce car repairs. Maybe you make gourmet meals, whereas I sling hash. In each of these many cases, if we say people should get income in proportion to the value of what they contribute to society's pie, you would get more income than I would. But should you? Is it ethically warranted? Is it economically wise?

Why should your more productive inborn genetic characteristics—greater strength, beautiful singing voice, greater speed, amazing memory, or better reflexes, or your more productive work tools or more effective workmates, or even the fact that you produce a more valuable output, ethically entitle you to more income?

In none of these cases would giving you extra income reward some activity of yours, but, instead, it would reward only your luck in the genetic, equipment, workmate, or assigned product lottery.

In other words, suppose you are born with Adele's voice, Ronaldo's athleticism, or Chomsky's mind. You have been fantastically lucky in the genetic lottery. Should we then shower you with wealth on top of that good fortune? Doing so calls itself meritocracy, but is it?

Suppose you use a great tool that others don't yet have. Should that entitle you to more pay? Should we shower you with wealth because you were lucky in the tool lottery?

Is rewarding luck fair? Or does rewarding luck subvert fairness and our other values similarly to how rewarding property or bargaining power subverts them?

I should perhaps note at this point that a key thing about values is that they are not true or false. I can't advocate a value on grounds that I can prove it is true. Likewise, I cannot reject a value on grounds I can prove it is false. No one can prove any such thing about a value.

Instead, to choose among values and norms, the distinction has to be that I like what fulfilling one value leads to for society and I don't like what fulfilling another value leads to. This was true for our earlier choice to favor equity, self-management, solidarity, diversity, sustainability, internationalism, and participation, all of which we found likable. As we proceed we also need to find likable whatever refinements of those values we settle on to further guide our approach to organizing particular aspects of social life, and in the case of this book, to organizing mainly economics.

So, do we think an economy will be better if it rewards a person for their luck in inheriting traits like strength, speed, and smarts? Should exceptional ball players, singers, calculators, and what have you earn high income for special abilities?

If you think the answer is yes, as any advocate of giving people income for the value of their contribution to society's pie has to think, then be aware that top athletes who now sign contracts for as much as $40 million dollars a season are actually getting less than the value that they add to the enjoyment of people watching them. They get less? Yes, because much is taken by team owners, TV stations, shoe manufacturers, and the like who have sufficient bargaining power to do so. But let's consider a less extreme example.

Two farm workers go out in the field and work under the same sun, for the same duration, using the same tools. One is 6 foot 4 and really strong. The other is 5 foot 9 and of average strength. They both produce valuable output, but the bigger, stronger farmhand produces twice as much.

Do we then feel it is morally desirable to pay the stronger farmhand twice what we pay the weaker one? Might it be better if the workers get income according to a different norm? Is piling wealth on top of lucky genetic endowment ethically sound? Likewise, should we reward people for luck in the equipment lottery? I have better tools at my disposal than you. Should my hourly income be more in the same proportion that my tools let me produce more? Is society better if we reward luck in being with a more talented team of co-workers, or in being assigned to produce objects of greater value?

Socialists of virtually every denomination don't like rewarding property or bargaining power, but many socialists do favor rewarding personal output, at least until someone points out the full implications of doing so. In any event, we propose, instead, that a worthy economic vision should give income for how long one works, for how hard one works, and for the onerousness of the conditions under which one works as long as one is producing something that is socially valued.

With this approach, an average income would roughly equal payment for a workload of average duration, intensity, and onerousness. If I want more leisure than average, I should arrange to work less hours and get commensurately less income. And the same goes for the intensity of my work or its onerousness, where this onerousness, however, is limited in how much it might vary by the fact that we all have balanced job complexes, as indicated last chapter.

People claim capitalism is a meritocracy. They mean people earn its rewards fairly. But what that means depends on how we define fair. If fair means based on duration, intensity, and onerousness of socially-valued work, then anything one gets for some other reason—for example, for having property, for being powerful, or for having innate talents—is not fair. A meritocracy, in that case, would be an economy that rewards people for our proposed reasons, and not for property, power, or output.

It may help to look at this another way. Imagine we live in the old west and there is a lot of land to distribute. Boss Bonanza has everyone line up at some starting line and race to lay claim to parcels. Those who move fastest will get the best parcel. Those who arrive last will get the worst. Fast horse, better parcel. Better route, better parcel. Is that a meritocracy?

Too much luck you might reply. Too much horse. Okay, suppose we handicap the race. We somehow make all the horses the same speed. Everyone has to travel the same path. People take off. Is that a meritocracy?

What is interesting to note is that in the first case and also in the handicapped case, there are much better parcels, average parcels, and much worse parcels. The parcels wind up in the hands of different folks according to their time of arrival, but depending on the parcels the difference in reward can be huge even for minor differences in speed getting to the parcels.

It turns out even if you make the race itself fair, you will still get inequality—perhaps horribly vicious inequality—if rewards are excessively unequal. We conclude that a worthy meritocracy should have two aspects. Everyone should "race fairly." But also, outcomes should be sensibly equitable. It turns out what we propose, and not what people endure in a market system, is a worthy meritocracy. With our proposal you get more income if you merit it based on your outlay of effort. Fair race. But in our approach, the extra income you get matches the sacrifice of time, intensity, or circumstance that you suffer. Fair outcomes.

Still another way to look at our equity proposal is that each worker gets a work assignment plus an accompanying income. Equity says we should ensure that the sum of the debits and the benefits of one's work and of one's income taken together are comparable for everyone. If I work harder, or I work longer, or I work under more onerous conditions, the greater loss that I endure due to my particular efforts should be offset by my getting more income for my particular efforts.

But we still have a problem. Consider Donald. He gets that working longer, harder, and under more onerous conditions is reason for him to receive higher pay. So, Donald goes into his backyard, turns on a hose aimed at himself, and furiously digs holes and then fills them. Donald does this for hours on end. He endures a long workday, high intensity labor, and onerous conditions. He expects high pay.

Or consider Margaret. She gets that working longer, harder, and under more onerous conditions is cause for receiving more pay. So she decides to play tennis many hours, with great energy, and under a hot sun. She is not very good at tennis, but she is intent at it. She expects high pay.

It seems our norm has a loophole. "Yes! It does! Dump the whole vision now," screams a detractor. But no, we have simply not taken into account the full norm. Donald and Margaret have ignored the phrase at the end that remuneration is not just for working longer, harder, and under more onerous conditions, but that remuneration is for doing so to create socially valued product. Donald can't get paid to dig and fill holes. Margaret can't get paid for work she cannot do well enough for her effort to be socially valued.

This actually harks back to the idea of the Commons offered when talking about productive assets. There is a natural, a produced, and also what we might call a human commons in society. That is, there are resources given by natural history, there are technologies and infrastructure given by past human production, and there is also an accumulation of skills, knowledge, and talents held by humans. When such factors are employed intelligently and effectively in production and are not squandered on useless undertakings or used in a manner that is less beneficial than other ways they could be used, or literally squashed out of existence, our society benefits.

Working to produce something no one benefits from or using resources, tools, and skills in ways inferior to how they could be used is wasteful. It does not contribute to the social pie. It is not or perhaps more accurately it should not be socially valued. And less obviously, but for the same reasons, working at something ineffectually also fails to produce what people value for some of your duration of work time. So the full advisory or norm is that the economy should remunerate for the duration, intensity, and onerousness of socially-valued work. Notice, to answer what determines what counts as socially-valued work has to wait as the answer depends on the economy's method of allocation, a subject taken up in our next two chapters. What we know, however, is that the answer needs to be true to the values and other features of our emerging economic vision.

The participatory equity claim is that if workplaces (and allocation beyond workplaces) can enact this approach to income distribution then remuneration will be economically fair, as well as highly consistent with the other values we favor. However, even if we agree that this would be true, it would do no good to propose a formally fair approach that, however, would be either unimplementable or if implemented would leave everyone impoverished due to generating insufficient production.

So we must ask, can equitable remuneration of what we might call a workplace's overall "payroll" among all its workers even be arranged? And if it can be, what institutional steps would it require? And if we were to organize an economy to remunerate in the proposed fashion, would there be negative implications so severe that they would offset the ethical and other gains of the approach?

The Measurement Problem

The claim that equitable remuneration makes ethical sense but could not be successfully implemented arises from a belief that it would be too difficult to measure duration, intensity, and onerousness of each person's work or too difficult to know if a person's work was properly socially valuable. Or it arises from a belief that to make such determinations would, even if possible, require some kind of authoritarian, judgmental approach that would violate solidarity and self-management.

First, workers presumably wouldn't be welcome to change their own involvement in workplace activity willy nilly, simply on their own choice. If I wanted to work longer hours, perhaps because I want more income for some special purchase, I couldn't unilaterally just stay late every day and do extra work since that would leave less work for others. I would have to get collective agreement from my workmates who would be affected. The same goes for piling up intensity and onerousness points.

In any event, let's call the amount a worker earns for working at an average intensity at a job with average onerousness for an average duration, the average or basic income. Then each actual worker would earn either the basic income or some higher amount due to having worked longer or more intensely or under worse conditions, or some lower amount due to having worked fewer hours or at lower intensity or at a job that had above average quality of life effects.

I assume we can agree that counting the hours a person works would be easy, even if it wasn't the case that one would have to arrange in advance for any significant variation in hours. Likewise, instances of significant difference in job onerousness would be modest, though perhaps this would arise with dealing with crises that arise. More difficult, it might seem, would be measuring intensity. We must first note that the precise methodology for allotting income inside workplaces among their workforce need not be the same from workplace to workplace. Adherence to the norm is what would be universal, not a particular specific approach to the nuts and bolts of its implementation, which would be collectively self-managed, as with other choices and perhaps different for different workplaces, or even for different work teams in one large workplace. That said, to demonstrate feasibility, here is one possible general approach that some workplaces might opt for.

Each worker receives a kind of "evaluation report" from their team or perhaps from their whole workplace or from just a committee established for the purpose where the report indicates the income they should receive to be used for consumption expenditures. This evaluation report might, for example, indicate hours worked, intensity of work, and onerousness of conditions, yielding an overall "effort rating" in the form of a percentage multiplier. If the rating was one, the person's remuneration would be the social average for the workplace. If the rating was 1.1, it would be a tenth more, if it was 0.9, it would be a tenth less. What would explain a person getting higher or lower remuneration is the person having worked productively more or less hours or at a higher or lower intensity of effort or onerousness.

But who would judge these differences, and by what form of evaluation? This might well be a zone of variation from workplace to workplace. One workplace might opt to have a highly precise numeric rating system where people are graded to one or even two decimal places above or below average. Another workplace might less precisely and I think more realistically and desirably designate "above average," "average," or "below average," with the designation meaning average income, or a tenth above or a tenth below with the options, maybe three as stated here, or five, say, having been agreed by the workers council of the workplace to be the only variations permitted without special needs.

If those two approaches, more and less precise, did exist in an economy, which would you prefer for your workplace? Given that everyone is doing well in any event, that we have balanced jobs, and so on, I have to say I think I would prefer the looser to the tighter option. At any rate, the judgment might be made by a workplace committee (all members of which, of course, have balanced job complexes) or in a small or modest sized workplace, instead by a vote of whole councils, or by whatever other means each workplace opted for. For those wondering, quite reasonably, what prevents a whole workplace from exaggerating their effort so that everyone receives more than they deserve, regrettably the full picture of the overall system in action depends on all institutions and their interactions. Regarding that particular concern, for example, the means of allocation in our new economy is an essential factor, so the question must wait just a bit, but the key idea is to remember the proviso that to be remunerated work has to be socially-valued. So the workplace in question, as a whole, earns a total income for its whole workforce in accord with its socially-valued output in light of its productive assets and workforce, which overall "payroll" is then internally apportioned to its members by way of their judgments about their relative efforts and sacrifices. The internal evaluation only impacts how the workplace's overall allotment is divided among its members. The overall allotment which we can call the total payroll the workplace's workforce earns to then be apportioned among those workers, is determined by the economy's allocation system. The within-each-workplace step is our current focus. The overall allotment to each particular workplace becomes a focus when we turn our attention to proposing a new means of allocation for our proposed new economy.

Another choice that might be prevalent for some workplace's internal apportionment of payments could be for a workplace to assume that barring exceptional cases and prearrangements, everyone works at an average intensity level so that for the most part income will vary only with hours worked. The only exception to that, a workplace might decide, would be by petition to the council—either by a person claiming to deserve more, or by workmates who are convinced some person deserves less, each of which would, in this model, presumably occur only infrequently. Another quite different choice some workplace might prefer is to implement a much tighter rating system that would yield a significant number of employees getting various different amounts more or less than average. But the main point is that since circumstances and opinions would differ regarding the best and most accurate means to calibrate effort and how closely to do so in different workplaces, not least due to their having different jobs and conditions, different workers councils would be free to opt for different systems—the choice having significant impact on the involved workforce but virtually no effect on anyone outside. A workplace might even opt to allot some payroll to a fund for collective benefit rather than individual income. Assuming different workplaces did opt for different methods of work evaluation, workers might well make this one of the factors they consider to select a job in the first place. And most important, however different various procedures might be, they could not lead to extreme income differentials since there could only be so much variation in time worked and intensity and onerousness in any event, even if workplaces accommodate different preferences on this score.

Note that the above discussion of remuneration only describes how a workplace in a new participatory economy could conceivably remunerate its overall payroll in a just and equitable way. It does not yet argue that doing so would elicit desired quality and output of work or foster the other values we favor, or that there wouldn't be negative side effects that mitigate benefits, to be addressed next. Nor does it indicate how the total payroll of different workplaces would be equitably established, a prior step that has to be addressed after later proposing new means of allocation.

The Incentive Problem

The concern that negative effects would outweigh benefits generally arises from the belief that equitable remuneration for duration, intensity, and onerousness of socially-valued labor would not provide needed incentives to get good results. Our persistent critic Margaret Thatcher returns to point out that if workers are only paid for duration, intensity, and onerousness, then workers can't earn way higher incomes for any work they do. And, she continues, in that case people will not become, for example, surgeons, engineers, accountants, or lawyers. And her claim is almost universally accepted. If young students couldn't earn ten or more times what they could get for other pursuits, they would not become surgeons. Moreover, once in a job, not being able to earn a really high income would mean folks would not give their best. And if Thatcher's claims were true, or even partially true, it would be a problem, perhaps even a vision-destroying problem for our equity norm. Point being, Thatcher is right that it wouldn't be a big gain, or arguably any gain at all, to create an equitable society in which, however, no one was motivated to do any creative work that requires a lot of training, or for that matter, to be productive at anything. But is it true?

In reply, the proponent of remuneration for only duration, intensity, and onerousness of socially-valued labor says that with equitable remuneration the economy's incentives are just what they ought to be. Income earned for duration, intensity, and onerousness of socially-valued labor provides an incentive to work longer (but not so long that the loss of leisure outweighs the gain in income), harder (but not so hard that the losses due to exertion outweigh the gain in income), and, when need be, to complete really onerous tasks that prove necessary outside of balanced job complexes (but not when the pain due to the onerousness exceeds the benefits due to the gain in income).

In contrast, when remuneration is for property, the incentive effect is perversely to exploit others and to amass ever more property with which to exploit others ever more aggressively in the future. Likewise, when remuneration is for power, the incentive effect is for the powerful to amass more power so as to have steadily more means to accrue wealth, again in a steadily escalating spiral. When remuneration is for output, it is a mixed situation. Incentives to school oneself and become more productive have a potentially positive aspect, but that aspect is often vastly inflated beyond what is needed for the purpose. And payments for having talents—not for the training that goes into developing talents—have no useful incentive effect. I cannot change my genetic endowment due to the fact that a great singing voice or tremendous reflexes and strength are highly rewarded. How long I work, how hard I work, and my willingness to do onerous work is what I can myself decide, in part in light of income offered.

But what of Thatcher's view that we will have fair incomes if we have equitable remuneration, but we will have no doctors? If true, that would be disastrous. The reply is that while this parrots what Econ 101 tells everyone and what all of popular culture ratifies, it is nonetheless self-evidently false. Doctors now earn, let's say, $500,000 a year. The critic claims they receive their high income not because they have the bargaining power to take it, but instead because we would have no doctors if doctors earned a fair salary based on duration, intensity, and onerousness of socially-valued labor. This observation gets repeated so much and is taken for granted so prevalently, that nearly everyone comes to sincerely believe it without giving it any thought. We have to pay doctors vastly more than dishwashers because otherwise doctors would opt to wash dishes. But consider for yourself, if you could choose between a rote and repetitive job, on the one hand, say on an assembly line, and being a doctor in a hospital, or some other coordinator class job, on the other hand, which would you prefer—even without a salary difference?

Suppose you are just getting out of high school and have to decide whether to report for work on an assembly line or to go to college and then to medical school, and then be a lowly intern, before becoming a full-fledged doctor. Would you need to get ten times the income to suffer the incredible hardships of going to college instead of straight to an assembly line, and of going to medical school instead of to an assembly line, all en route to working in a hospital instead of on an assembly line (not to mention that the schooling/training would be free, in fact that it would earn an income in our proposed equitable system)? To ask the question is to answer it—but no one ever asks because every message in media from cradle to grave tells us not to think carefully about such matters. You may still not see it. Okay, you are facing the choice. Go to college to become a doctor or engineer, or whatever, for $500,000 a year. Or go directly into a rote job for $50,000 a year. Now imagine I start to lower your likely doctor salary. How low do I have to reduce it so you will reject becoming a doctor, or whatever other coordinator level job, and take the rote job? $400,000? Will you switch now? How about $300,000? $100,000? $50,000? Or will your reply be like that of every student group, including those who are pre-med, I have posed this too. Which is to say, as the rate dropped, before answering would you pause and ask how low an income you could survive on as you would only switch if survival was in question?

Some other concerns about equitable remuneration exist. The first goes like this. I work very hard but I don't think I should receive extra income for it. In fact, I find the prospect of getting extra pay for my hard work degrading. I work because it is a part of being a full and worthy person. I don't want to sully that motivation with remuneration for the effort that I give because I want to give it. Well, that's actually not a problem. You needn't take all payment you are entitled to. There is no reason lurking in this possibility, supposing it even exists, to want to disallow others from doing more labor to earn a bit more in order to get something valuable that they want.

Will people refuse remuneration in the suggested manner? We can only guess, but in a participatory economy where everyone will earn average and then a bit more or a bit less due to contributing above or below average exertion or duration, the (very rare) person who offers the above complaint about not wanting more pay for longer hours in our current society is typically someone making way above average rates of payment who doesn't feel right getting still more for work they eagerly do. Were their base income to become like everyone else's base income, and were they to have a balanced job complex like everyone else, it is quite plausible that they and their family's view of what they deserve for extra effort would alter—though, again, it would be no problem if it didn't.

A second confusion is more subtle. If you can earn more for working longer, or for working harder, or for working at more onerous tasks, the critic says—you have a reason to do all those things. As a result there will be a drift toward a longer work day, toward more intense labor, and toward worse working conditions. This is a perverse incentive, says the critic. We will wind up with too long work days, too harsh work conditions, and too intense job conditions. Is this true?

In an established participatory economy we all have balanced job complexes, comparable status and influence, and, let's say we also, at time zero, have equal incomes because we all work the same average work week. With our average income we get an average share of the total social product (after some goes to free goods, investment, and income for those who cannot work).

Now suppose all of us want more stuff than the current average. Is that conceivable? Yes, I suppose it is, and if it was the case, we would need to produce more stuff, which means we would need to work longer, or harder, or perhaps at some additional sufficiently productive tasks that were quite onerous. But this result, if it were to occur, would not be perverse. If we all want more product, as a whole tendency/desire of the broad population, then a good allocation system, as we will soon see, would let us know the human, social, and ecological costs, and if we still wanted more, even taking those into account, and despite having to work longer to generate it, so be it.

Now, is it likely we will all want more? The predictable truth is likely the opposite, and this is actually the one criticism of this type of remuneration system leveled by mainstream economists who understand the issue. With our new approach such economists point out, people are highly likely to want more leisure (just as people now do) rather than more stuff—and there is nothing in the proposed new economic arrangement, the economists add—unlike capitalism's drive to accumulate—that would prevent the new economy's workers from deciding to enjoy relatively more leisure by working less, which would in turn cause total output to drop. We can see this is highly likely even without taking into account what will be accurate considerations of ecological impact and even ignoring the impact of near equalization of shares of the product, and of revamping the product to not squander gigantic productive capacity on weapons and other antisocial products, and of having sensible, durable collective goods, and of having no pernicious status effects of consumption, and of having enlarged non consumption means to fulfillment.

But what about a particular individual? Could I work longer, or harder, or perhaps even doing some extra onerous tasks, to get more income? Yes. In the approach we are proposing I could do so. Is there anything morally or economically wrong with that? No. The extra income would be warranted by my actions and if properly agreed and organized would have no ill effects on anyone else's situation. Would having this option mean I would drive myself to dissolution in a mad pursuit of additional income? Of course not. Would it mean I could work as long or as hard as I want at tasks I choose without anyone else having any influence? No, because my choices have to mesh compatibly with other people's choices.

At this point, another realm of issues arises. What about the whole workplace's motivations? What about its incentives? Do whole workplaces want to sell as much as possible? Do they use false and tricky advertising to do so? Do whole workplaces want to cut costs as best they can? Do they turn off air conditioning, allow fumes, work faster, to do so? Do whole organizations adopt the mantra, "accumulate accumulate, that is Moses and the Prophets"? Do they have an incentive to spew pollution on outside actors? Rather than answer all this partially now, and then more when we discuss allocation, we will leave it entirely for discussion of allocation when we can answer more fully except to now say the obvious. To avoid these perverse, very familiar possibilities, a new economy, unlike existing ones, will have to have an allocation system that properly accounts for personal, social, and environmental impacts of economic choices and that doesn't set up any actors with power to benefit from perverse choices in these matters.

The Anarchist Objection

Another set of critics of remuneration for duration, intensity, and onerousness of socially-valued labor, this time from the left, don't see the need for remuneration norms and methods at all. They don't actually think about a preferred remunerative norm. They feel there is no need to do so because they prefer to entirely avoid the hassle of tracking values, times, durations, or whatever. To that end, they say that in a good economy we should each work to our abilities and each receive for our needs—and that's it.

That is, they urge that even if equitable remuneration isn't horribly flawed, and indeed even if it is sound and moral, it is unnecessary and less than optimal. This type of critic says the norm "from each according to ability, to each according to need" is better. Less hassle. Better results. So is this the case, or is the "from each to each" norm flawed?

The "from each to each" norm is long enshrined in a few different political heritages as the height of radical, socialistic, anarchistic wisdom and desire. But what does the phrase actually mean? If we go beyond the slogan, beyond its worthy emotional mutually respectful connotations to its actual substance, what do we find? Well, there are a few possibilities, though they are rarely, if ever, fully described by the view's advocates.

Suppose I am working in a system operating under the "from each to each" norm. How long will I work next week? If I "work to my ability," odds are that I could manage to work 60 hours at a balanced job complex or even 70, 80, or more. Should I do that? Is that what working to my ability means? And should I work as hard as my ability permits as well?

It is incredibly unlikely that any advocate of this norm, much less those concerned about people overworking, has in mind the above literal meaning. But what else might the norm mean?

It could mean that I should work up to what someone else says is my ability. But again, surely no "from each to each" advocate favors that kind of authoritarian interpretation.

It could mean, instead, that I should work the average amount and intensity for society unless I feel able and willing to work somewhat more or feel I should work somewhat less. But then, on what basis do I arrive at such conclusions? If the only issue is the effect of the work on me, I will likely wind up working less than I would otherwise have done. If the only basis or even part of the basis is the effect on others, then I need to have some way of sensibly gauging those effects. How do I do that? We will return to that question in a moment.

Now what about consumption? With "from each to each" operating, I have to determine what I wish to have from the social product. According to the norm, if I take the words literally, I should pay no attention to anyone else's situation and no attention to my level of work, and instead, I should just consider my needs. I ask myself—not someone else, since to ask someone else would convey absurd authority to that other person—what do I need?

One interpretation of needs is that I need what I physically need to survive. This would mean everyone would survive on bread, water, and vitamin pills—hardly an attractive prospect. Alternatively, my needs might be taken to mean whatever I would like to have. And that would literally mean, as best I can see, that I should ask myself what do I like, and take that.

Well, I can't believe any "from each to each advocate" actually favors that. Even if we ignore the (and it is often the same) critic who, just minutes ago thought that if we remunerated for duration, intensity, and onerousness of socially-valued labor, the hunger for consumption goods would be so great that people would press on to longer and longer hours and higher and higher intensity, anyone being even a little consistent would surely have to agree that told they can have whatever they ask for, a person will want a lot more than is good for the overall society and a lot more than everyone can have. Why not?

The person thinks everyone else can have what they want, too. If nothing says having less is better and my desires say having more is better, I would be masochistic to not take more, more, more.

All right, let's ignore the two extreme understandings of consumption according to need. Suppose the norm means, instead, as I assume it must for those who favor it, that each consumer should use his or her best judgment to consume the social average, and then to consume somewhat more or somewhat less based on whether they have seriously pressing additional needs or not. We should each restrain ourselves, presumably, out of a social impulse. I do wonder why it is okay to assume not only that everyone will try to do this, automatically, and will succeed—but even if we assume we all desire to be responsible, how will we each know how much is appropriate to take?

This is essentially the same information problem the worker had. Whether the issue is a worker setting his or her level of work responsibly, or a consumer setting his or her level of consumption responsibly, being responsible requires knowing what is average, and then knowing whether one has legitimate grounds to deviate from average.

Here is the crux of it. First, by assuming there is a known earlier average we are assuming that in the past people have functioned with this norm and arrived at something sensible as an average. But there is no reason to assume that unless we say how it happened. Second, the "from each to each" advocate clearly wants people to engage in some kind of social exchange that provides them with information enabling them to settle on responsible levels of work and consumption. This is what it means to say people will act responsibly. They will have information and will act responsibly in light of it—though there is no pressure to do so. The irony is that that is precisely the type of information and setting that our new economy is conceived to convey. Our proposals provide, as we will see once we discuss allocation, a collective process of exchanging statements of desire about both work and consumption, personal and collective, where one learns what is socially warranted and what isn't, and one settles on socially desirable and warranted choices in order to be able to proceed.

The only thing the "from each to each" advocate who wants people to freely arrive at their own agreed levels of work and consumption could reasonably take issue with would be whether or not the information conveyed by participatory planning is the best that it can be, and whether trying to arrive at responsible choices and succeeding with a norm and institutions geared to helping one do so, is worse than trying to arrive at responsible choices and failing, due to lacking a norm and institutions able to help and to prevent violations.

Think about a busy intersection. We want every driver to navigate it making responsible choices about when to proceed and when to wait. If we just have people drive to it and look around as best they can and do as they will, not only will traffic be a mess but every so often there will be a crash even if people only have honorable intentions. Now consider we try to improve things with a stoplight system—go on green, stop on red. Someone might complain that the system is authoritarian because it constrains behavior. One might answer, the goal is for people at intersections to get through without crashing and with a relative minimum of disruption of a steady flow of traffic, and that that is what the light system facilitates. And if it does facilitate it, it would be truly weird to reject the lights as an authoritarian imposition, preferring that everyone approach each intersection doing whatever they choose with the resultant level of safety and flow depending on how well they coordinate despite not having any shared agreements or having good information to use in the process.

The allocation situation is similar though actually far less manageable in the absence of helpful aids and effective restraints. The problem with remuneration for need and work to ability is that those norms are either utopian on the consumption side and draconian on the worker side, or they involve someone other than those involved determining need and ability, or—and this is the most likely intention of the view's advocates since the other two interpretations are so completely devoid of positive aspirations—it assumes a mechanism which conveys to each worker and consumer personal and system-wide information that allows them to make responsible choices without imposing class divisions, violating the ecology, enriching the few, or unnecessarily hurting anyone. Of course, the irony is that what can provide that, and was literally conceived to provide that, is what we will propose, called participatory planning, plus remuneration for duration, intensity, and onerousness of socially-valued labor.

There are other problems with the need/ability norm, one of which is particularly instructive. Suffice it to succinctly say that to sensibly know how to invest for the future and even to know what we should prepare to produce more of or what we should cut back to produce less of in the present, one has to know the relative desires for things—not solely that people would like them or not. But you can't know relative desires—do we want more of this or more of that—if the only information conveyed by the system is that people want things but not how much they want things.

What about the claim that if people get income and expend work in light of our equity norm, then it will not be an economy based on and also creating mutual aid? Well, it is true that we don't assume saintly people. Instead, we propose institutions which would likely include, certainly at the outset, rather selfish and self-centered people—such as the people who we are now due to our training and habits—and lead them/us to become more empathetic practitioners of mutual aid.

Here is the idea. In this new type of economy let's say I am by virtue of prior training, or even by genetic disposition, a very selfish fellow. I can gain by enjoying less difficult burdens at my work, or I can gain by enjoying a greater share of the social product in my consumption.

So how do I seek such gains? On the work side, I have a balanced job complex so the only way the quality of my work is going to improve is if the quality of socially average work improves, or if I find a socially average job I happen to like better than the one I already have. The second route to a better work experience is straightforward. I seek a new job, I get it or not. There is nothing special involved and nothing antisocial or, for that matter, particularly solidaritous, either. But the first route is interesting.

For my job complex to improve ultimately entails that the socially average job complex improves—which is to say that everyone's job improves. Mine doesn't get better on its own, but only if others do too. How do they all get better and thus how does mine get better?

Well, it happens most dramatically when changes in the ways we work, or in the tools we use, or in the social arrangements at work, eliminate or make the worst tasks less bad since that can significantly improve the average across all tasks. That is, the average typically goes up most when the worst tasks are dramatically improved or even eliminated. So my personal and even selfish desire to have a better experience during my work days would lead me to want labor saving and workplace improving changes for the most onerous tasks—the same attitude that a sense of solidarity and mutual aid would favor, an attitude that seeks benefit for all. I don't benefit most by advocating modest changes in my own workplace. Rather, I benefit most if I am alert to everyone's situation and advocate changes wherever they will have the largest impact. This is precisely an economic system that generates solidarity by the responsibilities and options it gives people. Mutual aid becomes the natural way to get along, not something special that one must struggle to maintain against one's surroundings.

What about the consumption side? Well, my fulfillment from consumption depends largely on my private consumption choices, and there is nothing special in that other than that when I consume individually, I do so knowing that my acts require work and resources, etc.

How can I get more consumption? I can raise my income by working harder, longer, or at more onerous tasks assuming my workmates agree on an arrangement of such activities that is good in our workplace. That route teaches solidarity somewhat because I know, via the planning process, which we have yet to discuss, the human implications of my choices, and because my workmates must agree. But I can also get more if the total social pie enlarges and, indeed, that is the only route to more income for me and for everyone in society. And that route is one of solidarity and mutual aid. We all benefit together rather than competing for benefits. Making some change that increases productivity in my work place isn't the point. That doesn't lead to workers in my workplace and myself getting greater income. The point is raising the social output in sum total, and thus the fair share that we all receive.

The key observation is that in a good economy there should be no way to improve one's consumption or one's work life at the expense of others. There should be no opposed classes, nor even opposed individuals, at least in any damaging, persistent, structural sense. This can't be achieved by market allocation where everyone buys cheap and sells dear and nice guys finish last. This also cannot be achieved by central planning where we do what others decide we must do. Equitable remuneration and solidarity instead point toward needing a new approach to allocation. It will turn out to be that we cooperatively negotiate outcomes to enjoy gains and endure losses together, even as we also seek work and consumption that is best suited to our personal fulfillment. We will want a new allocation mechanism, like our other proposed defining economic features, to produce solidarity and to make typical kinds of anti-sociality literally irrational while abetting equity and delivering collective self-management. This would allow us to say that the new economy we seek would literally propel the values we favor. It is a tall order.

There is another point to make in this chapter dealing with who earns what. How do we propose our new economy would handle free consumption? Even in contemporary economies where there is little solidarity, the public sometimes allows individuals to consume at public expense on the basis of need. Since we believe one of the merits of an equitable economy is that it creates the necessary conditions for attaining humane economic outcomes, and since we wish to incorporate features designed to build solidarity in our allocative procedures, we can reasonably expect considerable consumption on the basis of need. This will likely occur in two different ways.

First, particular consumption activities such as health care, education, or public parks may be deemed free to all. This would not mean that they have no social cost, or that they should be produced beyond the point where their social costs outweigh their social benefits. We don't want unwanted medicine, training, or parks. Rather, the point is that individuals would not be expected to reduce their requests for other consumption activities because they consume these free goods. On the other hand, of course, the average individual consumption per person will drop when society as a whole consumes more free goods.

For example, if we produce more health care, education, or parks overall, we have less productive potential left for everything else. Basically, everyone who benefits from their availability presumably pays for free goods equally (due to the reduction of other outputs available), regardless of their direct participation in consuming the free goods. This occurs on the assumption that the benefits of the consumption are generalized, or that (with medicine, say) the costs ought to be universally apportioned rather than penalizing those in need. Of course, these like other details of future economic choices would emerge and evolve in light of lessons from future experience. Likewise, what items should be on the free list would be debated, presumably in consumer federations, but medical care is an obvious example.

Second, presumably people will also be able to make particular requests for need-based consumption to be addressed case by case. Occasionally, for example, individuals or collectives might propose a consumption request above the level warranted by their income accompanied by an explanation of what they regard as a justified special need. These requests would presumably be considered by relevant consumer councils and either approved or rejected. If approved, for example, the costs might be spread over the population of the council approving. The councils decide, as usual.

The other deviation from income for duration, intensity, and onerousness of socially valued labor occurs for those who cannot contribute socially-valued labor for reasons of health, age, or whatever else may be the case. In that case, we can guess that any humane future economy would provide a full income with society essentially collectively subsidizing those unable to work. Presumably the desirable economy we are seeking would decide to do likewise.

Conclusion

It has been a long survey. Do we really want equity? Not in a philosophical debate, but in real terms, in real situations? Since our answer is unequivocally yes, we finally arrive at our proposal for what we have called equitable remuneration. After deductions from the total social product for free goods, for income for those who can't work, and for agreed upon investments, we should allot income (which is a claim on the remaining social product) in proportion to the duration, intensity, and onerousness of the socially-valued labor each worker contributes.

Another question that we mentioned briefly earlier, now arises. We refer repeatedly to "socially-valued labor" but what determines whether this labor or that labor is in fact socially valued? What lets us do that which is socially valued and avoid that which isn't? What lets us remunerate the former but not the latter? More broadly, having to this point proposed new property, decision-making, division of labor, and income norms and relations—is there any way allocation can abide and actualize our emerging proposal? Can workers and consumers interconnect without compromising our emerging commitments? Can allocation not subvert and indeed support the features already proposed? Can allocation promote self-management, solidarity, diversity, equity, and ecological sustainability while it sensibly determines and apportions the inputs and outputs of economic activity? That is our next focus. First in a chapter on markets and central planning, both of which options we reject. Then in a chapter on participatory planning, which option we advocate.

6

Who Likes Markets and Central Planning?

There are horizontal links (Markets). There are vertical links (Hierarchy). What other dimension is there? There is no third way.
Alec Nove

Just as the functions of the bodily organs of plants and animals cannot be arbitrarily altered, so that, for example, one cannot at will hear with his eyes and see with his ears, so one also cannot at pleasure transform an organ of social repression into an instrument for the liberation of the oppressed.
Rudolf Rocker

In economies goods and services are produced and consumed. How much and by whom? Workplaces produce this or that. What and how much? We all have incomes. How much can any particular income purchase of any particular item? How does what people consume match up with what people produce? Allocation is the name economists give to how an economy determines relative worths of economic inputs and outputs, determines what and how much to produce, determines investments, and mediates what consumers receive from society's product as individuals and as part of groups.

Allocation As We Know It

Allocation typically occurs in today's world by way of either markets, central planning, or a combination of the two. So can our proposal for a new economy retain one or the other? Can we successfully combine either markets, central planning, or a combination of the two with the structures we have proposed to this point: no private ownership of productive assets, self-managing worker and consumer councils, balanced job complexes, and equitable remuneration? Can all these features together become mutually intersecting elements of a worthy and viable new economy?

For property and decisions we rejected private ownership of productive assets and authoritarian control, and in their place we proposed collective responsibility for the natural, built, and human commons by way of worker and consumer councils where people have a say in proportion to the degree they are affected. This was to overcome capitalist rule. It was also to overcome misuse of society's assets. We argued that the choice would retain expertise but not inequitably reward experts with power. It would not predetermine any particular approach to tallying votes or disseminating and deliberating information but would leave those affected to settle such determinations.

For the division of labor, we rejected corporate roles which empower 20 percent and disempower 80 percent. We proposed to combine tasks into jobs so each job provides all workers comparable social skills, knowledge of workplace circumstances, connections to others, and confidence. This was to remove the source of class division and class rule of coordinators over workers. It was to establish classlessness. It was to tap the creative potentials of five-fifths rather than only one-fifth of the population. It was to remove class strife and subjugation and enlarge society's productive capacities.

For income we rejected rewarding property, power, or output. We instead proposed that people receive income for the duration, intensity, and onerousness of their socially-valued work or, if they can't work, that they receive average income. We proposed to replace exploitation and inequality with equity. This was to eliminate profit seeking and power-brokering. It was to provide proper incentives for what people can actually themselves undertake.

That's all promising, but however much we may wish to

implement self-management, balanced job complexes, and equitable remuneration, an economy also has to accomplish allocation and allocation is complex. If we can pick an existing allocation approach to combine with our other proposed economic features, doing so would certainly speed up and simplify envisioning a better economy. But can we?

Rejecting Central Planning

Central planning was the choice of many self-titled "socialist" but really coordinator economies. With only modest differences from the society-wide version, central planning is also used within massive production units, like Walmart and Amazon, to allocate diverse products and tens of thousands of workers among many venues.

In central planning, a planning agency seeks and assesses information from workers and consumers. It proposes inputs and outputs for all economic units. The units then consider their instructions. They either carry them out or they register problems they think will prevent their doing so. The central planners then assess the predicted problems and issue new instructions and the cycle repeats. It arrives at its conclusion when the planners no longer seek responses but instead issue orders.

The process is down go questions to workplaces (seeking information), up go answers to planners. Down go draft instructions, up go concerns/problems. Down go orders. Up goes obedience. In practice, central planning has many additional details to make it work well, but it has nothing that fundamentally alters its down/up logic.

Having been a key component of most post-capitalist economies, central planning has been relentlessly criticized by advocates of capitalism who typically claim central planning requires collecting too much information and distorts incentives. It can't work. Those criticisms have been, for the most part, exaggerated.

In fact, in technical journals, though not in popular accounts, mainstream economists often acknowledge the workability of central planning. And during decades of operations, at least according to the critical mainstream economists' criteria, Soviet central planning actually worked rather well. Indeed, when comparing the Soviet Union over its first 6 decades to countries that had comparable development at the outset—for example comparing the USSR and Brazil from 1917 on—the Soviet Union's outcomes were superior in output, development, and many other indices. Finally, huge capitalist firms economically comparable to or larger than small countries have used central planning to internally allocate their workforces and internal products for decades, and again, at least by mainstream norms, have done so quite nicely.

That a massive public lie—central planning can't allocate without disastrous material results—could be told and sustained shouldn't be overly surprising. Consider the lie that owners are highly productive and need to receive profits for workers to benefit, or the lie that 80 percent of workers are intrinsically unable to do empowering work, or the lie that doctors and other coordinator class workers need huge incomes to avoid their choosing to do rote instead of empowering jobs. Clearly, massive lies routinely persist.

But, if central planning can get things produced and distributed, which it can, why not use it for our preferred economy?

Our answer is simple. In central planning, workers and consumers must ultimately abide the instructions planners generate. There is a narrow decision-making top and a wide decision-obeying bottom. Central planning clearly violates self-management and even majority rule democracy. More, central planners are not interested in having to overcome resistance coming from local units. Central planners therefore do not want workplaces and neighborhoods to be self-managed by workers who will resist planners' directives. Instead, they want workplaces overseen by people who have similar interests to them.

In other words, central planners, who are coordinator class, seek to communicate with others in the coordinator class. That is who they feel unity with, who they personally understand. That is who feels unity with and understands them. Dealing with coordinators instead of workers involves no undue friction. For that reason, inside firms in centrally planned economies, the old familiar corporate hierarchy and centralized authoritative decision making is vastly preferred and implemented. Looking forward from the present, a new centrally planned economy would retain corporate roles from the past, but central planning would actually generate a corporate division of labor if the past didn't provide it in full form (which was actually the case in the Soviet Union and China).

The point is that central planning subverts desires for self-management. It subverts balanced job complexes. It imposes coordinator class rule. Even if planners start out honest and are not immediately corrupted by their power, over time they come to view those they administer as subservient. They come to view themselves as worthy and exceptional. They then reward themselves, and also people like themselves, more than workers below. Why also reward "people like themselves"? Because their justification for their higher incomes becomes their greater education, training, skills, connections, and decision-making responsibilities, and if that justification is to be compelling for the central planners, it has to be honored for all who have those "credentials," which means not only for those who centrally plan, but also for those who are empowered within local units. The empowered even come to think of themselves as better able to spend extra income. They can enjoy finer things. The workers below, not so much. These paternalistic coordinator views of themselves and of workers below mirror the same coordinator class attitudes in capitalist economies.

In other words, the central planners need local agents who will hold workers to the norms the central planners decide. These local agents must be locally authoritative. Their credentials must legitimate them and must reduce other actors to relative obedience. Central planning thus imposes (or welcomes, or is established by) a coordinator class that rules over workers. Workers are made subordinate not only nationally, but also in each workplace. Thus central planning is not an option for a truly classless economy of the sort we seek. "Power tends to corrupt, absolute power corrupts absolutely" is not mere rhetoric.

Rejecting Markets

In that case, what about markets? To clarify, market allocation doesn't refer simply to all economies where people get stuff from stores. Indeed, that is true in all modern economies, not just some. It doesn't refer to all economies where people have incomes and make purchases for prices. Again, that is true in all modern economies, not just some. Markets are instead a particular way to accomplish economic allocation. With markets, there are stores, yes. There are prices and budgets, yes. But market allocation only exists in those economies wherein buyers and sellers compete to advance their own separate interests such that prices and budgets arise from the competitive interactions of the buyers and sellers. Can we carry competitive market allocation over for use in a viable and worthy economy? If we can, why propose something new? Why replace what isn't broken? Sadly, it turns out markets, like central planning, would subvert our other gains.

First, markets immediately destroy equitable remuneration since markets, even without private ownership of productive assets (and thus markets in what its advocates call market socialism but what we call market coordinatorism), reward output and bargaining power instead of only duration, intensity, and onerousness of socially-valued work. In fact, even if we could forego labor markets in a market economy without disrupting its overall logic—which we cannot—with markets, a workplace, worker, or consumer overwhelmingly receives what it's bargaining power allows, not what is ethically and socially warranted. Competition incentivizes that if I have a monopoly on information, skills, resources, equipment, venues, connections, or even on the inclination to rule, I have more bargaining power and I get more. If I am white or male and society is racist or sexist, I have more bargaining power and I get more. More, lacking such advantages, I seek them. Markets generate inequity.

Second, with markets buyers buy cheap and sellers sell dear. Each seeks to advance self. Each fleeces the other or is fleeced by the other. A workplace gets ahead at the expense of those it buys from, sells to, or dumps pollution on. Each workplace seeks to get ahead because left behind it risks going out of business. Nice doesn't pay. Nasty pays. My defense against your nasty is to be nastier. My alternative to being nastier is to be out competed. Markets punish cooperation. Markets foster anti-sociality. Workplaces gouge, dump, and downsize not only to profit immensely, but even just to stay afloat. Markets pressure everyone to abide and partake of that workplace behavior. We become less humane than we should be. Markets propel us to seek more stuff than we should have. In each transaction, in each economic choice, markets pressure people to be cold to the circumstances of others. They propel workplaces and individuals to consider only self. It is true for producers trying to make a profit or even just stay afloat. It is true for consumers with no access to information about others and a context that destroys means or even inclination to support others. Markets push us to calculate every choice solely for self. It is an exceptional, not a normal, person who even considers distant others, much less is moved by distant others, much less advances the needs of distant others. Markets make us individuals in the most inward looking atomistic sense. Markets are literally a system in which we are made and must be sentient social atoms careening about, looking out for number one and ignoring what we don't know. Markets make us insular, ignorant, and selfish. They describe the result as virtue. They don't just compel greed, they deem greed good. They worship greed. They crush solidarity. They generate anti-sociality.

Third, markets explicitly produce dissatisfaction because only the dissatisfied buy again and again which is what market actors pursue to accrue income. As the general director of General Motors' Research Labs, Charles Kettering, who regularly introduced model changes for GM cars put it: business needs to create a "dissatisfied consumer"; its mission is "the organized creation of dissatisfaction." Advertising doesn't try to inform consumers so they can decide what they do and don't want. Rather advertising cons us into buying commodities to meet needs the commodities can never fulfill. This is so if a capitalist class profits or if enlarged surpluses go to workers in more successful firms.

Fourth, and of massive consequence, market prices don't reflect all social and ecological costs and benefits. Market prices result from competitive buying and selling by immediate buyers and sellers. They account for the impact of power-mediated production and consumption on those immediate buyers and sellers. They do not account for their impact on people peripherally affected by pollution or, for that matter, by positive side effects. In other words, only the direct buyer and seller enter into market transactions—not those affected at a distance. As a result, markets bias heavily against collective and public consumption benefits even while they propel collective and public debits by routinely violating ecological balance, sustainability, and stewardship. Plastics proliferate. Water, air, and sound pollution proliferate. Public services atrophy. Markets destabilize ecology and deny life. Markets are society's suicide machine. Okay, but perhaps our other choices for property, division of labor, and remuneration can tame markets sufficiently for us to use them.

Bearing on that last hope, fifth, markets also produce decision-making hierarchy and squash self-management. This occurs not only when market-generated disparities in wealth give different bargaining power to different actors, but also when market competition compels even council-based workplaces to cut costs and seek market share. Though this dynamic is a little more subtle to see, with markets present, even workplaces wanting to maintain self-managing councils, equitable remuneration, and balanced job complexes have no choice but to compete with one another to stay afloat. To compete they in turn have to figure out what costs to cut and how to generate more output even at the expense of workplace and consumer fulfillment. And then they have to implement such choices. But who in a self-managed council of workers, each of whom has a balanced job, would be good at overseeing cost-cutting that turns off air conditioning for themselves, mercilessly speeds up production by themselves, lies to everyone but themselves, and dumps garbage on neighborhoods where they themselves live?

It turns out that to accomplish these and other steps that they have to take to compete in markets, workplaces have to insulate some employees from the discomfort that cost-cutting imposes and then also let and even cause those insulated actors to feel superior to other workers so the elevated few will propel competitive steps at the expense of the subordinated many but not at their own expense. In other words, to cut costs—and to otherwise impose market discipline—even starting with councils and balanced job complexes, market logic elevates a coordinator class which in turn accrues ever more power to itself to in turn obliterate self-management, equity, and finally balanced job complexes.

Pressured by market competition, that is, any firm I work for must try to maximize its revenues to keep up with competing firms. If my firm doesn't keep pace, then its workers lose their jobs. So workplaces dump their costs on others. Workplaces seek as much revenue as possible—even via promoting excessive consumption. Workplaces cut costs of production—even via reducing comforts for workers and unduly speeding up work. Forget about workplace daycare.

To relentlessly pursue these paths to market success, however, a few conceiving and coordinating the choices must not suffer the pains those choices induce so they will willingly impose them. So even in a workplace that is initially committed to self-management and balanced job complexes, if it operates in a market its roles will over time impose a necessity to hire folks with appropriately callous and calculating mindsets of the sort that business schools now produce. Workers would then have to give these new callous employees air-conditioned offices and comfortable surroundings insulated from the harsh conditions they must impose on the rest of us. We workers would finally have to tell them, okay, screw us. Cut our costs to ensure our livelihood in the marketplace. In other words, we would have to impose on ourselves a coordinator class, not due to natural law, and not due to some internal psychological drive, but because markets would force us to subordinate ourselves to a coordinator elite we would accept and welcome lest our workplace lose market share and eventually go out of business. This flaw of markets, like the inbuilt flaw of the corporate division of labor, would institutionally subvert our worthy aspirations for classlessness.

Markets destroy equity, subvert solidarity, violate ecology, under supply collective goods, manufacture dissatisfaction, and finally also produce class division and class rule. Mainstream economists often claim that all these market failings are not a product of markets per se, but of imperfect markets that haven't attained a condition of perfect competition. But this is a bit like saying that the ills associated with ingesting arsenic occur because we never get pure arsenic. We only get arsenic tainted with other ingredients. The non-pure ingredients, not arsenic, are the problem. On the one hand, calling for perfect markets ignores that in a real society there is literally no such thing as frictionless competition, so of course we will always get imperfect markets. Even more important, calling for perfect markets ignores that the harmful effects of markets do not diminish when competition is made more perfect—they intensify.

Historically, the closer economies have come to a pure market system—without state intervention and with as few sectors as possible dominated by single firms or groups of firms, and with as few unions as possible—the worse the social implications have been. For example, there have rarely, if ever, been markets as competitive as those of Britain in the early nineteenth century. Yet, under the sway of those nearly perfect markets, young children routinely suffered early death working long days in the mills of the time.

The point is, well-functioning markets most certainly accomplish various essential economic tasks, but they do not promote excellence in any form. They do not resist—and they even facilitate—material, cultural, and moral depravity. As a result, seeking an economy that can deliver equity, solidarity, diversity, and self-management not to mention classlessness and ecological sustainability means rejecting markets as a tool for allocation.

Put differently, imposing restraints on markets to reduce their ill effects and adding to market requirements to enforce positive effects are worthy steps. But markets will constantly intrinsically work against all such impositions. Markets will either overcome such restraints or be transformed into new shape, new logic, new form, by ever elaborating and enlarging alterations. It may seem hard to imagine, but if we are serious about our proposed values, the conclusion is inescapable. For the final vision, reject markets. Morph them, replace them, until we have something structurally and logically new. It is not a cute slogan to ignore in our practice. It is an existential necessity to steadily attain by our practice, albeit knowing that it won't happen over night.

Our Allocation Problem

Our contemporary allocation problem is that (as could be seen in the old Yugoslavia and Soviet Union) even without private ownership of the means of production, markets and central planning each subvert equitable remuneration, each annihilate self-management, each horribly misvalue products, each grossly violate the ecology. They each relentlessly impose antisocial motivations. They each unavoidably impose class division and class rule. This is precisely the kind of dynamic our approach to thinking about economics attunes us to. Particular institutions—in this case markets and central planning—impose role attributes that violate our aims. They are leaky life rafts. A worthy vision must transcend them.

The same observation held for private ownership of productive assets, the corporate division of labor, and inequitable remuneration. These institutional choices too violated the values we favor. That is why we had to figure out how to transcend them. And now our critique of markets and central planning shows that they too violate the values we favor. Such a critique isn't an intellectual exercise that we should forget about once we step back into our own work and consumption. Do we hold our values or not? If we do, then our critique of markets and central planning is deep, devastating, and agenda provoking.

The title of this chapter is "who likes markets and central planning?" The answer is anyone who thinks nothing else is possible and wants to avoid the chaos they believe rejecting markets and central planning would cause, likes them. And anyone who actually likes the implications of markets and central planning for society, including that a coordinator class dominates a working class, likes them.

Allocation is the nervous system of economic life. To allocate is both intricate and essential. We can't sufficiently describe what we want for a new economy without offering a proposal for new allocation. What we want needs a name and a broad definition. We don't need contextual details. We need key defining features.

Put differently, to round out our proposal for a new economic vision consistent with what we have so far urged, we must conceive an allocation mechanism that can: 1) properly determine and communicate as accurate and full information as possible about the personal, social, and ecological costs and benefits of economic options, 2) give workers and consumers self-managing influence over choices, and 3) actively promote solidarity, facilitate equity, support balanced jobs, seek sustainable ecology, and ensure classlessness. These are tall orders that we must meet.

An Anti-Academic Addendum

Perhaps you have had the experience of taking an economics course in college or have otherwise heard economists claim that markets permit producers and consumers to fulfill their desires without external imposition, without waste, and supremely efficiently. Economists even prove that a mathematical model that they say captures the essence of market exchange has these delightful properties.

The problem is that their model and the reality they say their model "models" diverge dramatically. Imagine that I model war as including many people, severe disagreement, a few guns, and no dying. Then I examine my model for the properties of war.

My model leaves out too much that matters. Economic theory is like that.

Briefly, the economists' model assumes—among other falsehoods—that market buyers and sellers are all small and weak and unable to themselves affect prices. It also simplistically models their behavior as maximizing profit or surplus and maximizing personal preference fulfillment, and it then proves the model will have various properties. For example, it won't waste things. Yet strangely, in our economy 40 percent of all produced food is wasted. That alone—and there are many such glaring gaps between claims about the model and facts of worldly outcomes—should terminate people pointing to such models instead of pointing to reality to learn about reality. It does that, at least to an extent, for some high-powered more realistic economists, but not for the economics we learn in economics 101 or from media pundits' rhetoric.

Further, and more instructively, even if reality did act like the economic models and thus did attain what the models call "efficiency," what is that? The word efficiency is used by economists and their business paymasters to rally support for whatever they favor, but the word is rarely carefully considered. We all like efficiency when we think it means attaining desired ends without wasting things we value. Who would oppose that? No one wants to not attain what we seek. No one wants to waste what we value. And so no one wants to be called inefficient. But here is the rub.

Efficiency really means attaining the ends you seek, whatever those may be. It means not wasting things you value, whatever anyone else may think about the things you value. So, if you seek profit and you don't value the lives of workers or the health of your workplace neighbors, you should cut workers' pay and speed up workers' tasks while you scrimp on their safety and simultaneously dump waste into neighboring water supplies or spew it into the sky. In fact, given market aims and what markets do and don't value, for workplaces to not impoverish workers and to not dump pollution would be "inefficient."

Typical economists overly abstract their models. They leave out workers' well-being, social relations, and the environment. They then use the label efficient to appear credible and curry favor. Economists who do this are either incredibly stupid, or they know better but have succumbed to the pressure of accommodating those who pay their salaries or publish their writings. It is an extreme, albeit common, tendency. Do you think I exaggerate? Consider what John Kenneth Galbraith, one of the foremost and most accessible economists of the past century, had to say: "Economics is extremely useful as a form of employment for economists."

Our alternative is to seek self-management, equity, solidarity, diversity, sustainability, internationalism, and participation. It is to account for all that is personally, socially, and ecologically affected. It is, to the extent possible, to attain our goals and not waste what we value. And it thus requires a new method for allocation.

7

Who Allocates What?

Nothing is yours. It is to use. It is to share. If you will not share it, you cannot use it.
Ursula K. Le Guin

The only possible alternative to being either the oppressed or the oppressor is voluntary cooperation for the greatest good of all.
William Von Humboldt

Allocation, this chapter's focus, is what economists call the procedure that selects from a nearly infinite list of every conceivable item that might be produced using every conceivable combination of labor, tools, and resources, a single final list of what economic actors actually do produce and consume.

Markets allocate via competition among buyers and sellers. Central planning allocates via commands from central planners. We reject both markets and central planning for reasons summarized last chapter. We instead favor "participatory planning." One way to conceive this third approach is to start from either markets or central planning and progressively alter each to better approximate desired aims, better accommodate and work with other favored institutions, and better ameliorate or eliminate inadequacies. In practice, in real social situations, that approach will undoubtedly be part of any systematic change with movements winning various changes. But to conceive and present an alternative that isn't constrained by the limitations of the two systems and that is able to provide focus and direction for practical real world campaigns and changes, it seems to us we are more likely to conceive what we desire if we simply start over, so to speak, thinking about how to do allocation in a participatory, classless, and self-managing manner. For that reason, in this chapter we describe participatory planning with a series of ever more revealing "takes" on its features. Each new "take" repeats in different ways elements of prior takes even while it also adds new dimensions. Each new "take" clarifies but also raises questions that each subsequent "take" addresses. Different readers may have different preferences regarding how many "takes" to assess.

Participatory Planning Take 1: Requirements

We have proposed that all productive assets be treated as a Commons. We have proposed that workers and consumers self-manage in councils and federations of councils. We have proposed that jobs be re-conceived to convey comparable empowerment. We have proposed that everyone who works receive equitable income in accord with duration, intensity, and onerousness of their socially-valued labor. And we have proposed that productive assets should benefit and be overseen by all who are affected by their use.

To achieve all that, given that we have also rejected markets and central planning, it follows that we must propose a new means of allocation that will let workers and consumers collectively self-manage what they produce and consume. A new means of allocation that will sustain classlessness. A new means of allocation that will elicit freely expressed desires and provide information sufficient for workers and consumers to work and consume socially responsibly. A new means of allocation that will foster solidarity/empathy. A new means of allocation that will take into appropriate account the full personal, social, and ecological implications of production and consumption. A new means of allocation that will at the start of each new year arrive at a plan and then during each year continually update it in ways that respect personal and collective desires, that efficiently use society's productive assets, and that allot income equitably. A new means of allocation that will avoid the flaws of markets and central planning and enhance the virtues of the proposed property, decision-making, division of labor, and income structures of our proposed new economy.

What can accomplish these many results? We propose that in a new participatory economy workers in different enterprises and industries, and consumers in different living units, neighborhoods, and regions, propose their joint endeavors in accord with revealed knowledge of one another's needs and capacities. Councils revise their proposals as they discover more about the impact of their proposals on others and the impact of others' proposals on themselves. Councils finally arrive at a plan for each new year, and cooperatively update and implement that plan as the year progresses.

But can such non-competitive, non-authoritarian procedures facilitate successful self-managed, equitable, sustainable, and classless allocation? Can a social, multi-step planning process collectively determine that workers proposals for what to produce are socially worthy, that consumers requests for what to consume are socially responsible, and that in sum their production and consumption proposals match sufficiently to implement?

We have already proposed that society's natural and built productive Commons should have no private owners, and indeed have no owners at all. We have proposed self-managing workers and consumers councils and federations of councils. We have proposed enabling actors to influence decisions in proportion as they are affected by them, by way of their prior training plus their working in balanced job complexes. And we have proposed equitable remuneration according to effort and sacrifice of socially-valued work.

It follows that to be consistent with all that, participatory planning must include individual workers and consumers, and also workers and consumers councils and federations of councils as both self-managing conceivers and enactors of plans. The councils are, after all, the venue from which workers and consumers develop and pursue agendas. One added actor we propose is what we call an "Iteration Facilitation Board" (IFB), which is just a group of people, a part of whose balanced job is to help tally and report data that informs allocation.

Looking at the above paragraph, it turns out that allocation procedures conceived to fit compatibly with the rest of our proposed economy will need to be a system of decentralized (not centralized) and cooperative (not competitive) negotiation that arrives at relative valuations that reflect individual, social, and ecological costs and benefits which in turn inform workers and consumers self-managed decisions about actual inputs, outputs, and procedures, and which equitably allocate income to all involved. That's a mouthful, but if participatory planning achieves less, it is hard to see how it could be consistent with the properties we seek for a new economy. So how might an equitable, self-managing, classless allocation system actually work?

Participatory Planning Take 2: Bare Bones

Consider a quick account of a hypothetical participatory economy's participatory planning process. Workers councils, in light of their prior year's activities and the final prices from last year, propose the outputs they would like to produce and the inputs they would need to use to do so for the coming year. At the same time, consumers councils sum and then report the proposed consumption of their members plus the whole council's proposed collective consumption.

The National Iteration Facilitation Board tallies all this information in mutually agreed and transparent ways and feeds it back to the councils along with updated guesses as to where prices—which are a product of the planning process itself, and not of competition, power, or central imposition—will finally arrive when planning is complete. The councils then consider reports of products in over or under supply as well as updated indicative prices. They adjust their expectations and enter new proposals for their own activity.

Individuals and councils are incentivized to arrive at acceptable outcomes. They have good reason to honor the instruction that their proposals must ultimately be consistent with prices/valuations. That is, consumers must make consumption proposals within their income/budgets and producers must provide desired outputs without wasting assets from society's Commons.

The back-and-forth process of refining proposals continues until what consumers propose to consume sufficiently matches what producers propose to supply to deem the plan able to guide economic activity for the new year. Additionally, prior steps employ the same basic ideas but in different contexts to incorporate ecological costs and benefits into the process and to properly account for earlier-settled longer-term investment plans.

The claims for participatory planning are that the impact of each actor is broadly proportional to the degree to which he or she is affected by the choices decided. Final prices admirably account for individual, social, and ecological implications. The year's plan is reached without undue delay. The year's plan establishes a responsible and implementable agenda. Methods for updating the initial plan in light of changes in tastes, needs, and availabilities as the year unfolds are easily undertaken consistent with guiding values. Behaviors called forth during planning and in ensuing economic activity are not only doable and mutually agreed by all involved, but also support and enhance solidarity among the participants because the benefit of each participant overwhelmingly depends on the benefit of all other participants. Finally, and most importantly, participatory planning's outcomes and behaviors support and are guided by the logic and practice of self-managing workers and consumers councils, balanced job complexes, and equitable remuneration, and thus also classlessness.

Participatory Planning Take 3: Adding Some Texture

The above bare bones specification is likely too streamlined to suffice for most who have read this far. Such folks will want more "takes." They may wonder, for example: How workers and consumers can possibly successfully utilize full knowledge of effects and exercise proportionate influence on decisions, all without undue hassle and time spent on outcomes?

So, to add a bit more clarity, note that at the outset of each yearly planning process the facilitation board announces what we call "indicative prices" for all goods, resources, and categories of labor—in other words, for what goes into production or is available for consumption. Indicative prices literally means informed guesses or predictions of what prices will wind up as. Producers and consumers use indicative prices to guide their path of proposals and thereby arrive at final actual prices.

Participatory planning's indicative prices are first offered at the outset of yearly planning based on the prior year's final prices (or relative valuations) and on broad knowledge of general changes expected for the coming year, for example new technologies coming into use, climate or other such natural changes, or new demographics. Consumers, consumer councils, and federations of consumer councils respond to the predicted prices in light of their understanding of social trends and their own preferences. They make consumption proposals that take the indicative prices as estimates of true valuations of all the resources, equipment, labor, and good and bad by-products associated with each good or service. Their expected budgets limit their consumption proposals. Indicative prices indicate expectations as to how much each item they propose to consume costs from their whole income. In these respects, the situation appears like now—other than where the prices come from and what they take account of and the sources of income. Given my expected budget, given the characteristics of available products, how much of this particular item do I think I want over the course of the year? How much of that item do I think I want over the course of the year? I decide.

At the same time, workers, workers councils, and industry councils offer production proposals that list the outputs they propose to make available and the inputs, sometimes produced by other workplaces, they would use to produce those outputs. They too take indicative prices, updated in each new round of planning, as estimates of relative prices of outputs and costs of inputs.

When the Iteration Facilitation Board receives public proposals from workers and consumers councils, it tallies excess demand or supply for each good and mechanically adjusts the indicative price for the good up or down in light of the new data and in accord with socially agreed rules for these alterations. Because their income is for their socially-valued effort, Iteration Facilitation Board workers have no way to manipulate price projections to aggrandize themselves.

Using new predicted prices, and of course taking account of the first round of production and consumption proposals, plus, if they feel the need, consulting relevant qualitative information, consumers and workers councils and federations of councils revise and resubmit their proposals for a second round of the process. The idea is that new proposals from workers and consumers move the process forward, and then do so again, and again, over each new round of the process, to a final feasible plan.

Essentially the rounds of back-and-forth procedure, which are called planning iterations, "whittle" excessive or enlarge insufficient proposals into a feasible plan in which what is offered by producers matches what is sought by consumers.

The whittling, to take another step toward understanding the viability and worthiness of the approach, is proposed to occur in two different ways.

Participatory Planning Take 4: Making Plan Proposals

Consumers who request more than their expected incomes warrant, or who together want more of some good than workers propose to produce, receive new indicative prices. All together the population needs to attain a viable final plan so that economic activity can proceed. New prices make new choices beneficial. Consumers reduce or shift their consumption requests in each new iteration to better accord with their anticipated budget.

In parallel, workers councils whose proposals have lower than average social benefit given the resources at their disposal or who are proposing less (or more) than consumers desire of their product, have reason to increase (or decrease) their efforts, effectiveness, or number of employees, to meet consumer desires and better use the assets at their disposal so their work will all be socially valued.

In other words, if you ask in a consumption proposal for too much stuff relative to your likely income, or if consumer councils want too much of some collective item, or if a workplace proposal doesn't produce sufficiently for its available assets, or if there is more desire than what a workplace or industry proposes to produce, then it is important that the participants have reason to raise or lower their proposals in accord. Every participant's goal needs to include getting his/her/their proposals to an acceptable range to be met so the overall process arrives at a viable and worthy plan to execute in the new year, along with, of course, fulfilling their own desires as best their situation permits, and receiving appropriate equitable income.

As each iteration of the planning process proceeds, by virtue of their induced refinements, proposals move closer to mutual feasibility while (and because) indicative prices converge toward ever more accurate representations of the final full relative benefits and costs associated with the production and consumption of each economic item.

Since no participant in the planning procedure has excessive income or has excessive say in a council, no participant has an advantage in influence over any other, and since each participant impacts the valuation of social costs and benefits like all others do, but with each exerting more impact on what they are involved in producing or consuming and less on what they are not directly involved in producing or consuming, and since each exerts more impact on what they care more about and less on what they care less about, the procedure simultaneously supports sensible use of assets and also self-managed decision-making.

Since the income of workers is for duration, intensity, and onerousness of socially-valued labor, the procedure also supports equitable remuneration. No one has a socially acceptable path to excessive gain. Working longer, harder, or doing more onerous tasks, each with the agreement of one's workmates and contributing to valued output, does earn more income, and rightly so, but trying to steal or exploit is made difficult and even counter productive. No one could hide excessive gain beyond what they can legitimately and morally earn. There is no such thing as being rich, so becoming rich by being a master thief can't lead to visible consumption or other gain that would immediately reveal the violation.

Neighborhood councils make requests for collective goods. In light of the implications of their expenditures on collective consumption for their personal budgets, individuals make proposals for their own private goods. Neighborhood councils then make overall proposals that include their members' summed requests for private goods, as well as their members' shared collective requests for the neighborhood's collective consumption. Higher-level federations of consumer councils (covering larger areas) make proposals that include the summed requests from member councils as well as the federation's collective consumption requests. Individuals make their private requests in light of earlier proposed higher level collective requests, both because the collective requests bear on their income and because the higher-level request—my neighborhood is seeking a pool so I don't have reason to privately want one—can affect their personal choices.

Similarly, each production unit proposes a production plan. Workplaces enumerate the inputs they want and the outputs they propose to make available. Industry federations aggregate individual workplace proposals. The Iteration Facilitation Board receives proposals and then reports excess supply and demand. It also reports above and below average workplace social benefits per social costs ratios, and refined indicative prices.

Having proposed its own plan, every individual and collective receives information regarding other participants' proposals and the response of other participants to its proposal and to the continually refined indicative prices, and, when helpful, accesses associated qualitative explanations. Each actor (individuals and collectives), then makes a new proposal.

Every participant navigates through successive "iterations." Consumers take into account especially their own expected budgets and of course their preferences for goods and services. Producers take into account especially the social benefits as compared to social costs of their proposed outputs. When it can help, each considers additional qualitative information made available on request. The overall process converges to a viable and worthy plan.

Participatory Planning Take 5: Some Preliminary Judgments and Questions

We next consider how a participatory planning process yields a viable outcome. The iterations proceed until within acceptable pre-agreed margins what is planned to be consumed is planned to be produced and what is planned to be produced is planned to be consumed. That sounds good, but a number of legitimate practical questions arise.

Can people, especially consumers, even make the called for proposals? Will doing so take too long? What if people change their minds as a planned year proceeds? What about unexpected events? Will pollution and other externalities be accurately accounted in prices? Will collective goods be properly valued and paid for? Can short and long-term investments be planned and then enacted and continually updated without subverting the virtues we seek to embody in this new type of allocation? And even if all this can be achieved so that participatory planning is viable, why should anyone think the resulting participatory plan would be desirable?

Please remember, as well, that our proposal for economic vision is intentionally far from detailed. It is a scaffold to build upon. We might therefore reasonably wonder, can our proposed scaffold of defining features sufficiently guide establishing a full system of participatory planning in an actual specific society? For that matter, by what steps will the scaffold fill in details as a participatory economy develops? Will the additions be controversial? These are questions additional "takes on participatory planning" could start to clarify.

So, to take another step toward clarifying, consider that as a consumer in a participatory economy your budget for consumption beyond free goods is a function of the duration, intensity, and onerousness of your socially-valued work (or, if you are unable to work, is average plus having your health needs met and receiving free goods like everyone else). To consume more than your budget covers, we can reasonably envision that you would have to have some excellent reason and get permission from your consumer council, presumably due to some special circumstance. Similarly, for a consumer council to consume in total more than its members' total budgetary allotment, it would likely have to get an okay from a still higher-level council.

As a worker, the output expected from your firm is a function of the productive capacity of the assets you employ and of your and your workmates' efforts. In the planning process, you are saying to society that you would like to utilize some array of items from society's Productive Commons to benefit society by the resultant products of their combination. When it arrives at a plan, the planning process perhaps says okay to your final proposal. Your proposal is responsible and it fits. However, if you were significantly underutilizing your assets, which could then better go to other purposes, the process would have revealed the problem and we can reasonably envision that you would need dispensation from your industry council to proceed in addition to it meaning your total of socially valuable labor, and thus the total payroll allotted to your workforce, would be proportionately less than average and corrective changes would need to occur.

An attained plan, by the requisites of the whole process, manifests actors' preferences roughly proportionately as they are impacted. By the same requisites, each actor benefits according to the same logic as all others. My income depends directly on the socially average income since I get somewhat more or somewhat less due to my contributing a somewhat greater or somewhat lesser amount of socially-valued effort and sacrifice than average, an option that all agree is fair. Likewise, how my job impacts me depends on the quality of the socially average job complex (since everyone able to work has a balanced job complex, with each job roughly equal to all others in its empowerment impact), or it depends on special degrees of onerousness of my work, which all agree should be remunerated. Even my benefit from any investment proposed by myself and my co-workers or by my industry for my own workplace depends over time on how that investment raises social averages for jobs or alters average income for all, by expanding the total social product that we all share in—and so does your benefit, outside my workplace, depend on the same implications.

Solidarity is enhanced by participatory planning because workers' and consumers' interests are entwined and our daily economic calculations occur in light of one another's situations. Even if I don't actively learn of situations beyond my own, for my income to go up, either I have to expend more socially-valued effort and sacrifice, or the total social product has to go up with everyone benefiting. For the quality of my work situation to improve, the quality of society's balanced job complex must improve, and thus everyone's situation must improve, or I have to take a job more suited to my tastes. More, to the degree that a particular implementation of participatory planning opts to convey active awareness of the qualitative circumstances of others, then to that degree mutual benefit created by making choices in light of participatory prices fosters, as well, a personal dynamic of growing awareness and empathy. Diversity, which is itself a guiding value of policy making, is a natural outgrowth as well, both for the benefits that accrue from preserving many options and to maintain checks and balances. Equity is guaranteed by the universally operative remunerative norm that income is for duration, intensity, and onerousness of socially-valued labor. Self-management is intrinsic to the allocation system's foundational logic and fostered by its every feature. In other words, we know that any plan that a participatory planning session settles on will be worthy because we know the surrounding economic structures require that the outcome includes self-management, equity, and classlessness.

To clarify still further, prices are "indicative" during the planning process in the sense of indicating the best current estimates of final valuations. Every iteration until the end is a set of proposals. Each iteration until the end is an exploration, not a conclusion. Indicative prices are not binding at each stage, but provide flexible guides. Everyone knows that indicative prices that pertain before the end of planning may change in a future round of planning. More, when called upon, if made part of the process, qualitative information can provide additional guidance that can in some situations lead people to act contrary to what then current indicative prices might alone provoke, thereby speeding arrival at a viable plan, and in other ways affecting the plan's outcome for the better. For example, perhaps the demand for something my workplace has proposed is way above what we anticipated. We receive that information and also new indicative prices, but we still find the size of the unexpected demand baffling. We decide to consult some qualitative information—we just click and read—and we find there is a really good, not a faddish, reason for the unexpected growth of demand. Instead of doubting its legitimacy, we quickly move to meet the demand. Or, in another case, perhaps 60 members of my local area vote on neighborhood collective consumption to put in clay tennis courts and 40 vote to put in hard-tru courts—but one of the 40 also includes the qualitative information that when a neighboring town put in clay courts, the annual upkeep was four times as much as for hard-tru courts. When the 60 access that info, half of them switch their preference. The point is, one can imagine quite diverse situations in which qualitative information on top of indicative prices and product specifications may yield better outcomes than indicative prices plus product specifications alone, though it is also quite likely that even participatory prices alone would guide excellent outcomes precisely because they account for all social and ecological factors and because indicative prices, up to and including settling on final rates of exchange, do not stem from competition between buyers and sellers trying to fleece one another, and are not imposed by authoritarian determinations biased toward the well-being of decision makers. Indicative prices arise, instead, from the interactions of workers and consumers who freely propose their own activities.

Qualitative information, to whatever extent it is incorporated into participatory planning, would of course have to come directly from concerned parties. Workers and consumers would then presumably consult it only when they feel that proposals or prices were so unusual compared to expectations that they want to understand whatever special unexpected circumstances might have caused the strange indications. We produce violins or air conditioners. Based on last year we expect demand for some quantity. First proposals show demand to be four times what we expect. We don't want to rely on just the reported under supply and the new prices we receive. We want to also access information that reveals why there is such an unexpected demand. We care about how our product is used. So society may opt to provide qualitative information partly to check on and to help keep its quantitative indicators as accurate as possible, and partly to develop workers' and consumers' sensitivity to fellow workers' and consumers' situations and thus to develop people's understanding of the intricate tapestry of human relations that determines what each of us can and cannot consume or produce. It is reasonable to think that consultation of such information might be infrequent, but quite useful in unanticipated situations.

Participatory Planning Take 6: Variations

The above five takes on participatory planning address many central aspects. They do not, however, provide a detailed picture of either the planning "iterations" or of all the motives, actions, and institutions that make the iterations viable. They do not specify detailed day-to-day roles. They do not specify detailed social implications for workers and consumers during the planning process. Although such issues have been addressed in various places, the reason I did not yet do so here is not simply a matter of keeping things concise. Rather, I feel confident that there is not a single right way to do many specific aspects of participatory planning, just as there is not a single right way for a workplace to internally enact equitable remuneration of its overall payroll to its workers or to collectively settle on balanced job complexes, and there is not a single right way for consumer councils to ascertain collective desires, or for the overall plan to price external effects that occur beyond direct producer and consumer.

As one relatively simple example, instances of participatory planning could differ regarding the extent to which they utilize qualitative information along with indicative prices, instead of using only indicative prices during the rounds of planning. At one extreme, each participant—consumer or producer—might consult only numeric prices and of course descriptions of the product, with no qualitative accounts of the situations of workers or consumers made available, and might therefore make decisions consciously thinking solely about its own circumstances. Consumers and producers would know the qualitative properties of items for sale, of course, but they would know nothing qualitative about other participants' situations and choices. Alternatively, in another implementation, qualitative information about participants' choices could be made available for access, particularly when such proposals diverged significantly from expectations. Likewise, means for communication among councils, as compared to communication only within councils, might be facilitated more in one implementation than in another. Similarly, specific means for assessing the impact of externalities on constituencies that they affect, and thus the cost to be charged to firms that pollute and paid to citizens who suffer from the pollution, may differ somewhat in different implementations, or even in different cases within one participatory planning process. And of course use of qualitative information, of communications between councils, and of modes of determining how to price external effects are only three of many elements that could conceivably vary from one implementation of participatory planning to another. The Iteration Facilitation Board's mandate might, for example, be another example, as might the precise mandate of agencies that help people change jobs, or that propose possible investments for firms or industries, or that assess grievances.

Presumably, future participants in participatory planning will choose among possible details based on the lessons of their experiences and also on the circumstances of their economy, community, or industry. Considerations of what methods to employ regarding qualitative information and externalities, for example, would likely include concerns to simplify and speed up planning iterations on the one hand, as well as concerns to enrich mutual understanding among producers and consumers and to attain maximal accuracy in accounting external effects on the other hand.

The main point, however, is that balancing what is produced by firms and industries and what is consumed by individuals and groups in light of the full human, social, and ecological costs and benefits that go into and that emanate from each part of the dynamic can be achieved better cooperatively than via competitive or authoritarian procedures that pervert motives, distort personalities, and bias outcomes—and that produce class rule. In other words, allocation can be accomplished in accord with self-management. It can foster diversity, solidarity, and equity. It does not have to violate our values. It does not have to produce class division. It does not have to be done by markets or by central planning. It can be done by participatory planning.

But allocation is undeniably complicated. So, for those who wish to dive still more deeply, our next take considers a few additional aspects of accomplishing participatory planning.

Participatory Planning Take 7: Information and Communication

So far our picture of participatory planning is built around workers and consumers making and refining proposals in their councils. But what do workers in a council need to know to sensibly and even to optimally propose their production in light of its effects on themselves, on other workers, on consumers, on society writ large, and on the ecology? And what do consumers need to know to formulate their consumption requests in light of their own needs as well as the needs of other consumers and workers and their social and ecological effects? And does participatory planning provide the needed information in ways able to inform decisions without incurring damaging delays?

For optimally informed collective self-management:

- The proposals of participatory workers should account for the gains from working less or using less productive though more fulfilling techniques, against the consequent loss of consumer well-being due to lower output.
- The proposals of participatory consumers should account for the benefits of increasing their consumption requests against the sacrifices that would be required to meet those requests.
- Participatory workers should be able to distinguish a responsible production proposal that properly utilizes labor and infrastructure from a production proposal that falls short.
- Participatory consumers should be able to distinguish responsible consumption requests from ones that are excessive or, for that matter, unnecessarily modest.
- Everyone should make choices in light of the full social and ecological costs and benefits of what they desire to consume or produce, including the quantified and, when/if beneficial to consult, the qualitative causes and

consequences of their choices.
- The procedures of planning should not waste time and should propel actors toward responsible proposals and, when necessary, intervene to prevent indefensibly irresponsible ones from being enacted.

Allocation mechanisms provide means to decide among options. Should certain productive assets from the societal Commons be used to produce peanuts, prison cells, autos, or shoes in any conceivable combination of options? Likewise, given that such products are produced, how much of one should exchange for another? If I consume so much of one, how much of my income will I have expended that I cannot then spend on another?

Economists call a key concept in sensibly making such choices the "social opportunity cost" of doing any particular thing. If we produce peanuts, how much of other things will we forego because we have used labor, land, and facilities in peanut production? Likewise, if we produce autos, what do we forego from not having used the involved assets to produce public transit or violins? Given people's preferences, are we putting productive assets we receive from the Commons to their best socially-valued use? To get decisions that account for actual costs and benefits, prices need to account for full opportunity costs. Prices should tell us if we do x, how much of y could we have done instead, and therefore, do we really want to do x or would we prefer doing that much y?

If an economy functions perfectly, its prices will take into account the full effects of both the production and the consumption of its inputs and outputs. The full range of actual made choices in the economy, which is the actual final production and consumption that result from allocation, will determine the social opportunity costs of every single item among the totality of possibilities. This is a difficult but important point to understand.

In participatory planning, things don't have built-in objective values or costs. Rather the values of things result from and simultaneously determine contingent choices and outcomes. It is a circular relationship. The total quantities produced of shoes, autos, peanuts, and everything else and how they are apportioned in sum determine the relative value of each particular item which in turn determines the totals produced and how they are apportioned.

The economists' way to look at this is that an economy will ideally produce peanuts up to the point when producing any more peanuts would entail losing some other item more valuable to society than the extra peanuts, which is to say in economic lingo, it will produce peanuts up until the point when the social opportunity cost equals the benefit from the last peanut. Obviously, in the real world of human interactions there is no such perfect accounting, but approaching this situation is beneficial in precisely the sense of meeting needs without wasting means by taking them from pursuits where they would yield greater benefit.

As we proceed in light of this observation, however, it is important to realize, again, that a real economy isn't a mechanical wind-up system that functions however we might abstractly model or even instruct it to. If allocation ignores important factors, like market processes ignore externalities not to mention the well-being of employees, then when such allocation arrives at its final determinations of what is produced and what is consumed, those final choices won't, in fact, have properly accounted for full social benefits and costs, much less balanced them. We get way more pollution, for example, than had pollution been accounted for.

We churn out pencils. When do we stop churning? Pencils are useful, but the more pencils we produce, the less is the value of each new one we add to the pile, at least after a point (and this is true for most but not all products). Moreover, we certainly do not want to use up so much of our labor and resources churning out pencils that we start to forego things more desirable to us than our growing pile of pencils—say, milk. We also shouldn't want to do it beyond the point where we pollute so much as to outweigh the value of more pencils.

Ideally, again, assuming excellent prices that account for personal, social, and environmental effects, the economy will churn out each of its products to a point where the benefit of the last item of that output is equal to its opportunity cost, remembering that both the benefit and the cost depend, again, on the final allotments. To produce another instance of the item would then incur the same or a bit higher cost, and would have the same or a bit less social value, so that by not producing that item we could, at least in theory, use our productive capability to produce something else that would benefit us more. That is the professional economist's central message about arriving at efficient allocation. On the surface, it may seem a bit grey or mechanical but the message is instructive if the allocation's accounting has been inclusive. So the big question becomes, what do we count when we count? That is, do we count the workers' circumstances, the impact of pollution, or even the impact of the changes in consciousness associated with different choices? The problem in the mainstream profession's insight is that economists typically accept bad prices as if they were good. They ignore, or more accurately they downplay, the presence of factors inadequately accounted for even in their models, much less in actual social settings.

Let's return to discussing what is needed for a perfect, which is to say, an unreal but in some ways instructive situation. Producers and consumers must use numeric prices as a shorthand way of discerning the relative value and cost of various choices. This is so because it would be impossibly time-consuming to make all decisions about what to consume and what to produce absent a mechanism for summarizing massive volumes of information—and this is what numeric prices accomplish, better or worse, depending what they account for and what they leave out.

Numeric prices are ideally a social measure of what society wants and what it doesn't want, and how much in each case, where "society" is hopefully taking into account the full implications of contending possibilities. Numeric prices have worth, therefore, to the extent that an allocation system's processes—market competition's buying and selling, central planning's dictated and accepted instructions, or participatory planning's iteratively updated proposals—generate sufficiently accurate estimates of the full personal, social, and ecological costs and benefits of inputs and outputs.

In a participatory economy, prices, or relative valuations, arise in the process of participatory planning. Along the way, indicative prices serve as shorthand guides for making preliminary proposals and evaluations. The social character of the final emergent actual prices—their emergence from the preferences, circumstances, and social interactions of economic actors—not only in participatory economics, but in all economic systems—is important to understand.

Too often theoretical economists using the discipline's tools say little about the social origin of prices and make it sound like they are objective quantitative measures that represent an intrinsic, objective, non-contingent reality which can be found technically by an analyst solving equations. In the literature on central planning, for example, prices are too often seen as emerging from a cut-and-dried mathematical calculation. In neoclassical literature, market prices are too often said to arise from plugging fixed preferences and given technologies into some complex equations while assuming producers maximize profits and consumers maximize something called utility. Used carefully, this sort of thinking can shed some modest light on some limited questions. But used indiscriminately, it can be very misleading.

Real people's preferences arise in social interactions. They are not innate and fixed, but social and malleable. What we want and how much we want it is contextually and historically dependent. Not only do the outcomes of the clash and jangle of different people's preferences depend on what those interactions are like, but the very preferences that people bring to their decisions and that lie at the basis of economic results depend on people's interactions in that self-same economy. Our preferences influence and are influenced by our institutional circumstances and situations. Our institutional circumstances and situations influence and are influenced by the nature of the economic activities we undertake. Cause is effect is cause is effect. With different allocation systems our activities differ and different preferences and prices emerge. Emergent preferences and prices often deviate greatly from what we could reasonably call freely expressed desires and full measures of social and environmental costs and benefits.

In thinking about allocation, therefore, we should remember that for estimates of social costs and benefits to be optimal they must arise from realistic social, communicative processes that, as closely as possible, account for all the involved factors. To propose positive approaches for allocation, we have to propose processes that give people no incentives to dissimulate regarding their true desires. We have to propose processes that give people equal opportunity to manifest their feelings in determining outcomes. We have to propose processes that help people arrive at choices that are not perverted by impositions contrary to their freely expressed desires.

It is precisely because our participatory planning process differs in many respects from the flawed communicative processes of market and centrally planned allocation that its prices differ as well. Even the same population, with the same infrastructure, with the same everything except for having participatory planning and other participatory economic structures or, having say, markets and other capitalist or market coordinator structures, will arrive at different prices and outcomes. In fact, even for the same population and same productive Commons and the same participatory planning apparatus, matters of happenstance at the time of planning could cause a different plan to emerge. So how can we say that one set of prices is better than another? Prices are what the totality of choices make them.

The answer is that we can give a poor grade to a system's emergent prices when we can show that they don't take into account factors we think ought to have been accounted for, such as external effects like pollution. Or we can give a poor grade when we can show that prices were imposed, such as with central planning. Or we can give a poor grade when we can show that participants had inappropriate levels of influence, such as due to having different bargaining power. Or we can give a poor grade when we can show participants' preferences were warped, such as due to advertising or due to a bias against collective goods built into procedures that mis-assess collective goods.

Participatory planning's accounting procedures and the other defining elements of participatory economics consciously reduce all these distortions of final valuations or prices. More, indicative prices in a participatory economy derive from cooperative social proposals and refinements of proposals which can, if desired, be qualitatively checked when actors are confronted by unexpected reports. This addition can enhance the likelihood that quantitative indicators remain as accurate as possible. It can also help develop workers' sensitivity to fellow workers' situations and thereby sensitize everyone's understanding of the intricate tapestry of human relations that determines what we can and cannot consume or produce.

Yes, as critics will emphasize, the burden of distributing

information in a participatory allocation procedure can be somewhat greater than in a non-participatory economy because the latter simply disregards such matters. This is particularly true for adding qualitative information to databases able to be accessed when folks feel the need, so that then the 'bare numbers' that are prices can be considered in light of their 'real world' human context. While not being negligible, this would not entail everyone writing long essays about their work and living conditions. In fact, the whole approach could be optional. If pursued, it would presumably mean having a few people in each industry whose jobs included the task to generate concise accounts of unusual situations to correct for the fact that not everyone can personally experience every circumstance. It might be particularly helpful to consult such information when consumption or production proposals deviate greatly from expectations. In such cases, instead of seeing only a proposal that makes unexpected requests, we would be able to access reasons for the unexpected requests. This would increase our understanding of why producers of something we want more of are reluctant to meet that demand, or why consumers of something we want to produce less of are reluctant to reduce their requests. It might speed our ability to respond with refinements of our own proposals.

Part of a full critique of markets is that they cause buyers and sellers to become steadily more concerned solely about self, and steadily less concerned about others. In a market system there is every incentive to behave thus, and there is often no way to do otherwise. Even with no attempt to make qualitative information available, participatory planning would do vastly better than markets because even if workers and consumers in participatory planning only explicitly concern themselves with their own condition, the prices they act on nevertheless take account of impacts beyond buyer and seller. But at least in one sense there wouldn't be improvement because even though participatory planning's prices take into account other people's conditions, and even though arriving at a participatory plan solely using its prices would respect other's conditions, still, if people actively consider only their own situation, the process would not explicitly involve each actor ever self-consciously taking into account the situation of others. Account would have been taken, automatically, by virtue of being built into vastly improved pricing and decision-making, but not due to being built into the personal roles in planning. As such, I suspect planning with only numeric information would have significantly less positive impact on who we are and how we see others than would planning with occasional access to qualitative information, so I would lean toward opting for the latter even at the expense of some additional time spent.

Participatory Planning Take 8: Allocation Organization

In a participatory economy, as we have now seen in a number of successively deeper and also more complex and difficult "takes," our proposal for economic vision is that every workplace and neighborhood consumer council participates in the social allocation method we call participatory planning. But besides workplace councils, participatory planning will also undoubtedly involve industry federations of workers councils and a national producer council. And besides neighborhood consumer councils, it will also involve ward, city, county, and state federations of consumer councils as well as a national consumer council. Moreover, in addition to all these councils and federations of councils, participatory planning would likely have various agencies that would facilitate information processing for collective consumption proposals, determining the pricing of externalities, proposing and evaluating innovations and investment projects, handling workers' requests for changing their place of employment, and aiding individuals and families looking to find membership in new living units and neighborhoods, among other functions most of which will be discovered by future experience.

Finally, during each year at every level of the economy appropriate agencies, designed and operating based on future insights and experiences, might also help units revise proposals and search out the least disruptive ways of modifying plans in response to unforeseen circumstances. And we should remember that all workers, including those with such roles in industries and neighborhoods as well as those at the Iteration Facilitation Board, would get income for duration, intensity, and onerousness of socially valued labor, and thus would have no way to accrue excessive wealth. All this, taken together, is profoundly important but also too detailed to elaborate further for a visionary scaffold. However, we can at least ask, for clarity, what more specifically might be included among participatory planning's possible steps, and possible personal roles?

Steps of Participatory Planning

In participatory planning regarding day-to-day affairs over the course of a year, we propose that every individual or council at every level propose its own activities, and, after receiving information regarding other actors' proposals, and receiving the response of other actors to its proposal, that each individual and council then make a new suitably altered proposal, and that this recurs until a plan is adopted.

Thus, each consumption "actor," from individual consumers up to large consumer federations, proposes a consumption plan. Individuals make proposals for private goods such as clothing, food, travel, toys, etc. Neighborhood councils make proposals that include approved requests for their individual members' private goods, as well as previously approved requests for the neighborhood's collective consumption that might, for example, include a new pool or local park. Higher-level councils and federations of councils make proposals that include approved requests from member councils as well as the federation's larger collective consumption requests. Indeed, collective proposals precede personal ones as they impact each actor's personal budget by indicating how much each actor is "charged" for their share of collective consumption.

And similarly, each workplace council proposes a production plan. Workplaces enumerate the inputs they want and the outputs they propose to make available. Regional and industry-wide federations aggregate proposals and track excess supply and demand for the industry's products.

As every individual worker and consumer council navigates through successive iterations of participatory planning, they alter their proposals in response to the information they receive. There is no center or top. There is no competition. There are no excessively self-aggrandizing paths to pursue. Each actor fulfills responsibilities that bring them into more cooperative rather than into more antagonistic relations with other producers and consumers. Over the course of the planned year everyone is remunerated for effort and sacrifice. Everyone has a proportionate influence on their personal choices, as well as on those of larger collectives they are part of and on the whole economy. Updates flexibly occur as each year unfolds. It sounds viable, but can people actually make the called for planning proposals? And will the proposals be responsible? And will the process converge on a worthy plan in an acceptable time frame?

Preparing First Proposals

Suppose we kept records of the production and consumption that took place in the just completed year. Then with each new year we would have information about the prior year's enacted plan. Suppose the prices that wound up embodying the relative social costs and benefits last year were also recorded. Then each year we would have a set of final prices from the prior year to use to begin this year's estimates. If we also stored last year's full plan, access to additional relevant information could be made available to all actors in the planning process who choose to consult it. By accessing such information, each unit could easily see what its own proposals were in the prior year's planning process. With all this information available, how might workers and consumers councils make their first proposals for the coming year? Actual finely detailed and contextually efficient procedures will emerge and undoubtedly be steadily refined in practice in ways real-world lessons illuminate. We here suggest one possible, but not required method. We offer it to aid in understanding possibilities without drifting into thinking we can or must discern much less decide all aspects now.

For each upcoming year's plan:

1. Workers councils, individual consumers, and consumer councils first access relevant data from last year.
2. The same planning participants simultaneously receive information from the Iteration Facilitation Board estimating this year's probable changes in prices and income in light of existing knowledge of past investment decisions and changes in the labor force.
3. Planning participants also receive information from production and consumption councils regarding long-term investment projects and collective consumption proposals already agreed to in previous plans indicating the continuing commitments for the coming year.
4. Planning participants optionally review changes in their own proposals made during last year's planning to see how much they had to scale down their consumption desires or their desires to improve their quality of work life, and to remember their past aspirations in these regards. They also look to see what increases in average income and improvements in the quality of average work complexes are projected for the coming year, and

consider how they might best enjoy these gains.

5. Finally, using estimated prices as starting indicators of social costs and benefits, planning participants develop a proposal for the coming year enumerating what they want to consume or produce, and also—if society warrants doing so—providing qualitative information about any major deviations from expectations. Each proposal then enters the mix with all others, feedback arrives, and revisions are made. This occurs iteration after iteration, until a final plan is reached.

Please note, the above does not mean that individuals or collective consumption councils must specify how many units of every single product they need all the way down to size, style, and color. Goods and services would instead undoubtedly be grouped into categories according to the interchangeability of the resources, intermediate goods, and labor required to make them, as well as the easily predicted variation of preferences for optional features like size and color. For planning purposes, consumers would only need to request types of goods—shirts, vegetables, fruit, books, vehicles—from which workplaces could deduce based on past experience how many of different instances of each type of good would be needed to let everyone later pick a preferred size, style, and color, etc., to actually consume.

At any rate, individuals would present consumption requests for main categories of goods to neighborhood councils, which would by some agreed procedures collectively check for any significant problems in the requests and organize them into a total council request for the total of individual goods for all their members, along with the neighborhood's previously agreed collective consumption request, to become the total neighborhood consumption proposal.

Neighborhood proposals would be added to consumption

requests from other neighborhoods and then to full ward proposals, city proposals, and so on. Having the next higher-level council able to approve or contest lower-level requests until they are ready to be passed on could likely save considerable planning time and, in any event, might be advantageous for assessing collective implications, so might well be introduced into the process.

In the same way, on the production side, similar procedures would unfold. The workers council of a firm would freely access summaries of its last year's production, including what was initially proposed, changes made during planning iterations, and what was finally enacted to make separate proposals. It would access the IFB prediction of this year's requests based on extrapolations from new demographic data and last year's negotiations. Workers would presumably consider this information, perhaps guided by suggestions from some workers specially assigned to the task, discuss ideas for improving work life, and debate proposals that would finally settle on the firm's first proposal for inputs and outputs.

Proceeding from One Proposal to Another

Suppose in some participatory economy the first proposals are in. Workers councils have entered how much they want to work and consumer councils how much they and their members want to consume, all in light of their own very possibly overly optimistic assessments of possibilities. Do the first proposals constitute a plan or must we have another round? To decide, it is necessary to collect all the proposals and compare total demand and total supply for every class of final good and service, for every intermediate good, and for every primary input. In a first iteration, where consumers propose in part a "wish list" and workers likely propose output in hopes of some substantial improvements in their work lives, while some goods may be in excess supply, we can reasonably predict that for most goods initial proposals will reveal excess demand.

In other words, initial proposals taken together will not equal a feasible plan. As the next step, every council would receive new information indicating the goods in excess supply or demand and by how much, and how the council's own proposal compares to proposals of other comparable units in the same industry, as well as new estimates of indicative prices.

At this point, consumers would reassess their requests in light of the new prices and would likely, in most cases, "shift" their requests for goods in excess demand somewhat toward those whose indicative prices have fallen because they were in excess supply or at least less in excess demand than others. Consumers' councils and individuals whose overall requests were higher than average, and especially higher than anticipated budgets would warrant, would feel obliged to whittle down their requests in hopes of making their proposals responsible and viable. Why do consumers make changes toward operating within budget? Because when the final plan is settled, their budget sets a limit on their consumption choices.

Equity and efficiency would emerge simultaneously from each round of consumers' refinements. That is, the need to win approval from other similar councils in the form of a meshed plan that all could then commence implementing, plus the need for one's own plan to be within budget, would together provide reason for councils whose per capita consumption request is significantly above the social average to reduce their overall requests into accord with their budgets. But the need to reduce could be met by substituting goods whose indicative prices have fallen for those whose prices have risen. Attention would likely focus on the degree to which council proposals diverge from projected averages, and on whether their reasons for doing so are compelling, in which case exceptions might be warranted.

Similarly, workers councils whose ratios of social benefits of their outputs to social costs of their inputs were lower than average, which is to say after consideration of mitigating explanations whose proposals weren't adequately utilizing their assets and inputs, would come under pressure to increase either their efficiency or their effort in using assets from the Commons, or to explain why the indicators were misleading in their particular case. Before increasing their work commitment, workers might substitute inputs whose indicative prices had fallen for inputs whose indicative prices had risen, or substitute outputs whose indicative prices had risen for outputs whose indicative prices had fallen. Why do they do this? Because they want their activity to be socially valued so it can be remunerated and because they need to wind up with a responsible, implementable, workplace plan so they do not instead wind up having their agendas thwarted by a need to re-conceive the use of their workplace assets, as well as their total payroll reduced due to some of their effort not being socially valuable.

Each iteration of planning would yield a new set of proposals. Taken together, these proposals would yield new data regarding the status of each good, the average consumption per person, and the "benefit to cost ratio" for each firm. All this would allow calculation of new price projections and new predictions for average income and work, which would in turn lead to modifications in proposals, all of which dynamics would recur in additional planning iterations until a feasible plan is reached. And when is that? When does the planning process conclude with a collectively agreed plan? When the gap between supply and demand of each item falls within some socially agreed range (including provision for some slack production to ease accommodating subsequent modifications of preference and actions). Notice, participatory planning is an entwined process of all producers and consumers, assisted by information agencies but entirely self-managed. No top. No bottom. No center. No periphery.

Flexible Updating

Converging on a plan during a planning period, and then updating the proposed initial plan during the year in light of changes in preferences or circumstances could each take advantage of the large scale of the whole planning process. For example, assume we have settled on a plan for the year. Why might we need to update it during the year and how might this be done with the least disruption?

Consumers would begin each year with a working plan including how much of different kinds of food, clothing, meals at restaurants, trips, books, records, tickets to performances, and so on they have proposed to consume. What if after some weeks, someone wants to substitute one item with a different one? Or what if she wants to delete or add items to what she had expected to prefer for the year? Or what if she changes her mind and wants to save or borrow more than she planned to, and to thus reduce or increase overall consumption?

She belongs to a neighborhood consumers' council that in turn belongs to a ward council, a city federation, and so on. Some changes that Tony and Thalia in one neighborhood opt for will cancel each other out when taken together with changed requests from all the consumers within their neighborhood (some people increasing requests for a particular product, other people decreasing requests for it). Other variations will cancel out at the ward level, and so on. As long as consumer adjustments cancel each other out at some consumption federation level, production plans need not change. The same overall array of goods is headed to the councils, or rather made available for purchase by the council's members online or while browsing at local store outlets.

Indeed, facilitating adjustments without disrupting production plans could be one function of consumer "adjustment boards." But what happens if aggregate demand for a particular item significantly rises (or drops) as it undoubtedly would in some cases? Suppose as one possibility, individuals record their consumption on "credit card" computers that automatically compare the percentage of annual requests "drawn down" with the fraction of the year that has passed, taking account of predictable irregularities such as birth dates and holidays, seasonal variation and the like. This data could be processed by planning terminals that communicate projected changes to relevant industry councils that, in turn, communicate changes to particular firms.

The technology could be similar to that used in contemporary computerized store inventories, where store sales are automatically subtracted from inventory stocks. In any case, what would presumably follow is that consumer federations, industry councils, and individual work units would negotiate adjustments in consumption and associated production, which might in turn entail adjustments in work assignments to account for changed demand. Such changes during the unfolding year could lead to work diminishing in some industries and increasing in others relative to the plan for the year, including possible transfers of employees, but there need be no more moving about than in other types of economies. In any case, the need for workers to change jobs or to increase or diminish workloads, and the ensuing impact of that on their lives would be a factor proportionately considered in the negotiations over whether and how to meet changed demands, though neither unemployment nor inequitable income would ever arise.

Notice also, since each firm's activities would have implications for other firms, we can confidently predict that if planned matches between supply and demand are calculated too closely, any change in demand of goods with many inputs could disrupt the whole economy. For this reason a "taut" plan would prove unnecessarily inconvenient since it would require excessive debating and moving. To avoid this and to simplify updating, we can pretty confidently predict that a plan agreed to should be loose enough to include some unutilized capacity for many goods. A practical knowledge of those industries most likely to be affected by non-canceling alterations would facilitate this type of preparatory slack planning, and is logically no different than planning in advance for medical, disaster or other needs that individuals alone can't predict, but that we can socially predict and plan for.

There is a related additional issue, however. During the planning period, there emerges a final array of anticipated exchange rates or prices based on planned inputs and outputs for the economy. At the end of the year, we will have had actual inputs and outputs for the whole economy. Due to changes in output of various goods from the initial plan to the final reality, final real prices will differ somewhat from initially planned prices. The same is true for incomes for work. A person could have benefited or lost, having paid the initial plan price but gotten items whose true value wound up somewhat higher or lower. A participatory economy could simply reassess people's overall expenditure, charging them accurately at year's end, leading to some debt or remittance compared to their initial expectations. For that matter, facilitation boards could release new price estimates every few months for those who wished to avoid any large variations by adapting their choices based on the new valuations. Or, a participatory economy might instead allow such errors to pass unaddressed on the experience-validated assumption that over many years they would average out to no one's undue advantage. The point here is that these are details that will no doubt be resolved in practice, perhaps in different ways in different implementations of participatory planning and due to different practical lessons. The same observations hold in only slightly different forms for detailed procedures by which industries would credit equitable total incomes to their various workplaces for their overall duration, intensity, and onerousness of actually undertaken socially-valued labor, total income that each workers council would in turn internally equitably allocate among its members. The same logic again, with some modest differences, would presumably apply to detailed industry federation procedures for requiring updated operations by member workplaces to ensure that they responsibly utilize Commons inputs. To assess a vision, the main thing to keep our eye on instead of such contingent details is how the broad institutional structures and properties of the preferred vision—the visionary scaffold—fulfill desired values for economic life.

Converging On a Plan

Realistically adjusting indicative prices in light of stated preferences to balance supply and demand is typically more complicated in practice than in economists' theoretical models. A product in excess demand in one planning iteration could, for example, overshoot equilibrium into excess supply as workers offer to produce more and consumers offer to request less to respond responsibly to indicative prices. Likewise, since each product's status affects many others, progress in one industry could disrupt equilibrium in another. To make the participatory planning procedure converge at an acceptable rate, therefore, it may be agreed that specific economies will incorporate flexible rules that facilitate convergence within a reasonable time but do not unduly bias outcomes or subvert self-management or equity. Procedures with this purpose might range from simple formulas carried out by computer that seek short cuts toward convergence, to adjustments fashioned and implemented by assigned workers who are experienced in facilitating convergence when particular situations arise. Devising and choosing from among such experience-informed possibilities may become a practical issue in implementing any actual participatory economy. Or perhaps such procedures will prove unnecessary due to the bare process itself easily converging.

Considerations that a choice between contending procedures might involve, include, for example:

1. The extent to which iteration workers could accidentally or intentionally bias outcomes.
2. The extent of reductions in the number of iterations required to reach a plan or ease of conducting each iteration, and ensuing time savings.
3. The amount of planning time saved through compartmentalizing subsets of iterations with special simplifying procedures.
4. How much more or less onerous to producers and consumers their calculations become with different options in place.

One thing to make clear about participatory planning and participatory economics in general is, as I have often emphasized, that there is not likely to be a single right answer to how to accomplish its various functions. As with capitalism and all other social arrangements, within a participatory economy different approaches to problems may be taken in different parts of the economy and in different institutions. Different approaches could exist, for example, for measuring labor intensity or onerousness, or for balancing job complexes in or across units, or for organizing council decision deliberation or tallying procedures regarding participation and apportionment of influence in different industries and workplaces. There could be differences as well regarding handling social consumption and among different instances of the latter, or regarding means of determining proper accounting of externalities, or means for determining income allocation to industries and workplaces, or for facilitating planning convergence while simultaneously promoting empathy, preserving social transparency, and encouraging participation.

The point is that an economy is a participatory economy insofar as it implements the essential features of a Productive Commons, council organization, self-managed decision-making, classless job definition, equitable remuneration, and participatory allocation, and insofar as it prioritizes the values of self-management, equity, solidarity, diversity, sustainability, and classlessness to guide choices among more detailed features that fill out the essential visionary scaffold into a full-fledged practical economic reality.

Participatory Planning Take 9: Some Additional Features

The above discussion focuses on individuals and consumer councils making consumption proposals and on workers and workplace councils making production proposals. It explains how proposals for what producers wish to supply and for what consumers wish to demand are conveyed and contrasted, and how, in light of distributed information, individuals and councils alter their proposals until a plan is reached. Embedded in the logic is how collective consumption and other complexities as well are handled. But even for this all too long chapter (though all too short presentation of participatory planning), we should perhaps further clarify some issues regarding collective consumption, externalities, income via allocation, and investment procedures.

Collective Consumption and Externalities

Suppose your neighborhood would like a new swimming pool, your town wants to expand its public park, or your state wants to overhaul its public transport system. One way to approach collective goods is for consumer councils to propose any or all of these as part of their consumption proposals. Here are two aspects to consider. First, if the collective consumption is to occur, it of course has implications for what must be produced.

This is no different than what holds for private consumption requests. Second, these types of collective goods are still, ultimately, consumer goods that benefit people, and they must be both charged to consumer budgets and considered for their impact on everyone they would affect.

At first glance, there would seem to be no new issues. A neighborhood council discusses the matter and decides to ask for a pool. How do the neighborhood's members register the desire and collectively decide to make the proposal? Via self-management, of course. If the proposal goes through, people in the neighborhood will be charged on their consumption budgets their fair share of the indicative price, which price in turn may alter somewhat during the plan's iterations. If the cost to be charged is too high, that is, if the neighborhood residents feel they will have to give up too much of their personal consumption allotments to have the collective pool, the neighborhood cancels the request. If given their desire for the pool, the amount they have to pay from their budgets to get the pool is acceptable, the neighborhood persists in its request.

Some problems arise. Larry and Lance both live in the neighborhood. Larry is going to swim but Lance is not. Are they both charged a share, or only Larry? Or, suppose the pool will be used and enjoyed by folks in the surrounding towns as well. Larry and Lance's neighborhood may have proposed the pool, but if it is going to be built shouldn't all those benefiting bear some of its cost? And what if the reverse is the case? What if the pool's effect on water delivery will adversely affect the neighborhood next door? How do people suffering repercussions from the decision to have a pool influence the decision to propose the pool to the planning process of a council they are not even in?

Or consider a somewhat similar problem on a much larger scale: how to deal with pollution. Suppose Michigan's citizens, through their councils and after due deliberations, decide to collectively request a hydroelectric dam to replace a horribly polluting series of coal-based electric generators. How do the people of Michigan decide to request this in the planning process? More, how is the dam's cost to be allocated against the consumption budgets of the people of Michigan? Do the asthmatic citizens who suffer hugely from coal-generated pollution pay more than the folks less bothered by that pollution? More, it turns out that the pollution from the coal plants afflicted Chicago and to a lesser extent other cities in Illinois. Shouldn't those citizens who will also benefit bear some of the costs of the new dam, and, if so, how does that come about? To what degree do they pay and what impact do they have on deliberations?

Or suppose the reverse is the case. The Michiganites are proposing some mass project which will not benefit but will instead adversely affect people in Illinois, say with pollution. Again, how do the citizens of Illinois have their appropriate impact? Even more complicated, suppose the rest of the country enjoys clean air. Is there an equity issue? Why should Michiganers, even if they are most affected, foot the bill if, in fact, they were enduring worse than average air conditions in the first place? Can participatory economic answers to these queries be rooted in the logic of self managing council-based organization and participatory planning, each understood as social deliberative processes?

- First, unlike with markets, we want decisions about goods to account for their *full* personal, social, and ecological costs and benefits. We want the final price of goods to reflect all their effects as best we are able to make that happen. One likely possibility. If a firm produces pollution, the planning process considers the pollution a product. However, unlike most products, it registers as a cost. Thus the victims of the pollution establish a price for each unit of pollution. If the production is agreed to go ahead, the firm is charged for the total pollution. The residents who endure the pollution are reimbursed.

- Second, we want all people affected to proportionately influence decisions. When a proposal affects large numbers of people, it is not just that we want the initially formulated proposal decided on properly. We also want the system to facilitate the proposal's improvement. If a proposal has negative external effects, in addition to properly accounting for them if they persist, we want means to first try to amend the proposal to reduce those effects or even completely offset their impact.

The participatory planning process should not only promote that all those affected decide on collective proposals, and likewise that all those affected determine the cost of externalities, for example pollution, but that all those affected be able to amend and otherwise improve the relevant proposals. When my neighborhood requests a pool or Michigan requests a dam, very likely the people involved do not have at their disposal the full awareness and insights of people in other neighborhoods or states. We do not want to incorporate only the decision influence of those other people, but, at least in some cases, also their ideas and ingenuity.

To these ends, in participatory planning, one possibility is that when the residents of a smaller council propose some desired collective consumption (a pool or a changed energy delivery system), the proposal has to not only gain support in their own council, but must also be delivered to more encompassing councils above. So a proposal may go from a neighborhood up to a town and then to a city, a county, and so on, and likewise it may go from a state to a region and on to a country.

If a pool is proposed in my neighborhood, or a new dam in my state, and if there will be beneficiaries beyond the area of the proposing council, then in passing up the proposal its advocates are looking for it to become a proposal of the higher-level council, with the hope that all who benefit at that next higher level will also be charged for its consumption, rather than only a subset in the smaller proposing council paying the whole cost.

If we have a proposal, in contrast, which has negative impact beyond our own council's citizens, then after passing it up, broader constituencies will presumably indicate their displeasure, and establish a price/fee—that is a price the producer has to pay, adding to their immediate costs of production, and a fee that they who breathe the pollution have to be compensated.

In this case too, perhaps the proposal is taken over by the higher-level council, but this time it is likely adapted through deliberations to rectify or otherwise account for its broader negative impacts. The point is that regardless of where proposals originate, collective goods consumption proposals could sensibly eventually be sponsored at the level where they have their overwhelming proportion of impact, and at that level could be massaged and refined before acceptance. With that approach, only then would the proposal be put to producers and other consumers.

What about the apportionment of influence over these decisions, and payment for the items? In the absolute ideal case, each individual is going to influence a choice in proportion to the extent it affects him or her. Likewise, each is going to carry a share of the cost proportionate to the extent that he or she benefits.

Members of a council make decisions by means that involve both information transfer about the decision's properties and about people's reactions to it, as well as deliberations over possible refinements, all via some agreed set of deliberations and then voting procedures.

Participatory economic principles say we ought to choose all these mechanisms to try to make most likely an outcome that accounts for all relevant information and effects, that is appropriately influenced by all concerned, and that takes time and energy commensurate to what is at stake, but not more.

It seems very likely that there is no single right answer that always applies to how to best achieve all this. One person might feel that with each decision we should try as perfectly as possible to represent divergent opinions. Another person might feel that over the whole planning process there are many such decisions and if we err a little in some of them, the deviations from perfection will average out. Why not do a good job, therefore, but save the extra time required to do a nearly perfect job in the knowledge that in sum and on average, small deviations from perfect accounting in each decision will more or less be made up for by small deviations in others?

There are other possible attitudes as well. But the point is that unlike in market or centrally planned systems where the outcomes are determined by elites with no attention to most of the relevant information or to most of the impact on others, or to the wills of most people affected, or to the merits of the methods utilized, in participatory planning all these considerations are central. This is not introducing unnecessary complexity. It is addressing actual complexity responsibly.

Take the case of the pool in the neighborhood. Perhaps it is proposed by someone living there, then supported by others, and then put forward as a specific proposal. We can imagine neighborhoods having settled on procedures for their members to express their reactions. We can imagine the proposal clearly fits into some broad category of decisions typically decided by a particular decision-making approach, let's say majority vote by the whole neighborhood. Suppose the proposal passes along with a plan for how the bill will be charged throughout the neighborhood. The proposal then goes up to the next council level. If folks in higher councils are adversely affected, they begin to consider anew, and they may reject the proposal, or, more likely, add various amendments that would make it acceptable by reducing or eliminating its adverse implications. There could be agencies with workers tasked with various steps in such processes. Debate between levels could also occur, leading to refinements as well. If the initiating neighborhood felt that broader constituencies should help with the payment, it would pass up the pool request not as a finished proposal, but as an entreaty that the higher level council adopt it as their proposal, rather than the smaller neighborhood having to go it alone. Or, perhaps in a different participatory economy, or even just in a different neighborhood, or for a different type of good, there is a higher premium put on streamlining the planning process, so people opt for different routines and procedures.

Or, for the example above, what if the original vote in the neighborhood council failed? The proposers have a number of options. We can imagine that those in favor might form a subgroup and join together to propose the pool as part of their personal consumption allocations. As with other personal consumption requests, if there were harm to others, the neighborhood could intervene; but otherwise personal consumption requests that are within budgets would be approved. However, because in this case these are personal consumption requests, the requesters would have to forego help with payment for the pool from others in the neighborhood. A second alternative that could be pursued if the original vote in the neighborhood council failed would be that the proposers could go to the next higher council to see if they could convince that body to fund a pool, though the opposition of the neighborhood council would be a strong count against doing so.

The situation is roughly the same for Michigan enacting a massive project that would affect people throughout the state, or also in Illinois. Each collective consumption good proposed in the planning process is addressed first to determine the appropriate council level to handle it to be sure all its significant positive and negative effects are dealt with appropriately. Next, research by relevant agencies discovers the properties of the proposal and its implications for various users or bystanders, etc. Reactions are presented. Deliberations take place. When there are negative effects, as with pollution, they are enumerated by agreed procedures, charged against the pollution producer, and used on behalf of the pollution "victim." Finally, decisions are made using rules chosen to be as suitable as possible to the case in question.

In the negotiations themselves, proposals are likely altered in an effort to arrive at refinements that are universally desired or at least overwhelmingly accepted. Take the Michigan dam. Suppose it would displace various people. The initial proposal (we might hypothesize) could have come from a city well away from the proposed site of the dam that was seeking better energy provision and cleaner air, and that might have ignored the harsh implications of the dam for those displaced. As the proposal goes up through the ascending council levels, the local people who would be displaced gain knowledge of it and join the deliberations. Given the huge impact on them, they would play a powerful role, being given a chance to make known their horror at the idea and the huge negative impact on them. The proposal might be changed to include reimbursing people from the dam region, providing them with new houses in locales of their choosing, up to and including reconstructing their town elsewhere, all as part of the cost of the dam.

The point of all this is that given participatory values, goods with substantial collective impact would be handled by social deliberations that arrive at choices that try to appropriately incorporate the wills of all the people affected, to massage and modify proposals so they become optimal, and to apportion payment for costs in accordance with benefits enjoyed, and, when need be, to correct for negative implications or make restitution for them. Moreover, as noted in earlier takes on planning, collective consumption proposals and investment projects and determination of externalities would all need to occur for items to be undertaken in a coming year, before that year's more basic planning process begins, due to the implications for people's budgets and workloads.

Is there only one way to accomplish such tasks? I don't think so. Is it all accomplished perfectly? Of course not. Are there disputes or mistakes? Of course. These are fallible social processes. Economists typically model these kinds of phenomena far more abstractly than they actually occur. But that is not without lessons. For example, we can imagine approaches that forego considerable cooperative negotiation and refinement and instead adopt simpler dynamics. Maybe such a choice would provide a template for various situations. Or perhaps collective goods planning and attribution of external negative and positive effects would remain complex and somewhat messy, but tractable. One key observation and goal will undoubtedly be to ensure that there is no bias and certainly no bias that snowballs with errors producing further errors in the same direction. Indeed, a large part of the contrast to markets and central planning is that in the participatory case not only will problematic outcomes arise less often, but the source of the problems will be different. Participatory planning problems will be due to ignorance or to actual error, not due to systematic biases that always elevate some groups and make others subordinate, that always incorporate only limited information, or that always employ authoritarian procedures.

Consider cigarettes. In the best possible world, the price of cigarettes should reflect not only the usual matters of the labor and other ingredients that go into cigarette production and the desire of consumers for them, but also their impact on those smoking them and on the health system that cares for those who become ill, and the impact on those in the vicinity of smokers and on the health system that cares for them. How does the price of cigarettes get set in participatory planning? How well does it accord with the best possible world where some cosmic process determines all those impacts perfectly? Who pays the costs and enjoys the benefits?

The adverse impact of smoking on health, society might decide, should be paid for by the smokers. Health care would be free, but why should everyone in society foot the bill for aspects of health care that arise due to predictable, avoidable choices? Then the external health costs of cigarettes would entirely enter the price of cigarettes rather than being apportioned to all citizens alike. On the other hand, what about sports injuries or even pregnancy? There are issues, obviously, about what aspects of a good's implications are the responsibility of its users and what aspects are properly a part of society's responsibilities. There is no need to explore all dimensions of all variants for all goods here. Indeed, to do so would overstep vision's proper mandate. We want to propose a visionary scaffold, not a visionary blueprint. What is important about participatory planning is the institutions that could arrive at assessments in such matters not the specific contextual policies and methods future experiences will lead future citizens to settle on and continually improve.

Thus, if the above particular prediction about what people would decide was appropriate, the price of cigarettes would include a component fee to cover the costs of health care for medical problems that arise from smoking cigarettes. The cost would be high. But what about second-hand smoke? Cigarettes are, in this respect, a good with massive external impact. If a local council proposes, in sum, to consume a total volume of cigarettes—5000 cartons, say, if their consumption was entirely unregulated—the adverse impact from second-hand smoke would be significant. Councils at many levels, wanting a healthy environment, might be appalled by the overall consumption request. What happens? As with the earlier examples, a procedure must determine the external effect.

The first possibility is to implement restrictions that would reduce ill effects, such as no smoking zones. A second option might be to charge fees that cover the costs of ventilation methods, and medical charges. A third possibility might be to alter the product itself to reduce its ill effects. A fourth possibility could be the more aggressive banning of the product entirely, on grounds that there is simply no way to reduce the ill effects sufficiently to permit its sensible consumption. Perhaps there are other possibilities. The point is individual goods which yield adverse collective effects might well be deliberated partly on a personal level, as in each consumer saying that they want or do not want cigarettes, like they want or do not want a new shirt, but also by larger councils that would consider the sum total consumption by all members and its broader implications.

Income Via Allocation

When we earlier addressed issues of income we focused on how it would be accomplished within workplaces by workers councils in accord with their own agreed procedures for revealing each member's duration, intensity, and onerousness of socially-valued labor. We presumed, however, that the total payroll for the workplace was already determined and that apportionment of the total allotted payroll among the workplace's workers occurred in light of that. One can reasonably ask, how is the total that is warranted for any particular workplace's workforce determined?

Put differently, once a total income for all the workers in a workplace exists, we discussed how an equitable amount for each separate worker could be agreed on by the workers council of that workplace and why doing so would have proper incentive effects. The workers equitably apportion income in accord with effort and sacrifice by evaluative methods they choose to a degree of accuracy they favor. But a prior question remains. What determines the total payroll for each workplace?

Consider the whole society's output for end user individual and collective consumption. If everyone were to get an average income, including those who cannot work, it would be the value of the total product divided by the total number of people. In that case, if an industry has n workers, as a first approximation the industry would be allotted n times the average income per worker for the whole society—unless, due to some special industry features, the particular industry's workforce deserved more or less compared to workers in other industries. This could be so, for example, if the particular industry's jobs were on average more onerous, or if on average its workers put in more time, or if on average they worked more intensely than in other industries.

Similarly, let's say that mining lithium was allotted some total industry income as per the logic above. It would have a new and perhaps somewhat altered average income to allot per worker (because for example, the lithium industry's work on average is more onerous or its workers work on average longer or harder). In that case, each lithium workplace would get income to distribute based on its number of workers times the average income per worker for the lithium industry—unless, again, due to some features, now a particular lithium workplace deserved more or less than the industry average per worker because, for example, that particular lithium workplace had some old onerous technology that had been updated in other lithium workplaces, or its workers put in more time, or worked more intensely than those in other lithium workplaces.

So, the idea is that the overall plan directly determines the average income per person in society, and thus also the average income per worker. Then industries are allotted a share of overall income based on their number of workers but with corrections whenever the industry deserves more or less than average per worker, due to its special attributes. Next, each industry determines the total payroll to be allotted to each of its workplaces as the average per industry worker times the number of workers in each of the industry's workplaces, corrected, however, if any particular workplace deserves more or less than average per worker due to its special features. And then each workplace's workers council allots its payroll to its members with the same proviso.

So new questions arise.

1. How does society make judgments about whole industries?
2. How do whole industries make judgments about their component workplaces?
3. How do firms make judgments about their member workers?

The third question we answered earlier. Each workplace determines a procedure to use to determine who has worked longer or less long, harder or less hard, or under worse or better conditions than average in the workplace, and employs it, to a degree of precision acceptable to the workers in the workers council in question.

Now take that logic up one level. Each industry determines a procedure to use to allot the industry total among all the industry's workplaces and employs it acceptably to the industry's federation of its workers councils.

Take it up another level. The societal council of all workers determines a procedure to use to apportion income to society's various industries that is acceptable to the whole population.

The procedures chosen determine if each or any industry or then if each or any workforce within an industry and then if any worker within a workplace endures above or below average onerousness, or works above or below average duration or intensity, or has above or below average means of production, or above or below average cost for inputs, or if workforces are above or below average in their actual productive capacity. One approach is that to determine the various factors, by whatever means experience shows agreeable and effective, each level assesses the social products and social costs of the industry, or of the workplace, or of the worker, to ensure that work that is socially valued or otherwise justified, is properly remunerated.

Since the above gets into some more complex aspects of how to have a worthy allocation system, let's try giving it another run through with a different slant. The issue we are considering centers on how participatory planning and council self-management together provide appropriate income. There is already clarity about what constitutes equitable income and how a workplace council can allocate its total allotted payroll to its workers. They do it, we have proposed, as they decide, equitably, and with incentives that work, and so on.

The question we are now considering is how it comes about that the income allotted to each workplace as income to divide among its workers—that is, as the total payroll for the workplace—is what equity for the various workers calls for it to be. In other words, how is the total income allotted for all workers in each workplace determined such that the total payroll is what it needs to be for each worker in the workplace to receive his or her equitable income? Our answer is that average income is settled for society by the overall plan. Divergences from average are then settled for industries, and then in turn for firms within industries, and then finally for workers within firms, each by the involved workers council structure at the level in question.

Imagine a workplace has workers all working average duration, intensity, and onerousness for its industry. In that case that workplace would be allotted the average income per worker for its industry times its number of workers, and each worker would receive that average and all would be well. But what if some of the workers in that same workplace in the industry work considerable overtime, or in another workplace some do not exert, or still another workplace in the industry has some unduly onerous conditions, and so on? What causes the total allotted to each workplace to be such that it equals the sum of what ought to be the income of all that workplace's workers even with many of them deviating from average inside the workplace, or because the workplace itself deviates from average in its industry, or because the industry deviates from average in society?

The first thing to notice is that at the level of industries in society, and of workplaces in an industry, it is rather like at the level of separate workers in a single workplace. So the whole planning process (society) establishes total income for society. Dividing by population gives average income per worker.

Then society allocates the total societal income among all society's industries. That is, it determines the total income for each industry—which is the industry's total of workers times the average workers income for the industry but with an industry correction for each industry (with lithium mining being more onerous than publishing, for example, so that lithium work gets higher average income). Now each industry has its own total income and its new average per worker within the industry which may differ from the overall average for society due to the industry correction.

Next, the industry has to apportion its allotted total among the industry's workplaces. Each workplace gets the industry average per worker, times the number of workers it has, but now with a possible workplace correction because some workplaces may differ from others in onerousness, intensity, or duration.

Finally, as the last step, each workplace has to apportion its allotted total among its workers. Each worker gets the workplace's average per worker modified by a correction if some in the workplace work more, some less, and so on.

So what are the corrections?

Each industry should receive the social average income for each of its workers if each industry had the same average duration, intensity, and onerousness of socially-valued work for its workers. So, the correction for different industries should account for each industry's deviation from that overall average. Then the same occurs for differences among workplaces within the industry. And, finally, it occurs, as well, for differences among workers inside each workplace.

Arriving at the specific determinations is a bit complicated and more so when we take into account job balancing, but the relevant point is not the details but the overall aim and outcome which is remuneration for the duration, intensity, and onerousness of socially-valued work, while also providing the socially average income for those who can't work, and of course providing healthcare and diverse other public or personally free goods for everyone.

Investment

What about production of means of future production, which we call investment and which often requires years to complete and further years to have impact? Investment includes the dam discussed earlier but also things like new equipment or new factories where the aim is to increase productivity. It is hard to handle well for a number of reasons, not least that there are current and future consumers and they can be entirely different people with the latter not available to express themselves or not even born when investments are initiated. A key reality is that whatever assets we use for investment for the future we don't use for producing consumer goods for the present. And whereas current population benefits from consumption now, future population benefits from investment now to enlarge consumption later. We want methods that self-consciously protect and benefit both constituencies rather than sacrificing one to benefit only the other, or vice versa.

A second complication is that future preferences and production possibilities can only be guessed and that implemented plans continually change the setting of future plans. This means we are guessing future preferences and future effects of our proposed investments. Honest error is quite possible. In fact, to an extent, honest error is inevitable. So whenever we undertake an investment plan, it will very likely at least to some degree have flaws. Catching such flaws and revising plans in subsequent years is another essential need.

Proposals for investments in new consumer products would most often originate in the national federation of consumer councils. Indeed, these councils would not only be intrinsically more closely in touch with consumer needs and ideas, they would also likely employ workers to do research to inform such proposals. Similarly proposals for investments in new tools for production or for simply producing more familiar tools would likely come from workplace councils and ultimately from the industry and national federations of workplace councils. And the federations, and perhaps each workplace, would likely also employ some workers to do research to inform such proposals. The exact procedures to use to price such projects, to decide on enacting them, and to later account for their implications for production in yearly planning would certainly be more complex than more basic yearly planning, but would nonetheless be guided by the same values and the same need to function compatibly with the rest of the proposed economic vision. The same holds as for what we earlier called updating as a yearly plan unfolds but which in the case of long term investment becomes that we carry out year one of the investment plan, discover that things have changed from what we have predicted, and so now have to update subsequent years.

What about innovations that don't even fit within an industry but would instead generate whole new industries? Would this be left to university research? Or might society have an actual innovation industry whose mandate is to pursue and be a temporary home for such undertakings before they can stand alone as industries participating in planning? Or would both approaches exist? Or another? Time will tell but what wouldn't occur are approaches undermining self-management, equity, solidarity, diversity, sustainability, or participation.

To what extent can the yearly and multi-year investment planning processes work like the yearly planning process of negotiated cooperation among councils, and to what extent will it instead require a set of additional agencies based in federations of councils not only to generate proposals, but so that then a large-scale deliberation generates refinements, and then an overall vote arrives at investment plans which later inform yearly planning? It seems likely that such choices and perhaps other possibilities as well will emerge from future experience and its lessons. But for investment planning to provide part of the information for yearly planning, the main issue will be to ensure that it doesn't interfere with, and preferably that it further advances, solidarity, diversity, equity, sustainability, and self-management.

Conclusion

The point of the final sections of this chapter on participatory planning has been to give a loose introductory feel to some possible approaches to certain detailed pricing and deliberative properties of participatory planning vis-à-vis public goods and what are currently called externalities, whether positive or negative, as well as to allocative processes able to provide equitable incomes, and to some of the complexities of investment planning.

Participatory economics is a vision whose defining logic and features advance certain core aims and whose social processes will diverge from those aims only due to honest errors or perhaps the choice to save time by settling negotiations satisfactorily rather than more perfectly, but not due to some systematic incapacity or recurring bias that inexorably obstructs aims. On all these counts and particularly for technical aspects of participatory planning, a new book by Robin Hahnel, *Democratic Economic Planning,* referenced in our closing selected references, goes further into elaborating possible approaches to and proposals regarding some mathematical complexities than does this chapter.

For now, regarding our proposal for the essentials of a new economy, and thus for a visionary economic scaffold, it comes down to this.

Do we want people to receive income in accord with capital ownership, power, or the value of each person's personal contribution to social production? Or do we prefer to base any differences in workers' consumption rights only on differences in duration, intensity, and onerousness in producing socially-valued goods and services? In other words, do we want an economy that implements the maxim "to each worker according to the value of his or her property, or power, or personal contribution," or do we want an economy that implements the maxim "to each worker according to his or her socially-valued effort?"

Likewise, do we want a capitalist or coordinator few to conceive and coordinate the work of an obedient many? Or do we want everyone to have the opportunity to participate in economic decision-making to the degree they are affected by the outcome and to enjoy training and on the job circumstances that guarantee their capacity to do so? In other words, do we want to continue to organize work and preparation for work hierarchically, preserving class division, or do we want to balance jobs and utilize training for empowerment to attain classlessness?

Further, do we want a structure for expressing preferences

biased in favor of individual over social consumption? Or do we want to make it as easy to register preferences for social as for individual consumption? Do we want prices that mis-handle or ignore broad social and ecological effects? Or do we want prices that account for personal, social, and ecological costs and benefits? Do we want economic decisions to be determined by individuals and groups competing against one another for well-being and survival, where the enhancement of each is attained only at the expense of some other? Or do we want to plan our joint endeavors democratically, equitably, and efficiently, with all actors having self-managing influence and each benefiting in parallel with the rest? In other words, do we want to abdicate economic decision-making to the market or central planning, or do we want to embrace the possibility of participatory planning?

In sum, do we want to continue either capitalist rule and production for profit or coordinator rule and production for surplus, both with ecological decay, inequity, and class rule? Or do we want to attain classlessness, self-management, equity, and attention to full social and ecological implications, and thus to ecological and social sanity?

It may sound melodramatic, but do we crave class rule or classlessness? Do we desire anti-sociality or solidarity? Will we have barbarism or participatory economy?

8

Participatory Economics and Other Sides of Life

To see a world in a grain of sand and heaven in a wild flower. Hold infinity in the palm of your hand and eternity in an hour.
William Blake

I am only free when all human beings around me, men and women alike, are equally free.
Mikhail Bakunin

A new world needs a new economy. A new world equally needs new relations for other sides of life. Proposing a new economy, we therefore need it to compatibly support new relations elsewhere, and vice versa. Here are just a few suggestions for what change might include in some other parts of society. Here are also some intersections of participatory economics with those other parts of society.

Participatory Polity and Participatory Economy

Consider how society accomplishes the key political functions of legislation, adjudication, and the implementation of collective agendas. If participatory economics proves valid, then similar values will likely have simultaneously informed new polity. New polity will therefore likely seek to implement self-management and justice, as well as to promote solidarity and diversity. In reverse, new political relations would likely require an economy that abides political participatory democracy, that "produces" workers and consumers able to participate politically, and that does not "produce" conflicting classes that would subvert desired political aims to advance their class agendas.

To succeed, in other words, a new polity will presumably need a population prepared and inclined to participate fully. It will also need its own operations to function without class rule or even class division. One could imagine—as does the well-developed participatory political vision that has been offered, for example, by Stephen Shalom—a participatory polity built on neighborhood assemblies plus encompassing levels of federated assemblies, plus a dramatically renovated restorative judicial system, plus a new executive for implementing shared programs, such as a new Center for Disease Control. Such political innovations would in each case presumably honor self-management and equity and incorporate balanced job complexes.

To its political credit, participatory economics would "supply" to political life people who are well prepared by their economic activities for participatory political roles. Vice versa, participatory politics would need to similarly support new economic values and structures. Indeed, if political relations were to produce people expecting to dominate or be subordinate, or to produce people expecting to be enriched or impoverished, such people would find their expectations not only unmet but challenged by an accompanying participatory economy. Put differently, participants of economic life—people without class division, people empowered, people accustomed to self-managing would presumably be well-fitted to equitable judicial interactions, to shared political agendas, and to political assemblies which might even be consumer councils with a second focus. So far, then, so good. We need political vision, well beyond the brief comments here, and it should address the various defining aspects of political activity—for example, legislation, adjudication, and collective implementation. Whatever our political vision turns out to be, and I favor Shalom's proposals for a participatory polity, we can be quite confident that a just participatory political vision will support and be supported by a participatory economy.

Participatory Kinship and Participatory Economy

Next, consider the ways societies accomplish key gender/sexual/familial functions including procreation, nurturance, education of the next generation, household maintenance, and diverse choices for daily life in living units. We can sensibly predict that however all this is precisely and diversely accomplished, the new revolutionized kinship—perhaps it will be participatory kinship, for example, as it has been envisioned by Lydia Sargent, Cynthia Peters, and Savvina Chowdhury—would of course seek to prepare children for the most multifaceted, creative, and caring lives they might choose to pursue. It would presumably treat men, women, trans, and people of different familiar and of new sexual preferences and practices alike.

What changes might eliminate the hierarchies among men and women, and the toxic masculinity and subordinated femininity those hierarchies enforce and depend on? One change might be that participatory kinship relations would overturn the familiar familial arrangement wherein men father, women mother, and young girls and boys seeing and experiencing that division of responsibilities become imbued with patriarchal habits, inclinations, and desires. To avoid that, perhaps participatory kinship would include that neither men nor women mother or father. Instead, people of all genders would parent.

Another possibility. Perhaps a feminist revolution will determine that activity involving directly, personally attending to the needs of others has such profoundly positive implications for personality and empathy that everyone ought to do a share of it. Rather than taking care of the young, the ill, or the elderly being something women overwhelmingly do, such activity would be considered so valuable and socially constructive of humane sentiments and empathetic capacities that it would be shared equally among men and women.

Participatory economics sees empowering activity as so important and so essential due to its effects on those doing it, that it must be universally equilibrated. Analogously, participatory kinship might see caring activity as so important and so essential, also by its effects on those doing it, that it must be universally equilibrated. If so, participatory economy would have to accommodate the message. Likewise, participatory kinship would have to accommodate the message from the accompanying participatory economy that empowering activity must be equilibrated not only in council-based and collectively planned work, but also in daily life activity. This would be an instance of intersectionality in a participatory society.

In any case, a new economy that functions in a society with participatory kinship would have to accept and promote full and equal participation from both women and men. Women and men would have to be equally powered and remunerated for their economic labors. Education would have to uncover and aid the development of the most multifaceted, creative, and caring young people entering new jobs and would have to provide jobs which would further rather than stifle all such young people. A new economy would also have to facilitate—were kinship to call for it—a fair and equal distribution of caring work. In fact, in that case it would ideally have to alter work so that caring for those beyond self was an intrinsic part of every economic calculation.

Looking at the above menu of requirements, it turns out that conditions for a good economy to fit with transformed kinship sound like a prescription for participatory economics. In this case, as with politics earlier—so far, so good. We need to win new kinship because changes in other domains would not alone liberate sexuality and gender as fully as desired. We can then be confident, however, that such new kinship can support and be supported by participatory economics.

But wait, not so fast. An additional and more specific

question arises. What about household labor? What about the oft-raised demand "wages for housework"? How might this clear intersection of economics and kinship be handled in a good society?

There is a context to first clarify. The wages for housework demand and its associated ideas were first offered decades ago. The aim was to address problems in the then current society, problems which are now somewhat reduced but regrettably still very much with us. But would the question of how to organize a new society benefit from a different answer than the question of how should we combat various ills in this one?

One way to respond is to say that in a good society raising children, furnishing and caring for a dwelling, cooking for one's housemates, and tending to one another's living group needs should be addressed like all work. We should not only offer wages for housework as a demand now, but we should also propose wages for housework for a new society. This may well be the view of many and perhaps most readers of this book. But is there any other answer?

We certainly want a new society to fix the injustices associated with past approaches to what we can call, for convenience, household activity. But is the path that wages for housework proposes, though it is possible, the best solution? Doesn't it present a pretty daunting problem when we think not about today's society and economy, but about one we would like to have for our future? What would it mean, that is, not as a demand for now, which is one thing, but if it was adopted as a feature of a new society and new economy?

An analogy may clarify the question. To today demand a $15 minimum hourly wage in the US is quite progressive. To today demand a $30 an hour minimum wage would be quite radical. But to say a good society with a participatory economy should have a $15 or even a $30 minimum wage would make no sense. In fact, a minimum wage would be meaningless in a participatory economy because there is no difference for anyone in the rate of pay for an hour of average intensity and onerousness of socially-valued work. There is no unwarranted difference in people's incomes and what differences exist due to different duration, intensity, or onerousness are not only warranted, they also cannot get too large. So, this is the sense in which one might ask do wages for housework make sense now and perhaps during transition to a better economy, but not make sense in an established better economy in an established better society?

In participatory economics work occurs in balanced jobs. Work is remunerated for duration, intensity, and onerousness for work that contributes to the overall social product. Work is collectively self-managed by workers councils. Work inputs are requested by workers councils in production proposals that are cooperatively assessed and refined by participatory planning. Work outputs are made available to consumers by participatory planning. All this is considered essential to have self-management, solidarity, equity, and classlessness. Would incorporating wages for housework be a positive addition?

Well, in a future participatory economy what would be the workers council for household work? Would a household want to have its activity assessed in any way by the planning process? Also, aren't the main beneficiaries of household work the members of the household? Does that make sense? Should those who do household activity receive wages not as an immediate corrective to present day injustices, but as a long term goal for a new society? Should they even want to receive income for cooking a meal for themselves, their partners, their parents, or their children, or for others in their living units, or for guests for that matter?

To see the meaning of the last question, notice that we wouldn't want participatory economics to provide income for violin workers who produce violins that they then take home at no cost for their families and friends. If we allowed that, then they would receive income and receive product. Nor would we want participatory economics to provide income for farmers to produce food for themselves and their family, and not for social consumption by others.

And if we did opt for such a possibility in the special case of bringing up children or maintaining a living unit, who would get to say that my spending a whole lot of time constantly redesigning my living room isn't worthy of income? Who would determine how much I can play with my kids? These issues could be handled by special provisions and features to enact a reform in the present, if we adopted providing income for housework as a corrective to current injustices, but would they be needed, or even make sense, in an established new society? Might they even be counterproductive in such a new society? If we look into such matters, will it turn out that wages for housework is like balanced jobs? We would like to have it now. And beyond that, we must have it for a good economy, and for a good society. Or will it turn out that wages for housework is more like a $30 minimum wage? We would like to have it now, as a corrective to current injustices, but it would make no sense in a participatory economy and participatory society.

To think about this, it seems most germane to ask, what is the problem, after all, that wages for housework hopes to reduce if enacted in the present? Isn't it that the unpaid time given to household labor is given overwhelmingly by women? And, that the same women have less income from other work, as well? More specifically, women around the world spend roughly four-and-a-half-hours per day on unpaid activity in the home, while men spend an average of a little under an hour and a half per day on the same kind of activity. As a result, over 600 million women report that unpaid activity has meant that they could not seek paid employment outside the home whereas about 40 million men said the same thing. And, then, on top of it, women wind up in more onerous jobs at lower pay, when they can work outside the home. The problem is obvious. Women hold up more than half the sky, and are made vulnerable and dependent while doing it. There is another consideration, as well. Working in the home, as compared to outside the home, has different implications for the person doing the work. While the caring aspect is positive, the isolating aspect is disempowering.

A different approach to addressing the concerns that wages for housework addresses might note that a participatory economy will empower and remunerate men and women equally, albeit that would occur outside the living unit. More, supposing household work isn't remunerated in a participatory economy, there would nonetheless be average income for all who can't work, so there would be full income for all children and for the elderly or ill who don't work. There would also presumably be free universal daycare. Medical care would presumably be free. Education would presumably be free. Presumably meaning we can reasonably predict that future people would decide in favor of these policies. In that context, wouldn't it be possible to recognize that activity in households—cleaning, caring, cooking, maintaining, teaching—is actually unlike activity in workplaces. Indeed, wouldn't it be so different from activity in workplaces that paying people to bring up their own children, to cook for their own living units, or to clean or make more welcoming and comfortable their own rooms would in some sense denigrate and not elevate the activity as well as contradicting the logic of equitable remuneration and participatory allocation? Would it make sense, for example, that people both get an income for household activity, called wages for housework, and that they also get the product of the activity for which they get the income?

I clean my house. I furnish it. I decorate it. I cook for my housemates. And yet I and they not only get the product, I and they also get income for producing that product for ourselves.

That is ruled out for every other kind of work. Why should this, if we decide to call it work, be different? And would it make sense that all this household activity, deemed work, and treated like all other work, would have to be part of society's production planning instead of its consumption planning, and that it would have to be conducted under the auspices of a workers council and a federation of such councils?

An advocate of treating household activity as work and therefore an advocate of wages for housework might reply, "yes, these observations do imply that we would need some special considerations for household work as compared to other work. But the fact remains, we can't allow women to be overburdened by household labors."

Exactly so. But consider a person who agrees that we can't permit that problem to persist but who also feels that to label caring for one's own children, spouse, living unit, and living partners "work," and to treat it like any other work in a new participatory economy (as compared to in capitalism to win a valuable change in the present) would be trying to solve a problem in ways that unnecessarily subvert other values? Would such a person be wrong to urge that unlike other work, household activity, though admittedly critically important, admittedly time consuming, admittedly productive, and admittedly horribly handled in current society, would not be properly handled in a new society by a workers council determining what gets and what doesn't get remunerated, or by folks having to seek inputs as members of the production part of the planning process rather than the consumption part, for cleaning their own dishes?

Is this person—say me, here—who is questioning wages for housework for an established good society just trying to avoid solving the problem of women holding up too much of the sky? Just trying to preserve male advantage? What if a person agrees that the sexist distribution of household activity needs priority solving, but the same person doubts the desirability of having household activity remunerated, planned, etc.? What if that person asks an advocate of wages for housework, why do you think that in a transformed future we will need economics to solve this currently horrible kinship problem? Economics isn't all there is. Why can't a revolution in kinship relations themselves, a revolution that transforms families, living units, and all sides of life, plus changes in the economy, together achieve the result of ending gender inequities in all sides of life?

Consider one example. In a participatory economy in a participatory society, imagine a young child or an elderly family member needs round the clock help. Of course, such help from care workers would be free to the recipient because it is socially supported, and of course those doing it would have balanced jobs, receive pay like everyone else, have a workers council, be part of planning, etc. So far, there is no issue. But suppose the mother of the child or the husband of the ill partner wants to provide the care. To do it, the mother or husband, or it could be the reverse, of course, must take off from her or his job. The advocate of paying the person wages for household activity might then reasonably say that since society was willing to pay for a care worker to do the care work in the home, why can't society pay, instead, for the mother/father or partner to do it? It could. But is that the best or even a desirable approach? Does the mother/father partner want to have to enter into the planning process as a member of the council of daycare or private care workers? Should the mother/father partner want remuneration for the care they wish to give? Isn't an easier and better approach which would accomplish the outcome sought at no loss of income for anyone, be that the mother/father partner simply retains their income from the job they have to take leave of to do the home care, more or less like occurs now for maternity/paternity leave—though in a participatory economy the funds are provided by the whole society?

Depending on what emerges from kinship transformations, both approaches are possible. A participatory economy could treat household activity as work like any other or treat it as work somewhat like other work, but with caveats and dispensations. Or a participatory economy could treat it as household activity revolutionized by participatory kinship. Whichever way this debate may go, surely we can see that participatory economics can fit well with participatory kinship. And we can also see that in the nearer term, any effective campaign to reduce the incredible injustices associated with household and caring activity and every other form of patriarchal hierarchy is both justified and able to help lead toward a transformed future.

Participatory Culture/Community and Participatory Economy

Next consider culture/community, or the ways society accomplishes the elaboration of holidays, rituals, language, and other ethnic, racial, national, and religious relations and interrelations among communities of people. Here too, society needs new, transformed social relations. The aim would not be, I think we can guess, to homogenize different communities into one big one that stands alone. Rather, the diversity that has always characterized ethnic, religious, racial, geographic and other cultural communities would be seen as something to preserve and even enlarge. But, at the same time, such new relations would presumably want to remove hierarchies among communities such that some dominate while others suffer deprivations. However this goal may be accomplished—for example, perhaps by an approach outlined by Justin Podur called polyculturalism, or inter-communalism that guarantees all communities conditions of self-preservation—presumably members of different communities would not enjoy privileges denied to others or suffer indignities and denials compared to others. As a result, new community relations will likely require of an economy that it not empower or remunerate members of any one community in any lesser or greater way than members of any other community. And of course participatory economics will easily comply since it has no mechanism to even allow, much less to cause, even any two individual actors to be treated economically unjustly or overly acquisitively—much less any two communities.

A more nuanced and perhaps somewhat difficult possibility exists when we consider impact in the opposite direction. Given the implications of renovated participatory economic life and prior education for the talents, skills, knowledge, and confidence of workers and consumers, diverse communities will have a hard time retaining their members if they cause some to predominantly dominate and others to predominantly obey in their cultural or other relations. Even as we preserve and protect communities and celebrate their diversity, would such internal community hierarchies operationally disappear due to this characteristic of transformed cultural/community-economic interrelations? I guess time will tell this like so much else. For myself, I like to think so. But, if not, I think we can predict that the participatory economy would in any event pose a problem for communities which have customs, holidays, practices, and the like that, for example, expect some members to be anointed and empowered, and others to be followers. Likewise, communities imbuing such inclinations and expectations in their members would pose a problem for a participatory economy that expects and wants all workers and consumers to be socially caring, self-managing, and freely initiating participants.

Participatory Ecology and Participatory Economy

Next, consider ecology, or the ways society interacts with its natural surroundings including using ecology's offerings and impacting ecology's evolution. To a considerable degree, this is an intrinsically economic matter. A sane, healthy, humane ecology is presumably one that continually sustains and even enhances both its human partners and its own diverse conditions. A transformed ecology would say to economy: one, you must account for the implications of your choices on me, the surrounding ecology, and how their impact reflects back on you, the human guests; and two, you should be eager to abide ecological constraints and aims that arise from ecological wisdom but require economic attention.

And so how does participatory economy reply to ecology? By design and necessity it says yes, the participatory economy accepts your requirements and welcomes your wise impositions. Participatory planning seeks to reveal and act in light of not only full personal and social costs and benefits of economic possibilities, but also their full ecological costs and benefits. More, participatory economy can and will eagerly abide any requirements born of ecological wisdom and brought to economy from without. Participatory economy will itself reverse excessive resource depletion, climate destruction, pollution, and more, and it will happily accept ecological instructions regarding habitats and relations it might otherwise treat wrongfully, thereby being an ecological or Green, and not just sustainable, economy.

Of course, we could talk much more about each of the above, or we could address more specific facets of a new society such as health and caring, sports and competing, science and exploring, or technology and investing—and we have in fact done so elsewhere and in some references that conclude this book—but keeping this chapter short and only indicative precludes such exploration. However, there is one additional area I would like to briefly address, precisely because its practitioners often raise an instructive concern about participatory economics that has not been widely addressed elsewhere: Art.

Participatory Art or Artistic Economy?

So, what might we expect for painting, filming, writing, singing, designing, dancing, and musicianship in a better world—and what implication might diverse artistic innovations have, or demand, from our future economy?

What is better art? Painter and participatory economy advocate Jerry Fresia suggests that in the eyes of current artists better art would be art that is undertaken non-instrumentally and personally expressively. It would be art that is inner directed. Art that is done as an end in itself, without pressures, without external constraints. Art accomplished for its own intrinsic virtues. Art accomplished to express self, find self, understand self, and enlarge self. From these desires for transformed art there arise some artistic concerns about participatory economics.

I have encountered, for example, many artists who say, wait a minute. You want artistic work to be done in accord with a workers council? You want other workers and consumers who are not artists to have an impact on what artists do? You want me to earn an income from my art, to be able to be an artist and survive, only if my art is deemed socially valuable? Come on. I don't want that. I want to be my own individual. I want to do as I wish. I want to enjoy and experience the wonder of creativity however I choose.

So a question arises. Is there a contradiction between what participatory economics would likely deliver for artists and what artists themselves say they want? Participatory economics claims to be a self-managing, classless, solidarity, feminist, caring, intercommunalist, and green economy. Can it also claim to be an artistic economy?

The concern artists often raise suggests that artists are special and, as a result, should not be subject to any external social dynamic. I empathetically see where this view comes from. In our world virtually everything, including singing, dancing, painting, filming, and writing, is commodified. Art is bought and sold. Its production is alienated by its commodification. With markets, art's aim shifts from personal expression and development to pleasing payers. Artists say, and I think rightfully so, in a better world art should escape all that alienation. But the advocate of participatory economics should reply, yes, but so should all other work, and indeed so should all other activity escape all that alienation. Is the solution for a good economy to treat art's escape from what has been called capitalism's "Cash Nexus" as fundamentally unlike any other work's escape from capitalism's "Cash Nexus"? Should art not abide the norms that other participatory work respects? Or is the solution for a good economy to give all work an artistic aspect and to then treat all work, including art, the same regarding norms that work should respect?

Participatory economics chooses the latter course. First, it entirely removes from society class hierarchy. It entirely removes power-mediated buying and selling. In fact, it entirely removes all buying and selling as we have known such activity. Second, participatory economics strives to make all work involve experiencing the wonder of engagement and the freedom and enjoyment of collective self-management. It strives to make all work involve the insight and learning that comes from expressive activity. But it also strives to make all work involve the pleasure and sociality of aiding others' well-being. It isn't that cleaning a research lab, an assembly area, a dance floor, a film studio, or a painting room is made entirely non-boring, much less entirely expressive. It is that self-managed work freely chosen to fulfill oneself and others—and not to fulfill just oneself or just others—is not work as we have known it. And with that change, the performing arts become another activity, like research, doctoring, designing, building, assembling, and mining. That is, art becomes work undertaken freely to benefit oneself and also society. It becomes work organized in balanced job complexes. It becomes work that receives equitable remuneration. And it becomes work that is subject to oneself but also to others who it affects.

In this view, the new economy recognizes that like all work art should include a non-instrumental moment of self-fulfillment and an expressive moment of self-discovery. But the new economy also incorporates that like all work that is undertaken as part of one's social contribution to economic output, art must also incorporate the desirability of benefiting and respecting the will of others beyond oneself. Or that is my expectation, at any rate.

Participatory economics differs hugely not only from capitalism but from coordinator market economics and coordinator centrally planned economics, each misleadingly often called socialism. This is not least because various prior conceptual frameworks have obscured rather than highlighted how monopolized empowered work establishes a class between labor and capital in capitalism, and elevates that same class above labor in coordinatorism. To incorporate a non-instrumental and an expressive moment into all work and to incorporate a social moment into all remunerated art makes all work into art and all art into work. And it may be that that is the ultimate capstone of paying attention to all dimensions of class and work relations in proposing a new economy.

At any rate, the upshot of this short chapter is that an economy can only exist affecting and being affected by society's other aspects. Vision for a transformed economy, polity, kinship, culture, or ecology requires that each be compatible with the rest. What we can say at this point regarding this requirement is that our proposal for participatory economics looks like, feels like, and reacts like it will have just such compatibility.

9

Winning A New Economy: Between a Rock and a Hard Place

Consider nothing impossible, then treat possibilities as probabilities.
Charles Dickens

Oh, the fishes will laugh As they swim out of our path And the seagulls they'll be smiling And the rocks on the sand Will proudly stand The hour that the ship comes in
And the words that are used For to get the ship confused Will not be understood as they're spoken For the chains of the sea Will have busted in the night And will be buried at the bottom of the ocean.
Bob Dylan

Is proposing a new economy an academic exercise or can our proposed vision inspire, orient, and inform current activism? Can we in time make participatory economics no longer a vision, but a new reality?

These two questions highlight strategy and in this last chapter we can at least offer a few thoughts.

Vision and Reforms

So, first, can our proposed vision matter for tasks we undertake now? Social change activists often debate reform versus revolution. Work in a limited present but seek a liberated future. Today, modest changes. Someday, full transformation. But how do we conduct activism for limited gains today, with the personalities and means that we have immediately available, and yet do so in ways that lead toward a liberated future tomorrow?

An answer arises quite naturally from advocating participatory economics. We can seek reforms, but reject reformism. We can fight for change now, but galvanize support to win greater change later. We can acknowledge and work in light of present limitations, but simultaneously chart a trajectory to where we wish to go.

We want participatory economics beyond capitalism. We want feminism beyond patriarchy. We want participatory polity beyond authoritarianism. We want intercommunalism beyond racism. We want ecological sustainability and internationalism beyond suicidal nightmare. We want to win limited gains now. We want to develop steadily more comprehension of, desire for, commitment toward, and means suited to winning greater gains later.

The problem is that our self-evident stance leaves us having to navigate between a rock and a hard place. The rock is reformism. If our words and actions don't challenge the permanence of basic institutions, our words and actions will enforce their permanence. If we tilt toward reformism, our aims will tilt toward suicidal compromise or sell-out.

The hard place is delusion. I remember how the chant "We want the world and we want it now" used to bounce off surrounding skyscraper façades many decades ago. It lifted us. It also made us think reforms were for cowards and sell-outs. If we tilt toward "ultra-leftism," our prospects will tilt toward holier than thou posturing.

Too much emphasis on respecting our limited present will preclude escaping our limited present. We must be bold.

Too much emphasis on attaining our desired future will preclude gaining a foothold to get moving at all. We must be practical.

The solution? Take manageable immediate steps, but conceive and implement those steps in a trajectory conceived to reach our desired future.

Suppose we seek to increase the minimum wage. We say we want, nay, we deserve, $15 an hour. We speak, write, chant, and focus unswervingly on the new minimum wage. We create ties, connections, and means to exercise pressure to raise sufficient costs and fears for elites that they relent, rather than risk greater losses. We mobilize. They buckle. Good. We win $15 an hour as a new minimum wage. But we win without any notion we should persist after we win. We don't raise long-term vision. We win but don't connect our campaign to other aspects of a full program. We win and we go home. We win and our words and acts have actually ratified the idea not just that many should have a still ridiculously low minimum income, but that there should be a minimum income at all.

A second way to approach the same situation is to not fight for such a demand at all. We claim that such a demand will ratify the powers that be. We say it will fail to seek a new world. It will be coopted. We will be coopted. So we take to the streets, courageous and committed, and we demand the world now. We look good. We sound good. We are full throttle. We learn nothing lasting. We build nothing lasting. We win nothing lasting.

We need a third approach, different than reformism but also different than entirely abstaining from the minimum wage campaign. So we seek the $15 an hour wage. We simultaneously convey a larger conception of what is a just, worthy, and warranted income consistent with our ultimate aims—for example, that people should receive income for how long they work, for how hard they work, and for the onerousness of the conditions under which they work, but not for property, power, or even output. Our proposed vision informs our chosen words and deeds. We mobilize, but more deeply, we organize.

In this third approach, we seek $15 an hour as a worthy advance. We also seek it as a step toward fully equitable remuneration. We build ties, connections, and means to exercise pressure that can win now. We also foreshadow, prepare for, and facilitate winning more later.

These three contrasting approaches exist for almost any campaign one might initiate. We can demand gains, talk entirely about their immediate benefits, and go home and celebrate their attainment, which tilts toward minimalist reformism. We can forego even seeking immediate limited gains on grounds they aren't all we want, which tilts toward maximalist "ultra-leftism." Or we can seek gains to attain and celebrate very meaningful advances now, but at the same time prepare to seek much more and advance much further later. It turns out that beyond fostering hope and allowing a positive tone, our proposed vision has immediate worth precisely to the extent that it inspires, orients, and informs this third immediate and long-term approach whether regarding property, decision-making, jobs, income, or allocation.

Vision and Organization

Or consider a related situation that is less well discussed than the need to avoid reformism and avoid ultra-leftism, but for which pretty much the same type of thinking, albeit in more contextually specific conditions, applies.

Imagine trying to set up a new institution or movement organization meant to embody the values of a desired future while it serves various purposes and needs in the present. A new but closely related choice between a rock and hard place arises.

On the one hand, we would want our new project to work well in the present, with current people, tools, and sources of support. On the other hand, we would want our new project to embody new values, aims, and structures, and even to have new features consistent with and able to melt into a better future. Too much attention to fitting the constraints of present circumstances and we might build a lasting project which would, however, so lose touch with its ultimate goal that the benefits of its successful establishment would be undercut by its failure to sufficiently plant the seeds of the future in the present. Too much fealty to the ideal goal and we might be true to our desires but not progress or perhaps not even survive, in existing circumstances.

By way of an example, consider a hypothetical large scale media project. Suppose the stated aim is:

1. to provide needed news and analysis
2. to develop new institutional relations able to define and sustain a new kind of journalism

On both counts such a project would hopefully seek to plant the seeds of the future in the present. It would hopefully try to enhance the amount and quality of needed news by virtue of providing a more amenable venue for it. How might those initially involved in such a project proceed?

First, they would have to employ people who are used to working in and have various habits and expectations molded in the present. Likewise, they would have to pay bills. For example, those involved would need income for their labors and other expenses would also need to be met, such as rent, equipment, fees for services, research costs, and so on.

Questions would arise. Where should funds come from? How should relations among people involved in the project be structured? What division of labor and what mode of making decisions? Likewise, how would the new institution interface with already existing alternative media organizations, or with its own audience, or with other institutions such as movements and the government?

For each choice, the general quandary would be how does one navigate between:

1. The need to establish the institution in the present, with

all the present's constraints, and to keep it functioning at a sufficient scale to accomplish more than the associated writers and other workers could accomplish if they were dispersed among other existing mainstream and alternative institutions, such as those that they already had jobs at before embarking on the new project, and,

2. The need to have the new project take shape and operate consistently with its longer-term aims rather than the project persisting but losing its identity and thus its merit in the process of persisting.

This conundrum should be very familiar to anyone who has created new institutions and/or worked at or interacted with them. It defines many hard choices whose resolutions depend greatly on views of what the implications of those possible choices are likely to be.

So, take for example starting the *Intercept* or *TeleSUR English* each not overly long ago, or, for that matter, starting Z Communications years earlier, or much more recently starting RevolutionZ, or, most important to going forward, starting new efforts.

A first decision that would arise, for example, is should we take advertisements?

The argument for doing so is simple. We need funds with which to pay bills. The argument against doing so depends on how we see the situation. We might feel that ads are bad only because they have bad content. In that case, we might think we shouldn't advertise cigarettes, but it would be fine to advertise good books or even just books generally. To pay bills, we should advertise what is not immediately horrible in its specific content, and what won't corrupt our thinking and lead via a slippery slope to violating our values.

A different analysis might say advertisements are intrinsically bad. They sell the attention of our users to corporations. Our audience becomes our product. Our content becomes a mere means of attracting that audience. And before long, we seek to attract not just any audience, but an audience with means to buy the commodities advertised. The ads we choose may for a time seek to sell only nice items, but we are really selling our audience to the corporations who buy our ad space, and, in so doing, we compromise our whole media project. And as an added debit, to advertise ratifies the practice of deception.

Such a discussion always occurs in some context. For example, should we employ other means to accrue funds? We might try to raise donations from users but that entails that we repeatedly ask for them, which can undercut outreach and degrade those who are asking and those who are asked. It can make it seem we care most or even only about money. On the other hand, if we can keep those ill effects to a minimum, to seek user donations might allow self-sufficiency while it raises pressures on our media project to meet audience needs rather than to sell audience attention to companies.

But what if our audience can't or won't donate sufficiently?

What about taking funds from large money donors, whether foundations or individuals? On the plus side, this can generate large chunks of cash, facilitating many useful endeavors. On the downside, this can generate dependence on sources who may in time impose implicit or explicit constraints on content. They tell you, "Your values are nice." Here is a big donation. We take it. We become dependent on that level of help. They then add: "Don't go too far or you will lose our support." We can't afford to lose it. The threat they raise need not be explicit to do major damage.

Consider a still more complex issue. We wish to create a media project, a political organization, or whatever. How will we make decisions? How will we organize our work? Analogous calculations arise.

As initiators we will need to make decisions and organize

the tasks composing our work. Any organization has to do both, of course. But, we may wonder, should we do it in ways that are familiar from current society and that match people's prior experiences and expectations? Or should we do it in new ways that attempt to move toward what we prefer for a new society, but that differ greatly from people's prior experiences and expectations?

The former approach is easier. We know that in at least some respects it works. It will be easier to get funding for the familiar. It will better fit people's prior habits. A hierarchical approach to decisions, for example, will get decisions made. A corporate division of labor in which some folks monopolize empowering tasks while others do purely rote tasks will get considerable work done. Donors will understand those choices. So will potential employees.

In contrast, to employ self-managed decision-making that apportions to all workers a say proportionate to their involvement will diverge from people's prior experiences. It will require training and experiment. It will alienate potential large donors. As compared to what people are used to, it will seek unexpected and unfamiliar participation from some folks and strip considerable authority from others. Similarly, arranging tasks into jobs so that everyone does a comparable balance of empowering and therefore also of disempowering work will require a kind of involvement people are not used to and which many may initially find quite foreign and some may consider burdensome.

The argument for the "plant the seeds of the future in the present" option of self-management and a new division of labor is twofold. First, the choice won't ratify existing relations that our long term aims should want to transcend. Second, while the choice will risk new kinds of problems due to clashing with old habits and expectations and horrifying big donors, it will also allow new kinds of benefits due to facilitating diverse opinions and better developing and utilizing all participants' talents. Third, there would be positive effects on a media institution's or movement organization's products and outreach.

Consider an analogy. Why should a media institution reject sexist or racist structures in its own organization? First, we easily agree, to do so will not ratify much less enforce what needs to be rejected. Second, we also agree, doing so will allow new kinds of benefits such as contributions from folks who would otherwise be alienated and diminished. And third, almost as obviously, if a media institution or movement organizing project is internally racist or sexist, over time its ability to address issues of race and gender outside itself will steadily deteriorate. It will become steadily harder to even perceive, much less critique those flaws outside of one's work when one is daily enacting and abiding those flaws inside one's work. Incorporate racist and sexist features. Rationalize doing so. Lose capacity to perceive much less oppose racism and sexism. The analogy is that the same insights hold for having internal authoritarian decision making or corporate divisions of labor. Incorporate authoritarian and corporatist features. Rationalize doing so. Lose capacity to perceive much less oppose authoritarianism and classism in broader society. The rationales that justify our internal choices will infect our values and perceptions and in turn will inhibit and even obliterate prospects for media coverage or organizing work to fully properly address power and class.

So, we deduce that for a media experiment or a movement organization, the issues we are considering become how do we raise finances, make decisions, and define jobs and rules for work? And what is at stake is twofold. Will editorial content or outreach organizing be compromised? Will the institution's structure itself not only survive but also serve as a positive model?

It can be hard to judge choices people make about such matters from outside the constraints and pressures they face.

But it ought to be possible to arrive at broad guidelines for such judgments. Win reforms but avoid reformism. Win reforms that benefit folks now, move toward ultimate goals, and also prepare and inspire folks to seek further changes later. Do the same regarding not just demands and how we fight to win them, but also when constructing our own organizing projects, organizations, movements, and new ways of conducting daily life. Live, learn, love, and otherwise sustain and enrich all lives today while seeking a better world for tomorrow.

Vision and Winning

But, we come to a second big question. Can we in fact win a new economy, a new society, and a new world? The only definitive answer to this question will be to do so. Final proof can only emerge from practice. But since we must win—because the cost of not winning is simply too much to even contemplate—there is a sense in which the question is moot. We try. We don't wait on proof that action will succeed. And, in fact, action will often seem to fail, but then we try again, until final success. But is this only a recurring act of faith? Is it only a wild recurring leap over, around, and through doubt? And is this leap based only on fear of failure and rejection of failure, and not on a real sense of success?

It could be thus. Indeed, I think, for transformative energies it often has been thus. But I don't think it should be thus. For two reasons.

First, it is too much to ask. Without a sense of direction toward victory, too many people will balk at the outset or fall away in time. A big dose of reasoned commitment, and not just courageous commitment, will greatly strengthen recruiting and member sustainability.

Second, a reasoned commitment based on a formulated path forward, with its features conceived and repeatedly tested, with its methods refined and repeatedly improved, with its structures implemented and repeatedly enhanced, is a commitment that has direction and is strategic, creative, and intelligent, and not only courageous.

For these reasons, an effective project for a better society will need a compelling vision of key features of the sought economy, polity, kinship, culture, ecology, and international relations. It will also need a conception of how to win that we continually update from our growing experience, and that perpetually gives us not just courage but also reason to believe in and guidance to attain our own futures.

A clarification may be needed. To win a new world does not occur in a flash. There will not be a day we are living in an old world, and a next day we are living in our sought new world. Even just considering economy, even just considering a new division of labor and a new allocation system, these changes will come unequally and take time. Full balanced jobs won't appear in a flash in all firms at once. The dwindling old corporate division of labor, under siege and saddled by restraints and mitigating structures, will for a time exist alongside steadily maturing new balanced job complexes. And the same will hold for participatory planning and markets. For some time participatory planning will persistently develop and spread while markets are forcefully restrained and replaced. We call this period of militant restraint of the old with vigorous construction of the new transition. What is most critical about participatory economic transition is that with the elimination of private ownership and during the forging of new relations, the corporate division of labor and markets are not considered solutions but are deemed problems to overcome. They are targets of struggle. They are targets for elimination. Without that guiding agenda, the transformation of economy would preserve and elevate the coordinator class above workers. It would put a new boss in place of the old boss. It would be coordinatorist. But deeming the corporate division of labor and markets as residual targets to fully replace, participatory economic transition will persist until it attains classlessness.

In short, we need to understand and share where we now are and what structures and obstacles around us as well as in ourselves enforce current reality. We need to envision and share the core features of where we want to wind up. We need to forge and reforge, share and re-share, and traverse and re-traverse a steadily updated path from what we have to what we want.

We repeatedly mobilize larger and larger, steadily more committed, steadily better informed, steadily more effective activism against current relations. We repeatedly organize ever more deeply to plant the seeds of the future in the present and to motivate and empower our means to construct the future itself.

The rest of *No Bosses* offers a conversational afterword answering some questions readers may wonder about the participatory economic vision, its history, and its prospects, followed by some references that may help with related tasks. In truth, though, I expect the most important references are still to be produced by new voices, including hopefully yours.

10

Origins, Prospects, and History of Participatory Economics

You may encounter many defeats but you must not be defeated.
Maya Angeliou

Listen revolution We're buddies See together We can take everything
Langston Hughes

Books are not very interactive. Someone writes. Someone reads. There is not much dialog. Perhaps I can improve that a little by here answering some questions I have received at talks or personal exchanges as if we were personally chatting. If you send additional issues/questions, maybe we can together make the experience of this book still more interactive not least via the book's website. You can reach me at sysop@zmag.org. I try for interaction, as well, with the weekly podcast RevolutionZ and, still more interactively, at the online School for Social and Cultural Change at sscc.teachable.com including a course on participatory economics.

Question 1: "Doesn't proposing social vision overstep our possible knowledge? Shouldn't social vision emerge from broad constituencies with lots of experience?"

Blueprint-like details of a future society are unattainable knowledge. To even try for a blueprint would be useless, pointless, and inappropriate. A blueprint is beyond our means. More important, future details are for people in the future to decide. At most now offering possible texture, beyond basic essentials, to make a vision more accessible and understandable, seems reasonable if such examples are acknowledged to be only possibilities.

And I agree that to be insightful, social vision should incorporate the ideas of many people with much experience. When small groups propose new vision, their aim should therefore be that larger groups improve their proposals. But does that mean it is too soon to seek vision? I don't think so. We have centuries of highly relevant experiences to consult. If not now, when?

Question 2: "But won't advocating vision close possibilities? Won't we advocate what we propose so tenaciously that we miss new insights?"

I agree. Inflexible advocacy would be horribly damaging. But the solution to inflexible vision isn't no vision at all, just as the solution to unhealthy food isn't no food at all. We need flexible, learning-oriented vision.

More generally, I believe sectarian irrelevance afflicts us mostly when we feel that to be open and flexible denies our integrity. In contrast, I believe we best avoid sectarianism when we recognize that to be open and flexible enlarges our integrity. It follows that our priority should be to improve our views, not to reflexively defend them. We should realize that finding and fixing weaknesses is more constructive than robotically preserving against change.

Question 3: "But why economics? What about everything else? Doesn't the pursuit of economic vision slight the rest? Are you merely a mechanical Marxist after all?"

Surely we can agree we need economic hope, orientation, and direction? Your question highlights that we also need political, cultural, family and kinship, ecological, and international hope, orientation, and direction.

It seems to me that to pursue economic vision while trying

to promote other vision does not slight other vision any more than the reverse. If all pursuers of vision take account of their efforts' implications for other pursuers of vision, surely we can intersect and mutually enforce our visions and actions so they work together for the benefit of all.

The Marxist tradition has had many virtues, but it has also had many very serious debits. One debit that you allude to is that it has often been economistic, elevating the importance of economics above all else. Another debit is that it has rarely taken seriously the need for vision. And a third, and for this book perhaps the most critical debit, is that Marxism has most often obscured or literally denied the existence of a class between labor and capital that becomes a ruling class in what we call coordinator economies.

Question 4: "What's so bad about capitalism?"

I am tempted to say let me count the ways, but to be comprehensive would take far too long. How about capitalism produces Herculean disparities of income and wealth and engenders anti-sociality instead of solidarity and mutual aid? It elevates authority rather than reason and it celebrates obedience rather than self-management. It produces isolation and alienation rather than mutuality and respect. We get war rather than peace. We get mansions above and cardboard houses below.

Capitalism commercializes everything until nothing remains sacred. Capitalist market madness reduces love, comradeship, artistry, and dignity to profit opportunities. Our limbs are smashed. Our minds are hobbled.

Capitalism is a thug's economy, a heartless economy, a base, vile, and largely boring economy. Capitalism mocks equity, rewards injustice, enshrines greed, and worships accumulation. Capitalism endlessly embalms spiritual and physical corpses.

Question 5: "But why not advocate an economic vision we already have? Why not advocate social democracy?"

I agree it would be easier to advocate a familiar model, but social democratic capitalism is capitalism with workers and what I call coordinators made somewhat more powerful. And, yes, realigning bargaining power can certainly temper some of the worst flaws of capitalism. Realigning bargaining power can also be part of a trajectory of changes toward a new economy. But realigning bargaining power can't alone eliminate capitalism's defining flaws, and those flaws, even reduced in impact, remain quite horrible.

Social democracy doesn't arrive at entirely new relations and for that reason its modest gains are revoked whenever capitalists regain full power. Unless we desire only stopgap reductions of contemporary horrors, we shouldn't advocate social democracy as our ultimate goal. We can certainly favor various short-run social democratic aims, as anyone sentient and caring ought to, but we should talk about them and organize for them as parts of winning a fully new economy, not as final ends themselves.

Question 6: "Okay, then why not socialism?"

The problem with adopting socialism as a vision is that the label is quite vague. Does socialism mean a "good economy," a "classless economy," an "economy with justice and equity," an "economy with self-management?" If it means those things, that's fine. I want those gains, of course. But I fear that using the label "socialism" can confuse people because every societal instance of socialism that has ever existed, and virtually every formulation of socialism carefully proposed as a vision, has had attributes that at best fall massively short of our sought virtues, and at worst resemble massive dungeons.

In actual practice, socialism has always meant public or state ownership of productive property, plus corporate divisions of labor, plus income for power or at best for output, plus allocation by class-propelling, personality-perverting markets or by central planning. Few who propose socialism have significantly deviated from these features. Socialism, as it has been specified, has most often been a class-divided economy with material and influential subordination for most of its actors. Some central ills of capitalism have certainly been reduced or even transcended, but new flaws have emerged and other familiar flaws have been aggravated. A coordinator class of empowered actors has repeatedly risen to ruling status.

Some socialists reply—"Wait a minute, what we advocate is a new socialism. We call what we favor, which is also what you favor, participatory socialism." I respond, if you agree that markets, central planning, a corporate division of labor, and remuneration for output all violate essential aims, and if you instead favor participatory self-managing alternatives, then we agree on substance and I would only add that I still doubt it is useful to use a term that needlessly confuses not just the rich, but also working people.

And then came Bernie Sanders, AOC and others, and suddenly the label socialism was somewhat retrieved from meaning statist, coordinator class ruled models. Is the break that Sanders initiated sufficiently large that advocates of a new economic vision can call it green socialism or eco-socialism or libertarian socialism or participatory socialism and not have those who hear them confuse what they are proposing with something they rightly reject? Maybe, but I admit I still have doubts.

Question 7: "But then why not Anarchism? Why do we need a new system with a new name, 'participatory economics'? This new system still has wages so it is wage slavery. It still has exchange so it is still market driven. Anarchism is better."

Anarchism is fine with me when it means people managing their own lives, enjoying classlessness, ending wage slavery and market competition, and reducing hierarchy to a minimum. But beyond those wonderful aspirations, I think anarchism proposes no system of institutions to accomplish production, consumption, and allocation in anti-authoritarian ways.

The second part of your question perhaps indicates why. Wage slavery is people selling their ability to do work for some time period to owners, or some other elite constituency, who then use their control over that period to try to get as much output from the workers as they can. That simply does not exist in participatory economics.

Participatory workers work, so that much is true. They contribute to the social product. That is also true. And they get income for their efforts, also true. But they collectively determine their work and the social product. They receive claims on the social product, but their share is allotted according to one norm for all: duration, intensity, and onerousness of socially-valued work.

Exchange happens in every economy. Exchange in central planning is regimented. Orders given, orders taken. Exchange in markets is competitive. You fleece me or I fleece you. Market prices reflect bargaining power. Market exchange is an alienated, mis-directed process. In contrast, exchange in participatory economics is cooperatively negotiated. We produce together. We exchange to mutual benefit. Prices reflect individual, social, and ecological costs and benefits. Participatory economics is actually the classless, self-managing, equitable anarchistic alternative to wage slavery and market exchange.

Just as I think participatory economics fulfills the best aims of socialism, so too I think participatory economics fulfills the still more encompassing best aims of anarchism. Suppose anarchists were to agree on this. Would using a new name remain important to add clarity that there is something new proposed? I think maybe so.

Question 8: "What makes you think participatory economics is so desirable and why should we believe it would actually work as you claim? What should people do about it, when they hear this vision?"

The key institutions of participatory economics are designed so there is no capitalist class and no coordinator class. There are only workers and consumers who each do their own special labors, each excel in their own unique ways, and each enjoy the same equitable opportunities and broad conditions.

I look at the system's features and see that each actor, to get ahead, has to behave in ways consistent with the well-being of others, rather than seeking to trample others' well-being. To earn more each actor must work socially usefully longer, harder, or at more onerous labors. Each job improves as the average balanced job complex improves. Outcomes abide the wills of the whole populace, rather than only the wills of elite sectors. Each actor in workplaces and in consumer units has appropriate influence over each decision from the smallest personal choices to the largest collective projects. Valuations reflect full personal, social, and ecological costs and benefits.

So I advocate participatory economics not as nirvana, not as the end of history, not even thinking it will do what it aims to do without need for continual improvement. Rather, I advocate it as an approach to economic production, consumption, and allocation that will foster sentiments, aspirations, choices, behaviors, and outcomes consistent with the best human potentials I can imagine achieving in the next stage of economic history.

But as to your believing any of that, well, you certainly shouldn't believe such claims just on my say so, or just on anyone else's say so, or even just because it would be very nice if the claims were true. To become a reasoned advocate, you would need to look at the descriptions and arguments in some detail and assess them in light of evidence offered and your own experiences.

The participatory economic vision is not trivial, but nor is it unattainably complex. Understanding participatory economics doesn't require massive training. If the participatory economic vision is presented in plain and clear language, anyone interested in comprehending and assessing its core properties should, with some effort, be able to do so. Participatory economics is outside the box. It is not outside our reach.

Question 9: "Do advocates of participatory economics have disagreements about it?"

Yes, of at least three sorts: stylistic, tactical, and perhaps even basic. Stylistically, some advocates write and talk differently than others. No big deal. We all agree we should seek utmost clarity.

Tactically, some advocates feel that in our current context to reach some particular audience or to highlight some particular aspect is especially important, where other advocates prioritize different audiences or aspects. For example, advocates sometimes differ about whether trying to reach left activists or to reach professional economists is more important. Or some advocates, in the view of other advocates, excessively over emphasize the importance of balanced job complexes or in the eyes of others some advocates excessively over emphasize the speed and ease of planning. Regrettably, avenues for reaching the broad public are not yet within reach, at least that I know of, and I am sure all advocates would welcome that chance.

As to more substantive differences, I can think of two that may exist, and perhaps a third. First, there may be differences over how detailed is too detailed. Some think we can reasonably assert more now, some think more can only be determined later by those implementing a participatory economy. This type of difference particularly involves participatory planning, but may also arise for other facets.

Second, differences may exist regarding the value of facilitating social interactions among workers and consumers, or at least regarding workers and consumers each having access to knowledge of circumstances beyond their own councils during planning. Informing that, there may be differences over the importance of streamlining planning procedures to reduce time spent, as compared to the importance of enriching planning procedures to increase solidarity.

Third, there may be a difference not only in emphasis on using efficiency as a guide, including worries about how doing so could interfere with features of participatory planning, but perhaps also differences over what is and what isn't efficient.

But, however real any such disagreements may be, none of them present a serious problem for the participatory economic proposal itself for the obvious reason that all of its advocates agree that, even accepted and enacted, the proposal would surely be refined and implemented in diverse ways that we can't now foresee, not only to fit different conditions and situations, but also to comply with lessons learned in coming years that extend beyond what anyone now thinks. In any case, differences make clear the need for further deliberations. And further deliberations can only be a good thing.

Question 10: "You have advocated participatory economics, sometimes called participatory socialism, for decades. I get that you think it retains merit. But no matter how valid, to have impact any proposal needs advocates. Why isn't the vision better known? Why aren't there more advocates? In their absence, why don't you seek a new project to pursue?"

These are fair and troubling questions, and I wish I could provide fully satisfying answers. I can't. I can only try to say something that might be useful. I do pursue various projects, of course, and all participatory economy's advocates do, but setting that aside, given that the participatory economic vision hasn't yet attracted wide support, I think your question is why don't I and other advocates jettison participatory economics as a priority?

You were too kind to add, "The reason participatory economics hasn't won more support could be that participatory economics is nonsense so there is no point spending any valuable time trying to evaluate its merits and debits, much less to advocate it."

I think the system's published critics, which is actually only a very few people, would probably say yes to your question, that is indeed participatory economics. And to me they might say, "Jeeez, Michael, let it go." But such critics have not convinced me nor, I suspect, any of the vision's admittedly still far too few serious advocates in the US, Scotland, Ireland, England, Sweden, Finland, Italy, France, Turkey, Brazil, Venezuela, India, South Africa, Australia, Japan, and elsewhere. Why not?

Participatory economics advances a few relatively straightforward ideas. Advocates believe those ideas make undeniable moral sense. No critic who I know of denies that. The basic ideas also seem, to the vision's advocates, to operationally hold together. They seem to be not only morally worthy but also pragmatically viable. If they are instead ridiculous, as your question gently implies, it should be simple for critics to demonstrate their flaws. However, what criticisms have been offered, often quite aggressively, and sometimes by very well-informed, creative, and even brilliant people, haven't seemed to me to even bruise the vision, much less dent it, much less bury it. Instead, critics have seemed to me to misstate the system's features and then to summarily reject what they misstate. Or, even less effectively, they don't even point to a non-existent feature to reject. They simply reject by fiat.

I and others have invited critique, given critique visibility, and tried to find critique compelling in which case we would be quite prepared to say, in line with this question's expectations, okay, we get it, we have had enough. The vision was a good try, but what else can we come up with? But, instead, as far as I can tell, so far criticism that has been offered has been rather easily answered.

The participatory economic vision has just five core components--a Commons of productive assets, workers and consumers self-managing councils, balanced job complexes, equitable remuneration, and participatory planning.

A compelling argument against this vision would demonstrate that attaining it would be unjust or have disastrous side effects. Or would demonstrate that what participatory economics claims to do would be nice, but it can't be done. Or, would demonstrate that once attained, the vision wouldn't hold together. People couldn't or wouldn't behave as it entails. Or would demonstrate that drastic negative side effects would offset modest benefits. Something like that. And such claims have certainly at times been raised by the few critics who have tried to seriously address participatory economy.

So, some critics have claimed that participatory economics would promote self-management, but would simultaneously incur widespread dumb decisions due to participation from weak decision makers. Or critics have claimed participatory economics would be a just but unproductive economy because it would have flawed incentives. Or critics have claimed participatory economics would remove the basis for class division, but at the same time, and for that very reason, would demolish quality and reduce output because it would require too many people to do what they cannot do well, or even do at all, and it would simultaneously underutilize the people able to do those things well. Or critics have claimed participatory economics would have participation but would, as a result, incur too many conflicting agendas and waste too much time deciding economic outcomes.

You can, and I hope you will, look for yourself at the debates and responses regarding all these claims, both the rebuttals that appear in this short book, and the longer treatments also available. For me, the concerns are real and fair, but once examined they melt into nothing. Indeed, the criticisms were all anticipated in even our very first book-length presentations, and our reasons for finding the criticisms un-compelling were offered even before the criticisms were ever raised by others. And then the anticipated criticisms were raised as anticipated. And then we advocates offered rebuttals. And then the predicted criticisms were re-raised with no response to the rebuttals. Over and over.

Speaking for myself, from the start I thought there would be at least some areas that advocates weren't aware of that would need serious and perhaps even fundamental correction, and not just modest tweaking. I expected those areas to be surfaced by critics who would show how our replies to their anticipated criticisms were wanting. But that didn't happen. More, the aspects that we knew at the outset were as yet insufficiently developed, such as clarifying ways to fully incorporate externalities in planning and clarifying how to best plan investment, weren't even called out by others. What we most often heard was instead threadbare old sores. Participation will take too long. People are too greedy. Participation will take too long. People are too dumb. Participation will take too long. People are too lazy. And, oh yes, participation will take too long.

I think the reason criticism has been weak was that on the one hand the participatory economic vision didn't overstep into details, and on the other hand its features are fairly simple and quite carefully conceived, so it just hasn't had overly serious problems. Or, maybe it is just that people have yet to seriously assess it and discover its problems—certainly only a few have tried.

Question 11: "How about, instead, the possibility that you and other advocates of participatory economics haven't given up because you have been too wedded to it, too vested in it, to hear much less to accept the criticisms that others point out? Have you been too enmeshed to see how blinded you are?"

That isn't for me to judge, but I will say that I don't think so. I think we have instead avidly and seriously welcomed, heard, and addressed criticisms. But what if the other side of the possibility that we advocates are too wedded, too vested, is—well, what if the vision is in fact sound? What if classlessness, equity, and self-management, as well as productive creativity in the sense of meeting material, social, and ecological needs and developing human potentials without undue waste would all be incredibly enhanced by the vision's proposed features? If I think that is true, don't I have to wonder, by this time, why aren't council self-management, balanced job complexes, equitable remuneration, and participatory planning widely advocated, or at the very least, widely considered? What obstacles other than their being ill-conceived might have impeded wider discussion, much less acceptance?

Have you wondered about that? Have you wondered, for example, whether critics of participatory economics have been too wedded to it being wrong, too vested in it being wrong, for them to even hear advocates' responses to their concerns, much less to accept the responses advocates offer?

Question 12: "I am not convinced. If participatory economics would efficiently and equitably fulfill economic functions of production, consumption, and allocation, and simultaneously take into account ecological, social, and personal effects, and if it would even convey collective participatory self-management and create classlessness—then why isn't it a widely shared vision for life after capitalism?"

Again, it's a fair question. One central reason has nothing

much to do with the participatory vision per se. That is, there are no serious institutional visions for life after capitalism that are widely shared on the left, especially in the US. Disinterest in all vision, not just this one, is thus an obvious factor. One explanation of why that disinterest is so prevalent might be that people doubt the possibility of anything better so doubt the value of thinking about vision at all.

A second factor in why the participatory vision in particular isn't widely advocated is that its features aren't widely known. The proposal has been around 30 years, yes. But it is not discussed much in left media, much less in the mainstream. So it is not so much that people have carefully assessed it and not gotten on board. It is more that people aren't even aware it exists as a visionary option, much less aware of its features.

Question 13: "Okay, those factors of course exist, I have to agree, but still a lot more leftists have heard of it than openly advocate it. So there has to be more to their reticence than not hearing of it."

I agree, there must be. And that does present a problem for advocates. But think of a left activist who is incredibly busy and committed. He or she reads some left literature, journals, magazines, and websites and never encounters serious mention of, debate about, or interest in participatory economics (or any other seriously elaborated economic or social vision). Absent that sort of indication that participatory economics (or any other vision) has some traction, he or she wonders, why give it any of my all too scarce time? Why pay attention?

The activist perhaps thinks, "I have things to do now so later for this vision, later for all vision." The activist hasn't assessed participatory economics (or any vision), understood it, and decided it is unworthy. She or he has so many things to do that vision doesn't appear worth the time to assess. Economic or other vision isn't directly on the urgent agenda of the activist's next meeting or event. As to longer-term importance, it is understandable for someone who does happen to hear of it to think, "if no one in the venues I pay attention to seems to care about it, why should I?"

Question 14: "Okay," the critic replies, "but even in that case, why isn't participatory economics addressed in left media? And what of the few people who have heard about it in some detail, but who haven't taken it seriously?"

Well, okay, you are pushing me to the wall. Let me push back a little. Do you wonder if any of participatory economy's critics, or those who just pass over participatory economics with a dismissive nod and no serious notice, ever consider the possibility that their dismissiveness owes to an implicit or explicit allegiance to wide income differentials between coordinator class and working class actors, or owes to their implicit or explicit allegiance to the idea that coordinator class members have innately superior decision-making wisdom and innately greater creativity for doing empowering tasks, or owes to their implicit or explicit belief that markets are forever, or even just owes to their not wanting to buck up against all those views?

And as to the media, the same questions arise. Do you wonder if few articles addressing participatory economics or reviews of books about it appear because such submissions are written but get rejected due to implicit or even rather explicit coordinator class interests, and especially due to unexamined coordinator class habits—just as, for a long time, and to a degree even still, serious content about race and gender has been rejected on grounds of white and male interest and especially habit?

No doubt many variables impact the low interest in, discussion of, debate about, elaborations on, and then acceptance or rejection of not just participatory economic vision, but also other visions for the economy, and even more so for polity, kinship, and/or culture.

But what about now? Has reading this book provided a clear view of participatory economics? Is that view such that you find the proposal eminently dismissible? If so, okay. Perhaps you will send your views our way. But if you don't find it eminently dismissible, are you motivated to pay additional attention to the participatory economic proposal and to debates about it? If you aren't, is it because you think having an economic vision is not worth the time, or is it because you have another vision which you think is better, or is it because there is something you have heard about participatory economics that repels you? And don't these same questions arise for proposed vision regarding political, kinship, and cultural institutions, which are arguably even less discussed than participatory or other economic proposals?

Isn't what we want for a better future as important to address as what we reject about out current situations? Don't we need to sufficiently know what we want to be able to plant its seeds in the present? To be able to point our actions toward it? To be able to avoid being side-tracked? To be able to be positive? And to generate hope and desire? If all that is true, why does addressing what we reject outweigh addressing what we want a hundred or even a thousand to one? Could it be that the dearth of attention to vision, even among committed radical activists, has to do at least in part with people deep down not really believing we can win and seeing no point in getting vested in something we can't ever attain? If so, then that is or ought to be a priority to address.

Question 15 "Okay, suppose I think it over and conclude that a participatory economy would work. What difference would that make? We can't win a whole new economy anytime soon, so what difference does it make if we advocate a vision for a whole new economy now? Is this all just an intellectual exercise?"

For many people hope and allegiance depend on vision. Our activist choices need to not only oppose what is, but to also build the consciousness, commitment, and infrastructure of what we hope to attain. In that light, supporting participatory economics has many implications for how to talk about current injustices and describe what we favor, as well as for how to organize ourselves to win the immediate gains we seek.

For example, with participatory economics as a shared economic vision, there would no longer be arguments about consensus versus majority rule. Rather, leftists would see self-management as the guiding principle for decision-making and realize that different methods of communication of information and of tallying support are just tools for attaining self-management, and that we should use different tools in different situations.

Participatory economics as a shared goal would likely also point us toward demands and processes that increase participation and transparency in allocation. It would push toward reforms like participatory budgeting and communal exchange that would improve lives now but also move toward participatory planning.

Participatory economics would likely also push us toward income demands that move toward remunerating effort and sacrifice. More, it would influence how we talk about income and seek to arouse desires for gains beyond immediate demands, and likewise for other campaigns. It would likely propel us toward building worker and consumer councils to pursue and implement diverse agendas. It would likely cause us to re-conceive the ways we organize our own institutions and campaigns so that in time we would no more tolerate movement organizations that embody corporate divisions of labor and market-oriented norms than we tolerate movement organizations that embody sexist or racist norms. Our organizations would likely move toward remuneration for effort and sacrifice, not for relative power, credentials, or productivity. And our organizations would move toward self-managed decision-making and, in particular, toward jobs balanced for empowerment effects rather than retaining the division of labor typically found in corporations.

Indeed we would understand the importance of the interface between the coordinator class and owners above them, and even more so the interface between the coordinator class and workers below them. This would in turn inform how we talk, what we demand, and how we organize ourselves. We would admire and pursue excellence and expertise, but we would not reward excellence and expertise with undue material wealth or social power. Nor would we mistake mystification for expertise. We would want current coordinator class members to support and seek participatory economics, but we would not prioritize attracting coordinator class members above attracting working class members.

There must be some way out of here, said the organizer to the activist—but it is very important that the way we choose doesn't lead us in a circle back to where we started, or take us to a new system that is still a dungeon. Having vision matters for where we wind up. Having vision matters for winning a new economy for a better world. Participatory economics is a proposed vision for one part of life. It is neither more nor less than that.

Selected References

The most potent weapon in the hands of the oppressor is the mind of the oppressed.
Steve Biko

Woe betide those who seek to save themselves the pain of mental building by inhabiting dead men's minds.
GDH Cole

Predecessors

A selection of works that preceded participatory economics but contributed, in hindsight, more than many other works.

Anton Pannekoek, *Workers Councils*, Melbourne 1951

Tjalling Koopmans, *Three Essays on the State of Economic Science*, McGraw Hill 1957

Andre Gorz, *Strategy for Labor*, Beacon, 1964

Herbert Marcuse, *One Dimensional Man*, Beacon, 1964

Daniel Cohn Bendit, *Obsolete Communism: A Left Wing Alternative*, McGraw Hill 1968

Herbert Marcuse, *An Essay on Liberation*, Beacon 1969

Murray Bookchin, *Post Scarcity Anarchism*, Black Rose, 1970

Peter Kropotkin, *Revolutionary Essays*, MIT, 1970

Noam Chomsky, *Government in the Future*, Open Media, 1970

Daniel Guerin, *Anarchism*, Monthly Review, 1970

Maurice Brinton, *The Bolsheviks and Workers Control*, Black Rose, 1970

Maurice Brinton, *For Workers' Power*, AK Press, 2020

Bertrand Russell, *Roads to Freedom*, Routledge, 1970

Shulamyth Firestone, *Dialectics of Sex*, William Morrow, 1970

Juliet Mitchell, *Women's Estate*, Pantheon, 1971

Bertel Ollman, *Alienation*, CUP, 1971

Cornelius Castoriadis, *Workers' Councils and a Self-Managed*

Society, Solidarity, 1972
Anton Pannekoek, *Workers Councils*, 1946/2002, AK Press
Rudolf Rocker, *Anarcho Syndicalism, 1938/2004,* AK Press
Peter Kropotkin, *Mutual Aid*, NYU, 1972
Wilhelm Reich, *Sex Pol*, Vintage, 1972
Sennet and Cobb, *The Hidden Injuries of Class*, Vintage, 1972
Howard and Klare, *The Unknown Dimension*, Basic, 1972
Stanley Aronowitz, *False Promises*, McGraw Hill, 1973
Ursula Leguin, *The Dispossessed*, Harper and Row, 1974
Steven Marglin, *What Do Bosses Do?*, RRPE, 1974
Simone de Beauvoir, *The Second Sex*, Vintage, 1974
Carl Boggs, *Gramsci's Marxism*, Pluto, 1975
Jeremy Brecher, *Strike*, SEP, 1977
Nancy Chodorow, *The Reproduction of Mothering*, UC, 1978
Murray Bookchin, *Remaking Society*, Black Rose 1990

Origins

A selection of works that preceded but foreshadowed and began to develop ideas key to participatory economics.

Michael Albert, *What Is To Be Undone*, Porter Sargent, 1974
Albert and Hahnel, *Unorthodox Marxism*, SEP, 1978
Patrick Walker, *Between Labor and Capital*, SEP, 1979
Ehrenreichs, "The Professional Managerial Class," *Between Labor and Capital 1979*
Albert and Hahnel, "More Locations on the Class Map," *Between Labor and Capital, 1979*
Albert and Hahnel, *Socialism Today and Tomorrow*, SEP, 1981
Albert and Hahnel, *Marxism and Socialist Theory*, SEP, 1981
Stephen Shalom, *Socialist Visions*, SEP, 1983
Albert, Cagan, Chomsky, Hahnel, King, Sargent, Sklar, *Liberating Theory*, SEP, 1986
Hahnel and Albert, *Quiet Revolution in Welfare Economics*, Princeton, 1990

Presentations/Elaborations/Parallel Efforts

Albert and Hahnel, *Looking Forward*, South End Press, 1991
Albert and Hahnel, *Political Economy of Participatory Economics*, Princeton, 1991
Roy Morrison, *Ecological Democracy*, South End Press, 1995
Michael Albert, *Thinking Forward*, Arbeiter Ring, 1997
Bookchin and Biehl, *The Politics of Social Ecology*, Black Rose Books, 1998
Michael Albert, *Moving Forward*, AK Press, 2001
Jeff Schmidt, *Disciplined Minds*, Rowan and Littlefield, 2001
Seymour Melman, *After Capitalism*, Knopf, 2001
Michael Albert, *Trajectory of Change*, SEP, 2002
Michael Albert, *Parecon: Life After Capitalism*, Verso, 2003
Michael Albert, *Thought Dreams*, Arbeiter Ring, 2004
Robin Hahnel, *Economic Justice and Democracy*, Routledge, 2005
Gar Alperovitz, *America Beyond Capitalism*, Wiley, 2005
Michael Albert, *Realizing Hope*, Zed Books, 2006
Michael Albert, *Remembering Tomorrow*, Seven Stories, 2006
Chris Spannos, *Real Utopia*, AK Press, 2008
Stephen Shalom, "Parpolity," *Real Utopia*, 2008
Cynthia Peters, "Kinship," *Real Utopia*, 2008
Justin Podur, "Polyculturalism," *Real Utopia*, 2008
Michael Lebowitz, *The Contradiction of Socialism*, Monthly Review Press, 2012
Robin Hahnel, *Of the People, By the People*, AK Press, 2012
Wilson and Thompson, *Parecomic* Seven Stories, 2013
Robin Hahnel, *Economic Justice and Democracy*, Routledge, 2013
Robin Hahnel, *The ABCs of Political Economy*, Pluto, 2014
Michael Lebowitz, *The Socialist Imperative*, Monthly Review Press, 2015
Michael Albert, *Practical Utopia*, PM, 2017
Michael Albert, *RPS/2044: An Oral History of the Next American Revolution*, ZNet, 2017
Anders Sandstrom, *Anarchist Accounting*, Routledge, 2020

Robin Hahnel, *Democratic Economic Planning*, Routledge, 2021
Michael Albert, No Bosses: *A New Economy for a Better World*, Zero Books, 2021

Some Websites

Participatory Economics at ZNet:
https://zcomm.org/category/topic/parecon/
RevolutionZ: https://www.patreon.com/revolutionZ
Real Utopia: Foundation for a Participatory Society:
https://www.realutopia.org
A Participatory Economy:
https://participatoryeconomics.info/
Parecon Finland: http://www.osallisuustalous.fi/
Parecon Sweden: http://www.parecon.se/org

CULTURE, SOCIETY & POLITICS

The modern world is at an impasse. Disasters scroll across our smartphone screens and we're invited to like, follow or upvote, but critical thinking is harder and harder to find. Rather than connecting us in common struggle and debate, the internet has sped up and deepened a long-standing process of alienation and atomization. Zer0 Books wants to work against this trend.
With critical theory as our jumping off point, we aim to publish books that make our readers uncomfortable. We want to move beyond received opinions.
Zer0 Books is on the left and wants to reinvent the left. We are sick of the injustice, the suffering and the stupidity that defines both our political and cultural world, and we aim to find a new foundation for a new struggle.

If this book has helped you to clarify an idea, solve a problem or extend your knowledge, you may want to check out our online content as well. Look for Zer0 Books: Advancing Conversations in the iTunes directory and for our Zer0 Books YouTube channel.

Popular videos include:

Žižek and the Double Blackmain
The Intellectual Dark Web is a Bad Sign
Can there be an Anti-SJW Left?
Answering Jordan Peterson on Marxism

Follow us on Facebook
at https://www.facebook.com/ZeroBooks and Twitter at https://twitter.com/Zer0Books

Bestsellers from Zer0 Books include:

Give Them An Argument
Logic for the Left
Ben Burgis
Many serious leftists have learned to distrust talk of logic. This is a serious mistake.
Paperback: 978-1-78904-210-8 ebook: 978-1-78904-211-5

Poor but Sexy
Culture Clashes in Europe East and West
Agata Pyzik
How the East stayed East and the West stayed West.
Paperback: 978-1-78099-394-2 ebook: 978-1-78099-395-9

An Anthropology of Nothing in Particular
Martin Demant Frederiksen
A journey into the social lives of meaninglessness.
Paperback: 978-1-78535-699-5 ebook: 978-1-78535-700-8

In the Dust of This Planet
Horror of Philosophy vol. 1
Eugene Thacker
In the first of a series of three books on the Horror of Philosophy, *In the Dust of This Planet* offers the genre of horror as a way of thinking about the unthinkable.
Paperback: 978-1-84694-676-9 ebook: 978-1-78099-010-1

The End of Oulipo?
An Attempt to Exhaust a Movement
Lauren Elkin, Veronica Esposito
Paperback: 978-1-78099-655-4 ebook: 978-1-78099-656-1

Capitalist Realism

Is There No Alternative?

Mark Fisher

An analysis of the ways in which capitalism has presented itself as the only realistic political-economic system.

Paperback: 978-1-84694-317-1 ebook: 978-1-78099-734-6

Rebel Rebel

Chris O'Leary

David Bowie: every single song. Everything you want to know, everything you didn't know.

Paperback: 978-1-78099-244-0 ebook: 978-1-78099-713-1

Kill All Normies

Angela Nagle

Online culture wars from 4chan and Tumblr to Trump.

Paperback: 978-1-78535-543-1 ebook: 978-1-78535-544-8

Cartographies of the Absolute

Alberto Toscano, Jeff Kinkle

An aesthetics of the economy for the twenty-first century.

Paperback: 978-1-78099-275-4 ebook: 978-1-78279-973-3

Malign Velocities

Accelerationism and Capitalism

Benjamin Noys

Long listed for the Bread and Roses Prize 2015, *Malign Velocities* argues against the need for speed, tracking acceleration as the symptom of the ongoing crises of capitalism.

Paperback: 978-1-78279-300-7 ebook: 978-1-78279-299-4

Meat Market
Female Flesh under Capitalism
Laurie Penny
A feminist dissection of women's bodies as the fleshy fulcrum of capitalist cannibalism, whereby women are both consumers and consumed.
Paperback: 978-1-84694-521-2 ebook: 978-1-84694-782-7

Babbling Corpse
Vaporwave and the Commodification of Ghosts
Grafton Tanner
Paperback: 978-1-78279-759-3 ebook: 978-1-78279-760-9

New Work New Culture
Work we want and a culture that strengthens us
Frithjof Bergmann
A serious alternative for mankind and the planet.
Paperback: 978-1-78904-064-7 ebook: 978-1-78904-065-4

Romeo and Juliet in Palestine
Teaching Under Occupation
Tom Sperlinger
Life in the West Bank, the nature of pedagogy and the role of a university under occupation.
Paperback: 978-1-78279-637-4 ebook: 978-1-78279-636-7

Ghosts of My Life
Writings on Depression, Hauntology and Lost Futures
Mark Fisher
Paperback: 978-1-78099-226-6 ebook: 978-1-78279-624-4

Sweetening the Pill

or How We Got Hooked on Hormonal Birth Control

Holly Grigg-Spall

Has contraception liberated or oppressed women?
Sweetening the Pill breaks the silence on the dark side of hormonal contraception.

Paperback: 978-1-78099-607-3 ebook: 978-1-78099-608-0

Why Are We The Good Guys?

Reclaiming Your Mind from the Delusions of Propaganda

David Cromwell

A provocative challenge to the standard ideology that Western power is a benevolent force in the world.

Paperback: 978-1-78099-365-2 ebook: 978-1-78099-366-9

The Writing on the Wall

On the Decomposition of Capitalism and its Critics

Anselm Jappe, Alastair Hemmens

A new approach to the meaning of social emancipation.

Paperback: 978-1-78535-581-3 ebook: 978-1-78535-582-0

Enjoying It

Candy Crush and Capitalism

Alfie Bown

A study of enjoyment and of the enjoyment of studying. Bown asks what enjoyment says about us and what we say about enjoyment, and why.

Paperback: 978-1-78535-155-6 ebook: 978-1-78535-156-3

Color, Facture, Art and Design

Iona Singh

This materialist definition of fine-art develops guidelines for architecture, design, cultural-studies and ultimately social change.

Paperback: 978-1-78099-629-5 ebook: 978-1-78099-630-1

Neglected or Misunderstood
The Radical Feminism of Shulamith Firestone
Victoria Margree
An interrogation of issues surrounding gender, biology, sexuality, work and technology, and the ways in which our imaginations continue to be in thrall to ideologies of maternity and the nuclear family.
Paperback: 978-1-78535-539-4 ebook: 978-1-78535-540-0

How to Dismantle the NHS in 10 Easy Steps (Second Edition)
Youssef El-Gingihy
The story of how your NHS was sold off and why you will have to buy private health insurance soon. A new expanded second edition with chapters on junior doctors' strikes and government blueprints for US-style healthcare.
Paperback: 978-1-78904-178-1 ebook: 978-1-78904-179-8

Digesting Recipes
The Art of Culinary Notation
Susannah Worth
A recipe is an instruction, the imperative tone of the expert, but this constraint can offer its own kind of potential. A recipe need not be a domestic trap but might instead offer escape – something to fantasise about or aspire to.
Paperback: 978-1-78279-860-6 ebook: 978-1-78279-859-0

the pursuit of POWER AND FREEDOM

KATHA UPANISHAD

Also by Pandit Rajmani Tigunait

Books

Touched by Fire: The Ongoing Journey of a Spiritual Seeker
Lighting the Flame of Compassion
Tantra Unveiled
Inner Quest: Yoga's Answers to Life's Questions
The Himalayan Masters: A Living Tradition
Why We Fight: Practices for Lasting Peace
At the Eleventh Hour: The Biography of Swami Rama
Swami Rama of the Himalayas: His Life and Mission
Shakti: The Power in Tantra
*From Death to Birth: Understanding Karma and Reincarnation**
The Power of Mantra and the Mystery of Initiation
Shakti Sadhana: Steps to Samadhi
Seven Systems of Indian Philosophy

*Also available in audio book

Audio & Video

Sacred Link™ Freedom from Fear Conference CD or DVD
  The Quest for Freedom and the Sacred Link™
  Sacred Link™ in Practice: Panel Discussion and Closing Remarks
The Spirit of the Vedas CD
The Spirit of the Upanishads CD
In the Footsteps of the Sages VHS
Living Tantra™ series – cassette or VHS
  Tantric Traditions and Techniques
  The Secret of Tantric Rituals
  Forbidden Tantra
  Tantra and Kundalini
  Sri Chakra: The Highest Tantric Practice
  Sri Vidya: The Embodiment of Tantra

the pursuit of POWER AND FREEDOM

KATHA UPANISHAD

WITH TRANSLATION AND COMMENTARY BY
Pandit Rajmani Tigunait

HIMALAYAN INSTITUTE®
PRESS

Himalayan Institute Press
952 Bethany Turnpike
Honesdale, PA 18431 USA

www.HimalayanInstitute.org

The paper used in this publication meets the minimum requirements of the American National Standard of Information Sciences Permanence of Paper for Printed Library Materials, ANSI Z39.48-1984.

Library of Congress Cataloging-in-Publication Data

Tigunait, Rajmani, 1953-
The pursuit of power and freedom : Katha Upanishad : commentary and translation / by Rajmani Tigunait.
p. cm.
ISBN 978-0-89389-274-6 (pbk. : alk. paper)
1. Upanishads. Kathopanisad—Criticism, interpretation, etc.
I. Upanishads. Kathopanisad. English. II. Title.
BL1124.7.K386T55 2008
294.5'9218—dc22
2008007569

Dedicated to the Sages of the Tradition

CONTENTS

Preface

If there is a single text that represents the complete range of yoga, meditation, spirituality, philosophy, and esoteric sciences of the East, it is the *Katha Upanishad,* recast here as *The Pursuit of Power and Freedom.* It is an ageless book, for it contains timeless wisdom. It presents us with fully mature knowledge pertaining to acquiring health, wealth, peace, and happiness without sacrificing the higher purpose and meaning of life. If all books and the information contained in them happened to vanish from the face of the earth, the wisdom of the *Katha Upanishad,* tucked away in the remotest corners of the human mind, would find its way to germinate, blossom, and reintroduce all the tools and means that a human race needs to build a civil society. The *Katha Upanishad* is the most precious gift that the sages of India gave to mankind.

I am a living testimony to this fact. Almost seven generations ago in my family lineage, a young boy died on the first day of his schooling. From that day a superstition took root that formal education for male boys in our family was inauspicious. Soon it was believed that anyone in our family who went to school would die on the first day, and so began a family tradition of illiteracy. Six generations later, my father dared to learn how to read and write, in spite of the displeasure of every member of the family. He did not go to school; some schoolteachers came to our home and taught him unofficially. Seeing that he was still alive in young adulthood, people began to remark, "Perhaps the time of misfortune that had befallen our family is over." I was the first person in my family who was officially enrolled in school.

My grandfather, who loved me very much, was no longer afraid of losing me, but he wished to play with me all the time. He always found excuses to divert my attention from studying. I followed him every chance I could. I would join him collecting mangos, milking cows, harvesting sugarcane, making raw sugar, spinning cotton, and making "sacred thread."

One day, when he was very old and we knew that he might die soon, I asked him, "Baba [a loving term for grandfather], what can I do that would make you happy forever?"

After a long pause, he said, "Tell me the story of Jamraj [Yamaraja], the Lord of Death, and what and how he told his student about heaven and hell, and attaining freedom from the cycle of birth and death."

I told him many stories pertaining to heaven and hell as described in Hinduism, but he kept saying, "No, no—not that one."

When I asked, "Then which story are you referring to?" he responded, "I do not know the whole story but I do know that there was a young boy who left his mother and father, went to the palace of the Lord of Death, and sat there at the gate for three days and three nights without eating or drinking. Then the Lord of Death came and gave him three boons. And I have heard that by listening to that story, one is freed from the jaws of death. I want to hear that story."

Until then, I had neither read nor heard this story anywhere. I tried my best to find the source, but was unsuccessful. One day I saw that my grandfather was on his deathbed. I was sad that I could not fulfill his desire. In the evening, in the course of conversation, I told him that I had not yet found that story. He responded, "Whenever you learn the story, tell me. You can tell me that story even when I'm sleeping, or even when I'm dead. A person who knows that story brings deliverance to seven generations before and seven generations after him. It is through that story you will deliver your love to me, and it is through that story we will talk to each other in the courtyard of our souls."

Not knowing what tomorrow would have in store, that night I lay in bed with my grandfather. In the early morning, upon awakening, I realized the warmth of his body was no longer there. He was dead. While people busied themselves with the after-death rituals, I kept trying to find the story my grandfather wanted to hear as his last wish. My intense desire to learn about that story took the tears away from my eyes—I had no time to grieve, I had no will to contemplate on death. My family thought that I had gone into shock, for I showed no emotions. My mother and aunt feared that I might lose my mind. They tried to give me extra attention, but I found their love and attention annoying, for I was voraciously reading all the books in my father's library.

Finally, my eyes fell upon the *Katha Upanishad.* There was the story of Yamaraja, the Lord of Death, and his student, Nachiketa, who waited at the door of his master for three days and three nights. In return, the master, the Lord of Death, granted his student three boons. With the first boon, the student, Nachiketa, was able to infuse the minds and hearts of his father and other family members with the complete understanding of life, and the resolution of all conflicts, leading to lasting peace.

I could not read beyond this point, for now the tears began to roll down my cheeks because my grandfather had been cremated. After hours of crying and feelings of regret, I went under the tree where three clay pots filled with water hung on a branch—a traditional way of performing ancestral rites for thirteen days after death. It is in these pots that the soul is believed to stay during the transition period while loved ones come and bid their farewell. I sat next to those clay pots and recited the entire *Katha Upanishad.* I hardly understood the depth of the text, but I was filled with the conviction that my grandfather, along with all of my ancestors, heard the story I recited. That was enough to make me happy.

Since then, I have read this scripture more than a thousand times. Each reading continues to add to the maturity of my understanding. And deep in my heart, I know that the remaining layers of ignorance will melt away once I read this scripture a few more times.

With this conviction, I offer the translation of the *Katha Upanishad* and my personal understanding of it to you. And I pray that this scripture casts its magic on those who read it, just as it did to me.

At the Crossroads of Power and Progress

ॐ

For ages, India embraced a unique culture—a culture that invested its resources more in meeting the needs of the soul than in fulfilling the cravings of the flesh. The sages, the founding fathers of this culture, continually affirmed that this world of ours has its source in a higher reality that is divine, eternal, and inherently beautiful. This reality is the Lord of the Universe, the Lord of Life. It is the primordial pool of intelligence, existence, and bliss. The world exists in its fullness because its source is perfect and full. In this ever-expanding universe, everything blossoms because the world is intrinsically connected to the boundless source of nurturance. Knowledge of this truth grants us freedom from bondage, and ignorance of it takes away the gift of joy that abounds in life. This is the message of the sages, and from this message the Vedic culture of India evolved.

Reality is one, all-pervading, beginningless and endless, and the world consisting of numberless forms is rooted in this single reality—this truth is the backbone of Vedic culture. The customs, beliefs, religious practices, and spiritual disciplines of Vedic times all found their justification in this ideology. Art, dance, music, and craft, as well as agriculture and commerce, found their expressions in response to the calling of this ideology. Ethics and morality, the concepts of vice and virtue, and even the basic principles of philosophy, mythology, and theology were crafted within the framework provided by this ideology. The relationship between humans and other living beings, and between humans and the celestial world, also had to conform to this basic ideology of the sages. Even religion and politics were no exception. Describing the dynamics of the ancient Vedic culture of India, Rabindranath Tagore, one of the greatest thinkers, educators, and seers of modern India, writes in his book *Sadhana*:

> The fundamental unity of creation was not simply a philosophical speculation for India; it was her life-object to realise this great harmony in feeling and in action. With meditation and service, with regulation of her life, she cultivated her consciousness in such a way that everything had a spiritual meaning to her. The earth, water, and light, fruits and flowers, to her were not merely physical phenomena to be turned to use and then left aside. They were necessary to her in the attainment of her ideal of perfection, as every note is necessary to the completeness of the symphony. India intuitively felt that the essential fact of this world has a vital meaning for us; we have to be fully alive to it and establish a conscious relation with it, not merely impelled by scientific curiosity or greed of material advantage, but realising it in the spirit of sympathy, with a large feeling of joy and peace.

This is what the philosophers and visionaries of the East identify as the spirit of India. As long as this spirit remained clear and strong, India thrived. Whenever this spirit declined, India became sick. Thank God, Indian culture has preserved the scriptures that describe not only the nature of this spirit but also the cure should this spirit ever wane. The *Katha Upanishad* is one of these scriptures.

Vedic literature is vast in volume and profound in content. This literature was composed over several millennia, and it was only four thousand years ago that a great adept, Vyasa, collected the writings of Vedic sages from different parts of India and compiled them in the order we know today. The most ancient portions of Vedic literature came to be known as the Vedas. Vyasa organized these writings in four books, known as the *Rig Veda, Yajur Veda, Sama Veda,* and *Atharva Veda.* These four books together form the most sacred texts of India.

Indians have always held the Vedas in the highest regard. According to them, the wisdom contained in these four books was revealed to the ancient sages. Clarity of mind and purity of heart enabled the sages to be perfect conduits for the knowledge that spontaneously descended on the horizon of their consciousness. Their retentive power enabled them to capture the flow of revelation and present it in a language befitting the glory and grandeur of the wisdom they intended to share. Their words spontaneously arranged themselves in perfect meters with rhythm and melody so impeccable that the minds and hearts of the hearers opened themselves effortlessly to those words. These words were called *mantras,* sacred sounds infused with powers of protection, guidance, healing, and nurturance.

The belief that every letter, word, and sentence in the Vedas was revealed was so ingrained in the Indian psyche that no change whatsoever was knowingly made in this literature. That is why, despite the fact that from time to time the Vedas were translated into different languages, the original always remained intact. Since Vyasa fixed their form no change has entered and nothing has been edited. The knowledge that the Vedas are revealed; that they have their source in the domain of the Divine; that they are self-evident, requiring no proof or any verification; and that the guardians of this wisdom have had no authority to alter even one single syllable charges us with confidence that the Vedas are a true reflection of the society and people that existed when they were written. Once written, it was as if they were set in stone, leaving just enough room for later philosophers and teachers to elaborate and interpret the contents by writing commentaries on these original texts. That is how Vedic literature continued to grow for the next several thousand years. The *Katha Upanishad,* although more than three thousand years old, is one of the latest texts in the Vedic tradition.

The Katha Upanishad in Its Social Context

From the beginning of its known history, India has been a primarily agricultural society. The people of the Vedic civilization farmed their lands and raised their cattle. Due to the high peaks of the Himalayas to the north and oceans in the three other directions, seasons were regular and predictable. The Indus Valley, the valley of the Ganga and Yamuna rivers, and the foothills of the Himalayas provided ideal land for farming. Those who lived deeper in the mountains and jungles earned their livelihood from hunting, and gathering fruits and nuts. Theirs was a life of simplicity, a life so meaningful and beautiful and so desirable that even the gods in heaven longed to live among humans.

What motivated them? Contentment. The people were happy with the rain that the clouds brought. They were happy that the seeds sprouted. They were happy that the crops ripened and gave plenty of food. Cows gave milk, calves played in the courtyards, and birds sang in the canopies of trees. The sun rose in the morning, driving away the darkness and inertia of the night. It set in the evening, filling the sky with endless colors. With a cool breeze and shining stars, night came and put them to bed.

Every night the ancestors and divine beings walked through corridors of twinkling lights in the sky, seeing that their children on earth were happy and well protected. Those with sufficient light in their minds and faith in their hearts saw these eternal souls, imbibed their guidance, and passed it on through art, dance, music, poetry, and folktales. To them, every aspect of nature manifested spiritual meaning. Every act of nature gave them a spiritual message. To them, every incident in life contained a promise of freedom. They had no complaints, for they were taught by their teachers, the sages, that life was a gift. It was to be prized. Living in the serenity of nature, they shaped a culture that revered life in all its forms.

The founding fathers of Indian culture also introduced a social system that rewarded the use of one's conscience. Their social, moral, and ethical laws stood on the basic principles of spirituality: life is sacred; hurting and harming anyone is a spiritual offense;

therefore, do not do to others what you do not want others to do to you. Compliance to the voice of one's own heart was the driving force for any moral act; refraining from hurting others only out of fear of being punished was, according to the Vedic sages, the mark of a low-grade person. Investing oneself totally toward one's own personal well-being and the well-being of others constituted the core of spirituality. Because this core principle of spirituality infuses everything else with lasting life, the sages called it *dharma,* the law of sustainability. The sages also called it *sanatana dharma,* the perennial or original dharma of mankind. Regardless of who we are and what we wish to become, practicing this kind of dharma is an absolute necessity.

The law of sustainability communicated by dharma constitutes the principles of duty, for such principles are charged with the power to lift the human spirit from a base existence to a civilized one. Without the principles of sustainability as a foundation, we cannot define right and wrong, good and bad, just and unjust. Unless we embrace the fundamental principles of dharma—sustainability in its broadest and purest sense—we cannot prevent our personal tastes and interests, and whims and ambitions, from colliding with those of others. And unless we see things in the light of this higher dharma, we cannot decide whose desires, goals, and ambitions are more valid. It is only in the light of dharma that we can grant justice to ourselves without being unjust to others. It is the understanding of dharma, therefore, that can bring the fight for justice to an end; it is the understanding of dharma that sheds light on our relationship with ourselves and others.

Right understanding of dharma makes us see how others' existence sustains our own existence, and vice versa. Once charged with this awareness, we are naturally compelled to protect those whose existence supplies life to us. We begin to understand the value of mutual cooperation and consideration beyond mere commercial gains. Thereafter, even our most mundane activities begin to bear spiritual fruits. In fact, the understanding and practice of this perennial dharma demolishes the wall separating the sacred from the mundane. We begin to experience freedom *in* the world and no longer find a reason to seek freedom *from* the world.

Tagore puts it beautifully in his book *Sadhana*:

> India knew that when by physical and mental barriers we violently detach ourselves from the inexhaustible life of nature, when we become merely man, not man-in-the-universe, we create bewildering problems, and having shut off the source of their solution, we try all kinds of artificial methods, each of which brings its own crop of interminable difficulties. When man leaves his resting place in universal nature, when he walks on the single rope of humanity, it means either a dance or a fall for him. He has ceaselessly to strain every nerve and muscle to keep his balance at each step, and then, in the intervals of his weariness, he fulminates against Providence and feels a secret pride and satisfaction in thinking that he has been unfairly dealt with by the whole scheme of things.

Thus the sages proclaimed, "*dharmo rakshati rakshitah*—the more you nurture dharma, the more it nurtures you." And it is on the grounds of this dharma—sanatana dharma—that the social structure of the Vedic people evolved.

The Evolution of Four Classes and a Caste System

During the early periods of Vedic civilization a caste system *(jati pratha)* did not exist in India. However, there was a class system *(varna vyavastha)*. In those days, people chose their professions based on their inclinations and skills. There were no rules or laws that prevented social mobility. Vedic society afforded equal opportunity to its members in every sphere of life. Faith and family affiliation did not serve as the grounds for any type of prohibition. But then there came a time when the caste system gripped the Indian psyche so tightly that race, class, and gender became the grounds for denying access to education, religious ceremonies, and spiritual practices, as well as the right to own property, and even to choose one's partner. During the worst days of the caste system, a prohibition was imposed on changing family trades. In those dark times, once you were doomed, for whatever reason, you were doomed forever. Understanding this evolution of Indian society from an open class system to a closed caste system puts the history of India's spirituality in proper context.

There is always a natural grouping of people living in a community. Some members of a community have a natural inclination for higher education, analytical thinking, research, scientific discoveries, and inventions. Some people within this group may be more inclined toward art, dance, music, writing, or teaching. Their distinctive love for knowledge puts them in one category. The sages called this group *Brahmana,* those who have a love for knowledge. There is another group of people who like to develop their physical might, love weapons, and find pleasure in enforcing law and justice. Their personality is such that they have to define their territory, invest themselves fully in possessing it, and find great pride in defending it, even at the cost of dying. They are *Kshatriya,* the warrior class.

Then there are people who love money. They love to trade, and profit motivates their actions. Their satisfaction comes from success in business and the name and fame that goes with it. The more objects they move around, and the larger the customer base they reach through their commodities, the greater the sense of accomplishment they find. They are *Vaishya,* merchants and businessmen. Then comes the final group of people—those who love to work. Intellectual stimulation, desire for power and position, and the tendency to dominate others do not make much sense to them. Their joy comes from seeing others benefit from their hard work. When they are no longer capable of working, they find no meaning and purpose in life. Theirs is a life of service. They came to be known as *Shudra,* working-class people.

These are the four classes, and everyone naturally belonged to one or more of them. The four classes, and the gray areas between them, were equally respected. People could switch their professions, and sometimes their hobbies, personal tastes, interests, and even simple curiosity could lead them to participate in the activities of a different class without much fuss.

During the beginning periods of Vedic civilization, people

belonging to each of these four groups worked together in mutual cooperation and consideration for each other. It was an organic society with everyone benefiting from each other. Teachers taught, for they knew that it was their duty. Warriors defended their community, for they knew that it was their duty. Merchants traded commodities between communities and made profit according to their conscience. Workers worked, for they knew that they were children of the soil. There were a number of subclasses within these four major groups, and everyone worked and discharged their duties while embracing a unique economic system known as *jajmani,* the barter system. Under this system, every person in the community or village was a client of somebody else. A weaver gave clothes to a teacher, and the teacher taught the weaver's children. A barber offered his services and, in return, received education from the teachers, protection from the warriors, and grains from the farmers. The nature of commerce in each village was somewhat fluid and decentralized. Respect for the family trade and the continuous refinement that generations added to it remained a driving force in the proliferation and success of "cottage industries." These family trades and cottage industries in no way restricted children from practicing different trades from their parents.

Then came the rise of precious metals—gold, silver, and copper—leading to the introduction of currency. This changed the entire nature of commerce. Commodities were no longer traded for other commodities; rather the exchange of precious metals became the ground for trading. This brought a total shift in the basic values of life. The basic things people needed to live a healthy and happy life lost their intrinsic value, becoming instead valued by how many coins they could fetch. Their ability to fetch coins depended on the supply and demand of the market; and supply and demand could be manipulated by those who had a greater stock of those metals. This gave a new interpretation to wealth and power. The more coins one had, the more power he could exert, not only in the acquisition of merchandise, but also in the mobilization of land and labor. This coin-centered power soon awakened lust for dominance among powerful members of society. With coins of precious metals they could acquire land, cattle—even human beings. With the power of money, they could influence not only the people of all four classes within their own community but also the people of other kingdoms. This set the wheel of consumerism in motion, only to spin with greater velocity as time passed.

Simple village bazaars turned into trading posts, trading posts into towns, and towns into cities. More trade brought more money, and money brought greed. Greed brought fear. Fear demanded protection, and the need for protection put warriors in greater demand, raising their value in society. From this warrior class emerged the *Rajas,* nobles and kings. The kingmakers—the business class—claimed the honor of being *Shreshthi,* the owners and masters of the highest and best.

Thus the rich and the protectors of the rich gained distinction in society, and they enjoyed this distinction—as we see even today—by displaying their wealth and power. The acquisition of power, position, honor, and glamour became the ground for a pervasive superiority/inferiority complex as the wealthy and powerful sought to protect their position. The classification of members of society that was previously based on the natural inclination for learning and cultivating unique skills began to evaporate. Wealth became the primary criterion to define status. As a result, the time-honored class system turned into the caste system.

With the rise of the caste system, the people in the lower strata of society were denied upward mobility. This created a circumstance where the poor kept getting poorer and the rich kept getting richer. The gap between the poor and the rich became a source of unrest in society. Now everyone was hungry—some hungry for food, others hungry for power and riches. And yet others fell somewhere in between. The great wealth of contentment that had once motivated celestial beings to descend from heaven and live among humans evaporated. A society that had once lived in harmony, that had worked in mutual cooperation, and that had prized consideration for others now began to manufacture *dasyu*—thugs, thieves, looters, and terrorists—a phenomenon that further fueled fear and the demand for security.

The people still had plenty of land. The rivers still brought rich soil from the mountains. The rain clouds still came on time. The soil still bore crops. The cows still gave milk. The sun still rose in the morning. The stars still lit the sky at night. But the people no longer had peace of mind. Their hearts became a battlefield. Everyone was fighting with their seemingly invincible enemies—anger, hatred, jealousy, greed, desire—all leading to an unavoidable fate: fear, insecurity, worry.

This grim state of society created a new market that had never existed in Vedic India: priestly business. The people of the Brahmana class, who once spent their lives in the pursuit of knowledge, joined the propaganda machine that the privileged members of society needed to manage the anger rampant among the underprivileged. In theory, the Brahmana were already members of the highest strata of society, but their status carried no weight, for they had neither power nor money. During this time of social upheaval—perhaps not by choice but because of the pressing needs of the time and out of ignorance—they joined the crowd that held power, prestige, money, and dominance in the highest regard. As the unrest accelerated, they found their niche in a society that was on the verge of collapse.

It is from this period of Vedic civilization that we find texts that promote kings as the incarnations of God, and rich merchants as virtuous souls reaping the fruits of their good deeds from past lifetimes. The people of the teaching class were also elevated to a distinguished position. They were exalted as the purest of the pure, flawless conduits for God's power and grace. The rich, the noble, and the people from the teaching community thus complemented each other. Greed and lust for power had spread its tentacles beyond the fields of politics and commerce all the way to the domain of spirituality that had once had the law of sustainability at its core.

This is how the spiritual tradition of the Vedic sages turned into a religion—a religion that discouraged reason, promoted blind faith, condemned simplicity, and cut off man's direct relationship with the Divine. This is when the ideas of vice and virtue and hell and heaven were introduced. Priests stood between humans and God. Rituals replaced inner inquiry. Life became complex, requiring an outside "expert" to interpret it. The display of power, prestige, glory, and glamour became the sole criterion of righteousness. The people from the Brahmana class issued ordinances regarding human values; the people from the merchant class gave their stamp of approval; and the people from the warrior class made sure the ordinances were enforced.

Who was left out? The people who belonged to the working class. Now this newborn faith proclaimed that the people of the working class must stay wherever they were; their job was to work within their family trades. Demanding anything more than what Providence offered them was considered a spiritual offense, a sin. Education for this class—especially spiritual practices that encouraged self-reflection—was portrayed as such a grave offense that it could bring misfortune to the whole society, and therefore it was the duty of the upper class to deny the working class access to education and spiritual practices. This brought the Vedic culture to its darkest hour, and this is when the *Katha Upanishad* was written.

The Day of Awakening

ॐ

The *Katha Upanishad* is a dialogue between an accomplished master, Yamaraja, and an ardent seeker, Nachiketa. Both teacher and student hold an important place in the spiritual and philosophical history of India. Since this scripture was written at least three thousand years ago—and both teacher and student must have lived even earlier—people today think that the dialogue between the two is mythical. According to the living tradition of this scripture, however, both Yamaraja and Nachiketa were real people. Just like us, they were born. Just like us, they had their share of life's gifts: pleasure and pain, success and failure, gain and loss, health and sickness, honor and insult, and all the experiences that come with the desire to live and the desire not to die. Just like us, they were curious to know what brings us here, what keeps us alive, how our body and mind function together, and what happens once we die.

As spiritual scientists, they were interested in discovering the anatomy of health and happiness, stamina and weakness, and joy and grief. In an attempt to find lasting peace, they tried to understand the source of fear and the way to eliminate it once and for all. Their limitless appetite for unveiling the mysteries of life enabled them to invest all their resources—physical, mental, and spiritual. This gave them access to a world filled with infinite possibilities—a world beyond our normal understanding. The *Katha Upanishad* is a written testimony to what transpired between such an adept and a student aspiring to learn and master everything that the adept knew.

Now I will tell you where and how the teacher and the student came to know each other, in what circumstance the student reached his teacher, and in what circumstance the teacher taught the student. The context in which the teacher gave the knowledge and the student received it will help you understand that our basic needs and the meaning and purpose of life have always been the same.

All of us want to be happy. In search of happiness, we are continually adding new nuances in the fields of science and technology, religion and politics, and trade and commerce. Experience tells us that the more we possess, the more fearful we become, and yet our desire for power and possessions forces us to exhaust all our energies acquiring everything possible. On the one hand, we want to be happy. On the other hand, we do not want to let go of that which makes us miserable. And yet we fail to see why we are caught between wanting and not wanting, freedom and bondage. How puzzling is our reality: We wish for heaven after death, but at the same time, we want to stay here forever. We can't decide what we want, and yet we want it. Yamaraja is one of those rare masters who transcended this dilemma, and Nachiketa is a student aspiring to transcend it. The great sage Vyasa compiled the dialogue between the two, adept and seeker, for those who no longer wish to stay in the limbo of wanting and not wanting and who wish to become decisive. This scripture is just for us.

The student, Nachiketa, was born into a wealthy family. His father owned a large property and was the head of one of the largest religious and educational institutions *(guru kula)* of his time. He was at the center of more than ten thousand students and hundreds of teachers and was considered to be one of the most pious persons of his time. Learned people throughout the land came to him seeking his advice on religious and spiritual matters. As the *Katha Upanishad* informs us, he enjoyed name, fame, popularity, power, and prestige. He had earned the title *Vajashrava,* the one glowing with glory. The hero of this scripture, Nachiketa, is the son of such a father.

Growing up in his father's home and receiving his education at his father's guru kula, Nachiketa mastered the arts and sciences that would enable him to carry on his father's legacy. He learned about agriculture, commerce, philosophy, social sciences, economics, religion, theology, and most important, the art of administering large institutions. But deep down, he was not happy with the lifestyle that his family and society had imposed on him. As a young boy, he had more than once questioned the value of the religious orthodoxy his family prized so highly. And each time, he was told to shut his mouth, for he was too young even to discuss such matters. He had noticed his father lecturing about family values, respecting others, and being sensitive to the thoughts and feelings of others, but this young man had also observed how at home his father's actions were totally contrary to what he was teaching. This bothered him. As a teenager, he confronted his father every once in a while and always got a flat reply: "While living under my roof, you'd better live by my rules."

Once he completed his formal education, Nachiketa was expected to take part in his father's work by teaching at the guru kula. He showed no interest in it. He told his father, "My education is not yet complete, for I do not know the purpose of life. To me, this world is a disappointment. There is no joy at home and no joy at school. Our work lacks vision. We are running after worldly success without knowing where this race will take us. Fear and doubt still haunt my mind. Therefore, give me some time, Father, so that I may discover the meaning and purpose of life, and thereafter I will join you in your work with love and respect."

Nachiketa's behavior created a rift in the family, but being a public man, Nachiketa's father managed his reaction as skillfully as he could. On several occasions the father tried to console his son: "What do you wish, Nachiketa? Tell me. You are my only son. Anything I own will eventually go to you. From where has this unrealistic thought of finding meaning and purpose in life entered you? What prevents you from enjoying all the comforts and pleasures of the world in favor of achieving inner fulfillment at this untimely age? Furthermore, the wealthier you are, the more good things you can do in the world. A destitute person cannot help others who are destitute. Be practical. Your duty as an obedient son demands that you relieve your aging father of his family and social responsibilities."

Nachiketa replied, "I understand, Father, the value of power and wealth. People salute money. Money commands honor. Money can buy comforts and conveniences. But I also know that money breeds vanity. Hunger for money erects walls between us. The more intense this hunger becomes, the higher and thicker the walls. What good is the money that splits apart our family? What good is the money that takes away our love and respect for each other? What good is the money that works against our basic needs of peace and happiness?

"I also see money as a source of fear. The more we have, the greater the fear of losing it. How can a person run by fear be happy? Our family is a living example of that. It pains me even more when I see the members of our prestigious family teaching others the lesson of fearlessness, whereas they themselves live under fear. We are believed to be the upholders of a spiritual tradition, but I see us simply as hypocrites. I do not want to kill my conscience by contributing to a tradition that I know lacks purity.

"I wish to bring back the wisdom that once enabled our forefathers to stand in the front row of the sages. We are descendants of the sage Gautama, a seer of mantras. His practice of austerity was unmatched, and in the act of selfless service he had no peer. His purity of heart and clarity of mind was such that even Lord Shiva felt honored to be born as his grandson; thus Shiva himself incarnated as Hanuman in our lineage. I know from the scriptures and stories of the tradition that gods and goddesses in human form have played in our courtyard. I wish to restore that legacy, not contribute to the one that holds name, fame, power, and prestige as the sole criteria for greatness and glory."

"Then go, Nachiketa, and fulfill your fantasies," his father said. "Come back whenever you are happy with your achievement."

Now Nachiketa began his quest, traveling from city to city, village to village, and cave to cave. Finally he met his master, Yamaraja, the Lord of Death. According to tradition, Yamaraja is the first human to solve the mystery of life and death and become immortal. That is why he is called the Lord of Death. This master is also known by two other names: Dharmaraja and Kala. Dharmaraja means he is Lord of Virtues, such as love, compassion, kindness, selflessness, forgiveness, patience, forbearance, and dispassion. He is also called Kala, for he is the one who first discovered the principle of time. He is a master who understood how time and space relate to each other, and how the relationship between cause and effect is invariably dependent on time and space. Because he understood the principle of cause and effect, he knew how our actions create our destiny and how birth and death and everything that exists between the two is a result of our destiny. This master is also unique in his knowledge pertaining to life here and hereafter. Nachiketa found this master to be the most promising of all he had encountered.

Once Nachiketa began to study and practice under the guidance of Yamaraja, an intimate relationship between the teacher and student naturally evolved. Living in close proximity, both physically and emotionally, Nachiketa realized that he had met a master whose wisdom and philosophy of life matched his own ideals.

In due course, Nachiketa opened his heart to his master completely and asked, "I know my father is very learned and well intentioned. In his actions, he is kind and giving. In his public life, he is generous and a source of inspiration to many. Being his son, however, I know a part of him that people outside our household have no chance of knowing. It is fear, not love, that rules our family. Values are preset and there is no room to question them. As children, we are taught to look good in the eyes of others. We carry a persona to meet the expectations of society. Sensitivity to our own feelings and our perception of ourselves is considered meaningless.

"The sincere and obedient son within me demands that I go back to the same old world, but I know that by doing so I will kill my conscience. I find myself in a spiritual crisis. It has taken away my peace of mind. How can I know, Gurudeva, when to honor and when to challenge the age-old values? How can I discharge my duties without slowing down my personal spiritual pursuits?"

The master responded, "Be strong, Nachiketa. This world is

not for weak and meek people. Don't run away from this world. Better you go back to the world and face the challenges that await you. It is young people like you who have the power to change and transform lifeless values and set new ones in their place. Great thinkers and reformers have been saying for ages that women deserve the same love and respect as their male counterparts. But society has made a decision to ignore such advice. The result is that the family life of a great many people suffers continually from a lack of harmony. Truth lies at the core of religion and spirituality, and this truth receives its life from compassion. There is misery in the world because people do not embrace truth, and even if they do, they do not infuse it with compassion. Remember, my son, failure to speak the truth is lying, but speaking it late is just as bad. Embrace truth in your thought, speech, and action, and conduct your life in the light of truth.

"Practicing truth in solitude is necessary only in the beginning stages of your quest. In a sheltered environment you can practice truth without too many distractions, but in that environment you do not have the opportunity to test your strength. Conforming to truth while living in the world is a higher practice. Once you conquer the adverse conditions there, you have become the master of yourself. The smaller the list of complaints you have, the greater the adept you are. While living in the world, how effortlessly you maintain your inner peace indicates how successful you are on the material plane. Now go back to your home, Nachiketa, and return to me only as a victorious, happy soul."

Nachiketa returned to his home and lived with his father for a while. What transpired during that short stay with his father is the beginning of this Upanishad.

Once upon a time, Nachiketa's father, Vajashrava, sponsored a grand ritual. According to the rules outlined in the scriptures, the sponsor had to invite all the learned people from throughout the land. He was expected to invite and honor people from all castes and creeds. As part of the ceremony he was supposed to give away all his possessions to charity. Since it involved renouncing his material possessions in favor of bringing peace and happiness to the lives of others, this ceremony was called *sarva-vedas,* the practice of sharing one's belongings.

The preparations for the ceremony began. The guru kula was completely renovated and cleaned, and fine touches could be seen everywhere. A magnificent ceremonial hall surrounded by altars of all different shapes and sizes was built in accordance with the scriptural injunctions. To match the grandeur of the ceremony, Vajashrava built new roads leading to the campus and lined them with trees and flowering plants. He constructed private houses for special guests and fitted them with all the amenities. News of this grand event traveled far and wide. Long before the grand opening, the crowd began to pour in, including traders, entertainers, artisans, and craftsmen. As the time for the ceremony drew near and the guests began to arrive, the drama began to unfold.

Although the organizers had put in place well-thought-out protocols, it was not easy to satisfy the high expectations of the dignitaries. As the oldest son of the host, Nachiketa found himself frequently managing unexpected crises on this solemn occasion. He wondered about the spiritual value of such a megagathering. He pondered, "It is a sacred ceremony. The purpose of this ceremony is to demolish the walls of selfishness, transcend our narrow feelings of 'me' and 'mine,' share our sorrows and joys with each other, expand our consciousness, and discover the sacred bond that holds our families, society, and all of humanity in place. Why is there so much emphasis on displaying our grandeur? What is this hunger for recognition? Who are we trying to serve, ourselves or God?"

The ceremony began. Tons of natural ingredients—herbs, grains, nuts, dried fruits, and *ghee* (clarified butter)—were being offered into the sacred fire. Priests recited their mantras, women sang their folk songs, and scholars displayed their academic knowledge as they debated each other in the formal assembly of experts. The several-months-long ceremony proceeded as planned and every day was filled with unique forms of rituals accompanied by distinctive types of charity.

Although the idea of coins as a means for trading was well established, in the field of religious practices, cows were still treated as the most valuable currency. Wealth, therefore, was assessed by how many cows you possessed. The worth of your charity was judged by how many cows you donated. On the final day, a large herd of cows was brought into a gigantic ceremonial hall. While priests made the official announcement of the cows being given as charity, poets read their poetry in honor of the donor, and the public cheered in astonishment. Thus, the ceremony concluded and the dignitaries poured in to congratulate Vajashrava on his successful completion of the ceremony.

Nachiketa, however, was absorbed in the world of his own thoughts. The honest observer and seeker of truth in him was becoming increasingly agitated. At the earliest opportunity, he confronted his father: "What is the use of giving away *these* cows? They have drunk their last drop of water, eaten their last mouthful of grass, been milked for the last time, and have nearly lost their limbs and organs. Definitely, the giver of such cows will go to the realm devoid of joy.

"Was it an act of charity, Father? I know our books say that cows given in charity entitle the donor to cross the formidable river Vaitarani that flows between earth and heaven. But, were they really precious cows, or simply a liability? Was it charity, or an act of tossing our headache to some unfortunates who couldn't say no? Has your name entered the list of virtuous ones? Has your conscience approved it?"

Finally, Nachiketa spoke his last words: "To you, everything and everyone is subject to possession—an object to be used and left aside when no longer useful. I am no different from anything else. So, to whom are you going to give me?"

His father snapped, "I give you to Death."

With this, Nachiketa returned to Yamaraja, the Lord of Death, his spiritual master, for his final studies and the direct experience of the reality that governs and guides our life here and hereafter.

Resolving Conflicts

Nachiketa arrived at the door of his teacher, Yamaraja. There he exchanged his greetings with the students and family members, and requested an audience with his teacher. Moments later came a cold reply, "Wait until I complete my work."

Years ago, Nachiketa had spent a great deal of time at his master's home. The love and affection, knowledge, and guidance he had received while living there had left an indelible impression on his mind and heart. In Yamaraja, he had found a selfless teacher with limitless knowledge and unconditional love: a mother with an incessant flow of protection and nourishment; a father with vigilant eyes constantly concerned with his child's well-being; and a friend who always stood on his side without judging him or the circumstances. Today, he was treated as a stranger. Yet confident in his resolve and trustful in his master's decision, he sat at the gate waiting for Yamaraja to call him in.

Three days passed with no word from the teacher. Nachiketa used these days to reflect. "During my stay with my master in the past, I saw how generous he was in helping me meet my worldly needs, but how skillfully he entertained my spiritual queries only after ignoring them for days and weeks, and sometimes even months. I know it very well—spiritual wisdom doesn't come easily. The master is definitely not here. He has traveled to the world far beyond ours—a world that keeps its doors closed to all except those with the highest degree of patience. I must not give in to impatience. No doubt he will return and lift me from this dull and heavy plane whenever I am ready."

Finally, the master returned, and before Nachiketa said a word, Yamaraja spoke, "Your resolve is commendable, Nachiketa. You deserve all honor and respect in this world. You have earned all my blessings. You sat at my door for three days and three nights without food or water. I'll fulfill three requests, whatever they may be."

Nachiketa responded, "May my father be filled with peaceful thoughts. May he be cheerful and free from grief and guilt. Upon my return, may he recognize me and speak with me. I ask this as the first of the three boons you have granted."

Yamaraja said, "You are too naive and kind, Nachiketa. You know how disappointing this world is; how inconsiderate people are; how unkind they are toward those who love them the most. You know from your own experience that love in relationships has been replaced by expectations and selfishness. Why do you worry about those whom you have left behind? Why do you cling to the welfare of your father who cares so little for you?"

Nachiketa responded, "I do not worry for the father whom I left behind. I am concerned with the father who lives in me—a father who can't touch and feel his own child. I'm concerned about a father who is barely alive, for his consciousness has shrunk to focus only on being a dominant male figure in the family and a power-driven member of society. I'm concerned about a father who has not only lost his fatherhood but also the benevolence of his soul that sees no limit to self-sacrifice."

"Your understanding of the human mind and family dynamics makes me exceedingly happy," said Yamaraja. "Your father will return to normal. After you are released by me, he will recognize you. Upon seeing you freed from the jaws of death, he will overcome his grief and guilt, and he will sleep peacefully at night." With this blessing, Yamaraja explained the secret of a happy and peaceful family life.

Love is the cornerstone of any relationship. Whereas selflessness nurtures love, expectations contaminate it. How selfless our love can be depends on how clearly we understand ourselves, for it is our own self-understanding that empowers us to understand others rightly. Misunderstanding is the mother of all miseries. Attachment to our self-image prevents us from examining whether our understanding is correct. Thus we go on worshipping our *asmita,* the sense of I-am-ness, which we hold so dear. Our failure to examine the validity of our understanding makes our asmita, the I-am-ness, swell to the point that we begin to lose sight of our soul. Eventually, this asmita matures into fully grown ego. That is when we become possessive—possessive of our self-image, possessive of everything around us. Ego has a limitless appetite. It can devour the knowledge of all the scriptures of the world combined. It can render all spiritual experiences inert. It can dull our intellect and blind our soul. Driven by ego, we abandon our loved ones, discard our teachers, trash our scriptures, and discredit the guiding light of God.

When we have not seen the face of truth, we operate on the

ground of ego. Ego is always self-righteous; it is always concerned with its image. And it is always accompanied by fear. To protect itself, it can go to any length—it can condemn others, it can harm others, and it can harm even those loved ones who try to awaken it to face reality and commit itself to positive transformation. It is this ego that has led kings to wars, and religious leaders to crusades. The worst among all acts of ego is to employ the power of intellect to manipulate tender human emotions and poison the collective consciousness through ideological cold war. But who is the first and the foremost recipient of the actions performed by our ego?

A person who has fallen into the trap of ego is the first and foremost recipient of his or her egotistical deeds. Even in the grimmest states of mind, there still flickers the flame of conscience. From the deepest recess of our heart, our conscience whispers, "You are hurting yourself. You are hurting others. You are marching on the path of self-deception. You are risking your peace and happiness to meet the cravings of your ego."

A weak person finds this whisper of conscience very painful. To avoid the pain caused by this bitter truth, a person with a swollen ego tries to escape from himself. The tragedy is that you can run away from the whole world, but how can you run away from yourself? From your own very essence that is your own conscience? In this situation, therefore, you are bound to suffer from inner conflict. This conflict takes away your night's sleep. You find no rest in life. But the soul demands nothing less than lasting peace. You have neither the vision nor the courage to turn your mind inward and find the peace that is in you, for you are afraid of facing your own inner demon, your own ego. Thus you run in the external world, seeking solace in temples, churches, mosques, swamis, priests, money, power, prestige, and recognition. But, alas, you always return empty-handed.

Fortunate are those who, like Nachiketa, have cultivated a clear, calm, and tranquil mind, and have nurtured a kind heart. Fortunate are those who are fully established in the principles of patience, fortitude, and forgiveness, for these are the virtues that can help us stand still and see our reflection in others and others' in ourselves without any fear or doubt. It is only upon nurturing these virtues that we can understand the dynamics of our mind, ego, and intellect, as well as the dynamics of our family, society, culture, and nation. And, ultimately, with that understanding, we can use our judgment in regard to managing the complex circumstances and situations of life. Indeed, these are the virtues that make us become a high-grade student destined to find a high-grade teacher fully equipped to impart the highest grade of wisdom.

Paradise of a Yogi

Just like any of us, Nachiketa had heard about heaven and hell. His culture had imparted to him the idea of good and evil. He was also familiar with the definitions of good and evil prevalent in the past. He had seen how priests stood between humans and their conscience, between the dead and their destiny after life. He had seen how direct experience gets replaced by blind faith, and genuine religious practices by mere superstitions. The trivialization of virtue and vice, of gods and goddesses, and of the ritual worship to propitiate them had always bothered him. He questioned whether God was really a petty-minded person who rewarded the doers of good and punished the doers of evil. Nachiketa seized the opportunity to discover the truth that had been shrouded in mystery, faith, doubt, disbelief, and personal preference.

He asked his master, "I have heard that in heaven there is no fear of any kind. In heaven there is neither death nor old age. Crossing the realm of hunger and thirst, a person in heaven enjoys pleasures that transcend all worries."

Nachiketa continued, "Tell me, Master, does heaven really exist? Is the heavenly world similar to ours? Is this world eternal and therefore not subject to any change or destruction? Do things in heaven always remain the same? How do we reach there after we die? Once we reach there, do we stay there forever? Do the residents of heaven have bodies like ours? Are all the souls in heaven equally happy? I have heard that there are seven levels of heaven and seven levels of hell. Who determines who goes where and for how long? Please unveil the mystery of heaven and hell as part of my second of the three boons that you promised."

Yamaraja responded, "To a confused person the idea of heaven and hell is very complex. However, to a person with a clear, calm, and tranquil mind, it is very simple: The state of mind free from fear is heaven. A fearful person lives in hell here and hereafter. The day you attain freedom from the fear associated with old age and death, you have created a heaven that cannot be destroyed by anyone. The day your actions are not motivated by hunger and thirst will be the day to build your lasting residence in heaven. The day you cross the realm of worries you will land in the kingdom of heaven."

The Journey Beyond Death

The idea of heaven and hell is as ancient as human civilization itself. In every culture, heaven is associated with the idea of pleasure, and hell with the idea of suffering. In the Indian tradition, just as in other traditions, it is believed that after you die you either go to heaven or to hell. Indian mythology gives a graphic description not only of hell and heaven but also of how we reach there.

During the time of death, all of us share a common experience of clinging to life. We do not want to die, and yet the reality of our death becomes evident. We do not want to let go of our belongings or loved ones. We do not want to lose our possessions. While alive, we do not want to share our possessions with others, fearing we won't have enough for ourselves. First, we try to accumulate wealth, sometimes even at the cost of killing our conscience. Then we try to hide at least a big chunk of it and invest the remaining as quietly as possible. We keep our investments secret even from our loved ones. When old age announces its arrival, we struggle hard to deny its presence. In a futile attempt to escape the reality of aging, we are confronted with fear and doubt, grief, and hopelessness. To remedy this pain, we visit our familiar domains of comfort:

vacations, parties, temples, priests, gurus, and gods and goddesses. Finally, death, the embodiment of fear, stands before us. In the shadow of death, our breath begins to tremble; our senses begin to crumble; our nervous system becomes paralyzed; our conscious mind is rendered inert. What becomes active? Our unconscious mind.

The unconscious mind is the storehouse of the subtle impressions of all of our past deeds. It is the treasury of our convictions and beliefs. Normally, the memories pertaining to the recent past disappear, giving room to long-cherished memories and habit patterns. At the threshold of death, as the nervous system, brain, and conscious mind collapse, our consciousness begins to sink into the vast abyss of our unconscious mind and its numberless impressions of the past. This is where the scriptures add the flavor of myth to the process of the journey beyond death.

At the time of death the devil of loneliness hovers over our head. In desperation, we seek someone to hold our hand. If we are lucky, we have our loved ones around to give their hands. At some point, even that comfort is taken away when we sink into unconsciousness. This is when our beliefs and convictions assume their distinct forms. Our vices and virtues come to life. Our unresolved conflicts begin to tear us apart. Guilt attempts to put our soul on fire. We are terrified to face our own conscience. This is when, as mythology explains, the Messenger of Death comes. Despite our unwillingness, he pulls our soul out of the body. He makes us follow him to the world beyond. If we resist, he ties us with his rope and drags us along the road. Before reaching the destination we have to cross a river known as Vaitarani.

Vaitarani is an amazing river. This river flows between two worlds—the world made of man-made concepts and precepts, and the world that transcends all. To virtuous people, its current is calm and its water crystal clear. To sinners, however, it is tumultuous, muddy, and filled with crocodiles. This river is simultaneously a living goddess of mercy and a demon of horror. It is miraculous in the sense that it presents specific forms and unveils unique attributes in response to the deceased soul's vices and virtues. Everyone must cross this river. Truly fortunate are those who wake up to the reality that this inescapable river is nothing other than our own mind and who befriend it long before the Messenger of Death knocks at the door.

On the other shore of this river lies the world of disembodied souls, a world that does not conform to the rules and laws of our time and space. This world is made of the likes and dislikes that propelled our actions while we lived on earth. It mirrors the perceived values we held so dear while we were alive. Its size and shape are exactly the same as the size and shape of our mind. For those who embraced the principle of forgiveness while they lived on earth, this world is ruled by the unfettered laws of mercy and kindness. For them, this world is heaven. It is filled with all the pleasures and comforts. However, this world is completely empty for those who busied themselves meeting the needs of their senses and running hungrily after power, fame, and worldly possessions. In this barren land they go hungry. For them it is hell.

No one outside us assigns us to heaven or hell, not even God. Our conscience is the judge who decides that we get what we deserve. In this respect, neither is heaven a reward nor is hell a punishment, but rather, going to heaven or hell is a choice that we make while we are alive. Those who mindfully attend to their human qualities and attributes and make a sincere effort to refine those characteristics create a heavenly condition for themselves here and now. In the attempt to become fully developed, they put themselves on the path of self-transformation. They examine their strengths and weaknesses, make an effort to overcome their shortcomings, and infuse their mind and heart with higher virtues.

As a result, they transcend their trivial self and rid themselves of their petty behaviors. This leads them to cultivate a taste for higher values. They are no longer attracted to the short-lived charms and temptations of the world. This is called cultivating the taste for heaven here and now. This is the process of self-transformation. Without this transformation, we remain victims of the lower tendencies of our mind and senses. Unless we upgrade our tastes to the higher values of life, we cannot comprehend the true purpose and meaning of life. Failure to know the purpose and meaning of life makes us run in this world blindfolded. This purposeless living and dying with regret is called hell. Thus, choices made carelessly assign us to hell, whereas actions performed mindfully entitle us to heaven.

Transformation here brings transformation hereafter. Unless we bring a qualitative change in our tastes and interests, we'll continue to make poor choices. What we call hell is simply a result of poor choices. To illustrate this, the sages tell this story:

In ancient India, there lived a sage known for his austerity, knowledge, and yogic powers. He was a worshipper of Surya, the Sun God. He had received several boons from Surya, including that Surya would appear to him whenever the sage requested. One afternoon, during his walk, the sage saw a mouse that had just fallen on the ground from the grip of a hawk that still hovered in the sky. The mouse was barely alive, and the sage was moved with compassion. He picked up the mouse and, using his yogic power, healed her instantly. Now this happy little mouse began to dance on the sage's palm.

The sage did not have any children. To experience fatherly joy, he turned the mouse into a little girl and raised her as his own daughter. As time passed, she grew into a beautiful young woman. Now the sage worried about finding a match for her. She described the mate of her choice—she would marry someone beautiful, strong, and respectful of her wishes.

Recalling the boon he had received, the sage invoked Surya and requested him to accept his daughter's hand. Surya agreed but said, "I'll marry her only if she consents."

When the father asked his daughter, she replied, "He is too bright and too hot. I would prefer someone stronger and better."

The sun said, "A cloud is stronger than I am, for it can easily block my rays."

With Surya's help, the sage called a cloud. Upon seeing the cloud, the beautiful young woman commented, "It is too dark and too wet. I prefer someone stronger and better."

The cloud said, "The wind is stronger than I am, for it can easily shatter me into hundreds of pieces."

Then the wind emerged. At the sight of the wind, the young woman exclaimed, "Not only is he unsteady, but he blows everything away."

The wind suggested the mountain for her husband. The mountain came, but before the young woman could open her mouth, the mountain said, "I know someone even stronger and better than I am. Someone who chews my foundation, makes holes in my body, even makes my limbs crumble, and I just helplessly stand and watch."

The young woman screeched joyfully, "Who is that?"

"It is the mouse," answered the mountain.

Then Mr. Mouse walked proudly in, and the young woman ran to embrace her dream. The sage stood in shock for a moment. Then, sprinkling sanctified water, he blessed the girl, "May you go back to your mouse-self and be happy with your soul mate, my daughter."

To be born as a human is a great gift. To die without knowing what this great gift is all about is the greatest loss. Human life brings with it the opportunity to recognize our potentials and to unfold them to their fullest capacity. As humans, we are endowed with a beautiful body with wonderful limbs and organs. How efficient and functional are our hands and feet. How quick and responsive is our nervous system. How developed is our brain; how alert are our senses; how fast and powerful is our mind; how sharp is our intellect; how crisp and well defined is our ego; how accurate is our intuition; and yet how poor we are in utilizing all these priceless gifts.

We abuse our body, misuse our senses, and exploit our wit. Intuition tells us that we are children of immortality, and yet we submit ourselves to the cravings of our flesh. We have been given the tools and means to fill our mind with divine thoughts and yet, due to carelessness, we let base emotions and primitive urges fill that sacred space. It is this carelessness that makes us forget that we are the creators of our destiny. Hell and heaven are a continuation of our hellish and heavenly conditions of mind, and those conditions are subject to change—provided we wish to do so.

Nachiketa's next question takes the discussion on matters pertaining to heaven and hell to a much deeper level. Upon hearing of the mind's ability to create a joyful world that continues to grow and eventually turns into heaven, Nachiketa asked, "So, is heaven only a figment of our mind? What about the reality of heaven and hell described in the scriptures? Once created in the mind, will they exist forever? We are also told that there are rituals that entitle us to heaven and protect us from going to hell. The sages proclaim that fire rituals are the surest means for getting to heaven. Is this proclamation only symbolic?"

The master, Yamaraja, answered, "This world is full of mystery. This mystery can be unveiled only upon entering the cave of one's heart. What people call spirituality or spiritual science simply refers to the process of lifting the veils that cover the cave of the heart. Deep in the heart resides the self-effulgent light of the soul, the light of absolute truth. Unless we lift all these veils one by one, face the light directly, and become one with the reality that shines eternally, we will continue manufacturing endless questions, and those questions will continue demanding answers."

This world is made of multiple layers of reality. The physical world, perceptible to our senses, is just one of those layers. This is a world of mortals—the souls that are born and must die. This physical world is called *samsara,* the place for migratory souls. This world is made of five gross elements: earth, water, fire, air, and space. Our bodies are also made of these five elements. Everything in this material world is constantly changing. Death, decay, and destruction are intrinsic attributes of this world.

The five elements constituting this world are inert in themselves. It is the mind that makes matter and the body made of it become alive. The mind itself is animated by the power of *prana,* the force behind breathing. Prana is the intrinsic force of the soul, the absolute consciousness. The unique association of the soul, prana, mind, and body is called the state of living. When *prana shakti,* the intrinsic force of the soul, puts the mind and the body together, it is called birth. And when this connection falls apart, it is called death. This is a complete biography of all living beings.

While living here, we have access to only a thin slice of the total reality. By harnessing the power of mind and by freeing ourselves from the fetters of matter, we can see a reality that transcends this material world. This is what is called yoga. In other words, a systematic practice of yoga allows us to see clearly the reality pertaining to the physical as well as the non-physical world. It also empowers us to see the relationship between the two.

While living on this plane, we can know what lies beyond. This allows us to face the reality that awaits in the life hereafter. This is called *moksha,* liberation, for we are no longer uncertain about our future. Freedom from uncertainty takes away our doubt. We are at peace here and now. We take this peace with us when we die, and it is this wealth of peace that breathes unique life into the non-physical world where we make our residence for a while. In layman's language, it is called living in heaven. In the language of yogis, however, it is living in freedom.

The physical world is subservient to the non-physical world. Knowing this fact is the first step toward enlightenment. Not knowing this fact is called ignorance. The physical world offers all the tools and means that we need to discover the dynamics of heaven, hell, and beyond. Similarly, in our body are found all the tools and means to discover the dynamics of the mind and the entire inner dimensions of life. According to Yamaraja, the master who has complete knowledge of the world here and hereafter, the science of sacred fire explains how to make the best use of all the gifts that are deposited in the material world as well as in the human body. In Sanskrit, this science is called *agni vidya.*

According to agni vidya, fire is sacred. Fire is the direct manifestation of the Divine. Emphasizing its importance, the scriptures say that it is the carrier of the gods, it is the mouth of the gods, and it is itself God. There cannot be a greater sin than trivializing this living god. In fact, the worship of fire and the worship of the Divine through fire rituals has been at the heart of spirituality in all the ancient traditions of the world. In the Vedic tradition of India, the science of agni vidya is divided into two parts: *bahir yaga,* external ritualistic practices, and *antar yaga,* internal yogic practices. If understood properly, the external ritualistic practices that center around fire can breathe spirituality into our mundane world; similarly, the internal yogic practices, while keeping fire the focal point, can make our body a gateway to understanding our mind and soul.

Agni Vidya: The Science of Fire

Agni vidya, the science of fire, is the greatest discovery of the ancient sages of India. Through continuous research, contemplation, observation, and experimentation, the sages gained direct experience of the sacred nature of fire. This experience led them to discover ways of using this knowledge to heal and nurture both the outer as well as the inner worlds. The aspect of agni vidya that focuses on bringing nature back to balance and nurturing the finer forces of creation is called *bahir yaga* (external fire ritual). Bahir yaga creates and maintains a healthy atmosphere in the external world, and *antar yaga* (internal fire ritual) does the same in the inner world. Antar yaga focuses on bringing our body, breath, senses, and mind back into balance, helping us tap into the vast pool of healing force that normally remains dormant within us.

There is a perfect equation between the inner fire and the external fire. The inner fire heals and nurtures our body and pervades and penetrates every single cell of our body. The fire in the external world is the source of healing and nurturance to all forms of life. Everything in the world is pervaded by this fire. From the tiniest speck of dust to the grandest mountains, from the core of the earth all the way to the edge of the planet's atmosphere, there is fire. The pervasive nature of fire is a shared knowledge of both physicists and spiritual scientists. However, they each look at fire from different angles. Physicists see fire as an inherent property of matter. It is a form of energy; it can be harnessed and put to use just as anything else in the world. To them, it is just another commodity—an object to be possessed, consumed, and exploited. Sages see fire in an entirely different light.

To the sages, fire is sacred. It is divine. It is intelligent. To them, there cannot be a clearer example of ignorance than putting a price tag on sacred fire. Just as fire resides at the core of our planet—and is the core of the planet—fire resides at the center of our existence and is the very core of our being. According to the sages, life is an extension of our soul—the body and mind are extensions of the sacred fire that the soul spontaneously emits. Due to the pervasive nature of the sacred fire, everything on this planet is sacred. Because the body and mind are extensions of the sacred fire, these, too, are sacred. It is in search of this sanctity that people of all cultures undertake arduous trips to sacred sites. It is in search of this sanctity that we adorn our bodies, purify our minds, and ritualize our acts of beautification.

The body is a living altar of the sacred fire. Within this altar, nature has built unique fireplaces called *kundas*. Wherever you see transformation occurring, there is a kunda. Thus every single cell in our body is a kunda, the locus for fire. The major organs, such as the heart, liver, kidney, pancreas, ovaries, and testes, and the sensory organs, such as the eyes, ears, and nostrils, are better defined loci for fire. The most significant centers of fire within us, however, are more subtle. They are called *chakras,* wheels of energy or concentrated fields of sacred fire.

There are seven chakras. The fire at each chakra is distinct, both in its intensity as well as in its quality. A comprehensive approach to the science of fire entails the study of these chakras, how to reach them, how to remove the ash that has been accumulating for ages on the fire in these chakras, how to reignite and refuel the fire, and how to channel the spiritually uplifting energy of these chakras to the highest plane of reality, which has made our crown its home.

The science of fire thus covers a vast field of self-understanding, including understanding our true self; its relationship with our body, breath, mind, and soul; its relationship with the absolute Divine Being; and its relationship with the larger world of which we are a part. This science also includes discovering the source of inner healing and nurturance—the elixir of immortality that lies in all of us. It contains the knowledge of here and hereafter—the ability to design a world compatible with our liking here and the ability to predict the nature of the world hereafter.

Gaining access to the fire within and propitiating it is not a simple task. It requires discipline, dedication, endurance, and patience. It requires the practice of yoga beyond the level of *asana.* It requires a mind trained and refined enough to clearly feel the flow of *prana shakti* through the *nadis,* the energy channels. It requires a mind quiet enough to hear the noise and commotion at each nerve center and chakra. It requires an intellect sharp enough to distinguish useful and spiritually uplifting thoughts from meaningless and spiritually degrading thoughts. It requires an ego enlightened enough to invest its willpower in a surrendered manner to serve the purpose of the soul. Thus, gathering all the prerequisites to light and propitiate the sacred fire within is initially a difficult task.

Therefore, the sages teach this science of agni vidya at a level accessible to all—the practice that centers around the sacred fire that is fed by firewood. This involves propitiating the Divine through fire offering, and by reconnecting ourselves with the inner healing force through external means. This aspect of agni vidya is called *karma kanda,* action-driven fire worship and self-discovery. It is an external ritualistic practice as opposed to an internal yogic meditative one. Yet it is totally different from the fire rituals routinely performed by perfunctory priests. It is a science, for it is grounded in definite rules and laws where precision determines the efficacy of the rituals.

The basic philosophy of fire rituals is the same as the philosophy of tantra. The philosophy of tantra proclaims that there is a perfect equation between the microcosm and the macrocosm. The laws that govern our personal life also govern the life of the planet and the life of the universe, and vice versa. The laws that govern the physical level of our existence, that is the body, also govern the material world. Every strand in the tapestry of life is fully intertwined. There is a link between an individual and the cosmos, between the inner world and the external world; and that link is unfailing and sacred. Honoring and reinforcing this sacred link that holds together every strand of the tapestry of life is at the heart of fire rituals. Thus, through fire rituals, we heal and nurture the primordial pool of the life force itself. Through fire rituals, we infuse our mundane level of existence with sacred awareness. Fire rituals are one of the surest ways to bridge the worlds within and without.

According to agni vidya, fire is the mouth of the gods. It is with this mouth that the gods eat. We offer oblations into the fire. The fire consumes the oblations. Upon this consumption, the gross form of matter is transformed into a subtler form of energy. Subtle properties of matter are now made available to the forces that preside over the different aspects of creation. Fire also transports the energy released from the oblation to its intended destination. Therefore, what we put into the fire and how we put it into the fire is the crux of the fire ritual.

Fire has seven tongues. Those tongues manifest in the form of flames. Each tongue has its unique characteristics and is designed to accept, transform, and transport specific kinds of oblations. In the performance of fire rituals, it is therefore important to know which tongue or combination of tongues of the fire to invoke. The decision regarding the invocation depends on the goals and objectives of the ritual. Since each tongue accepts oblations of ingredients that are compatible to the tastes of that particular tongue of the fire, it is important that we understand the unique qualities and properties of the constituent ingredients of the oblations. This requires a thorough knowledge of Ayurveda, herbology, and alchemy. Then we need to know how to capture and polarize the energy released from the fire ritual and make sure the fire takes it to the place it is supposed to reach. The power of mantra shepherds our oblations and assists the sacred fire in transporting them to the presiding forces of nature, or to the divinities within our bodies, or into the world outside us. Thus, agni vidya, the science of fire, at least in part, consists of the science of mantra as well.

The practice of agni vidya consists of three main components: the fire itself, the ingredients for the fire offering, and mantras. All these components bear fruit only when they are put together properly. Assembling them is possible when we know why we are performing the ritual and to whom the oblations are going to be made. Just as we have a personality, the finer forces of nature, too, have their personalities. To see a desirable result, we have to make sure that the overall nature of the ritual is compatible with the personality of the divinity who is being invoked and propitiated. Let us study each component individually.

The Sacred Fire

Not all fires are the same. There is forest fire, gun fire, arson fire, funeral fire, and chemical and industrial fire. All of these forms of fire share a common characteristic: they all burn whatever they contact, but none of them capture and transport the energy released by this consumption to a predetermined and distinctly defined destination. Fire is a ritual fire only when it is infused with sacredness. In part, this sacredness is engendered by the paraphernalia arranged around the ritual. And in part, it is our intention that breathes sanctity into the ritual fire. These are secondary causes that infuse fire with sacredness. Above all, it is the power of mantras and the proper way of invocating the benevolent forces of creation that make fire truly sacred.

To perform a fire ritual, first you build a kunda, fireplace. The nature of the ritual, its goals and objectives, and its presiding deity determine the shape and size of the fireplace. If general peace and prosperity is the object of the fire ritual, then a square-shaped fireplace is most appropriate. For other purposes, a fireplace could be triangular, circular, or hexagonal. Then you invoke the presence of the fire itself in the fireplace. Each step of the ritual acts is performed with the recitation of mantra, including the invocation of fire in the kunda. This invocation is totally different from carrying fire from somewhere and putting it just anywhere in the fireplace. There is a whole science about how to carry fire and how to place it at the most appropriate spot in the fireplace. Then, while repeating the mantras, you place sticks around the fire. Finally, you arrange the sticks in a manner that fire fills the entire fireplace.

Offerings are made first to the fire itself. There are specific mantras to propitiate and nurture the fire. It is only after the fire is fully ignited, ablaze, and strong enough to consume and carry the oblations that the offerings for the desired divinities are made. The nature of the ritual also determines the kind of firewood to be used. For example, you would never use bamboo in fire rituals where the goal is to propitiate and nurture the divinities that preside over our mind and senses. However, bamboo is perfectly fine as firewood if the goal of the ritual is to appease and honor our ancestors. To beget children, you would use pomegranate sticks; but for knowledge and dispassion, Himalayan cedar would be better.

The Ingredients for the Fire Offering

Each plant is unique. Not only the shape, size, color, and texture, but also specific chemical and medicinal properties make a plant appropriate for a particular purpose. The selection of herbs, plants, grains, and minerals as constituent ingredients for the fire offering is crucial. Equally crucial is how they are combined and the proportion in which they are combined. The most basic offering to the fire itself is *ghee* (clarified butter). Ghee, according to agni vidya, is food for fire. It supplies sacred fire with life instantly. Other forms of fat, or liquid fuel, such as kerosene oil, can do the same to ordinary fire, but not to sacred fire. Similarly, there are certain plants and herbs, such as sticks of Flame of the Forest and brahmi, that are more appropriate food for the sacred fire than many other important herbs.

The main function of the fire ritual is to make an offering to nature's finest forces and the divinities that fill the space of consciousness within us; fire is the carrier of the oblations to those forces and divinities. Therefore, selecting the ingredients for the offerings has to be done mindfully. We must know the name and characteristics of the recipient deity. We must know his or her personality. To ensure that the oblation is compatible with the liking of the deity and is offered appropriately into the mouth of the fire, we have to invoke that particular type of tongue of the fire. As mentioned earlier, fire has seven tongues. Each tongue has its unique quality. Similarly, all gods and goddesses, divinities, and nature's forces are grouped in seven main categories. The seven tongues of the fire and the divinities in seven categories match each other. The knowledge pertaining to their compatibility is therefore crucial in the selection of ingredients. The next important thing is the invocation of the particular tongue, which, as mentioned in the scriptures, is an exact science.

Mantras

In the science of agni vidya, it is through the power of mantra that a yogi awakens the dormant forces of fire and breathes sanctity into the fire. It is through the power of mantra that a yogi invokes the presence of nature's forces that for all spiritual purposes normally remain dormant. It is through the power of mantra that the nameless and formless is given a definition, and the infinite is assigned a respectful place during the fire rituals. It is through the power of mantra that the constituent ingredients of the oblation shake off their dormancy and make their subtle properties available to the one who is doing the offering. It is through the power of mantra that a particular tongue or combination of tongues is brought to life, and it is through the power of mantra that energy released from the consumption of the oblation is transported to its intended destination in a contained fashion. That is why every step of the ritual is accompanied by mantra recitation. The efficacy of the application of mantra, however, lies in its recitation by someone who is spiritually awake.

Sacred Fire and Heaven

This scripture, the *Katha Upanishad,* clearly states that sacred fire is a direct means to achieving celestial gifts. Many other scriptures, such as the *Bhagavad Gita,* provide details as to how, by worshipping or meditating on the sacred fire, we can become entitled to the gifts deposited in the celestial realms. In Indian philosophy, there are three worlds: *bhuh,* the physical plane; *bhuvah,* the space between the physical and the celestial planes; and *svah,* the celestial plane. The physical plane refers to our earthly realm—life on the planet and the laws that govern it. Life on earth is sustained by the forces of nurturance that flow incessantly from the celestial realm. Even the slightest disruption in the flow of energy emitted from the sun, moon, and stars can wreak havoc on life here in this world. The reverse is true, too. What we do here on earth has a great impact in the celestial realm. The relationship between heaven and earth, between a speck of dust belonging to our planet and a mighty star located a million light-years from here, is a known and mathematically proven fact of physics. What is not known to modern mathematicians and physicists is how our actions, especially the subtle ones, impact celestial bodies, such as the sun, and how such impacts reflect back on the earth. Let me explain a little further.

Every entity, regardless of its size and its distance from other entities, is exerting influence on everything that exists in any corner of the cosmos. There is a constant push and pull of repulsion and attraction between bodies of matter, regardless of where they are and how big or small they are. This phenomenon is succinctly described as the law of gravity. But whether the infinite number of discrete bodies of matter floating into an ever-expanding universe is dead and inert or living and intelligent is unknown to modern scientists. According to the sages, modern science, dealing only with the laws of the material world, is in its infancy. It has little or no understanding as to how the actions of a single individual or group of individuals performed here on earth can make any difference energetically elsewhere in the cosmos. Modern science has even less understanding of the effect of our thoughts and feelings, sentiments and intentions, on celestial bodies such as the sun, moon, stars, comets, and asteroids, and how we become recipients of what they deflect. People believing in the material sciences arbitrarily lump what they do not understand into categories like spirituality, mysticism, or mythology.

Fact or fiction, here is what the *Katha Upanishad* presents for us to examine and determine: Can agni vidya, the science of sacred fire, empower us to create a heaven here on earth as well as in the realm that stretches far beyond the territory of our earthly plane?

The nature of fire is to burn. Burning means fire consuming matter. Some of the matter turns into smoke. The rest turns into energy: light, heat, and millions of other forms of energy that are not detected by our senses, ordinary mind, or even a trained intellect. Once burned, this transformed matter is absorbed into the atmosphere. To understand this process of transformation and absorption, let us consider the analogy of the food we eat, the way it is digested, and its postdigestive effect on our bodies.

Certain objects and ingredients available in nature are edible and others are not. Edible food is digested, the nutrients are assimilated, and the waste matter is flushed out to be consumed by other entities—a natural cycle that goes on sustaining the web of life. But when inedible food by chance reaches our stomach, we feel sick. A gastrointestinal reflex forces bodily systems to eject that substance.

This is the case with what we put into the fire: If it is acceptable to the fire, it is digested and assimilated into the atmosphere, providing nourishment to specific aspects of life on the earth. The remainder is further utilized by the mysterious intelligence of nature. But when an unacceptable substance is put into the fire, the fire feels sick. Unlike us, it does not have a reflex to reject that unhealthy substance, but rather, following the law of its nature, it must burn whatever has fallen into its mouth. It must consume and deposit the essence of the matter into the atmosphere. This is an unavoidable, unchanging law of nature that the fire obeys unfailingly. Thus if you put sulfur and lead in the fire, the fire will make sure that it is fairly distributed in the atmosphere. If you put an herb in the fire, soon the healing properties will pervade the atmosphere.

The sages summarized this whole process in one word: *apurva.* Apurva means a totally new creation; something that did not exist before now begins to exist with its unique characteristics and functions. For example, once there was no acid rain, but as a result of people burning fuel containing sulfur, now there are clouds laden with sulfuric acid, which in turn give shape to a new reality—apurva. Or had there instead been a fire offering consisting of herbs, there would have been a totally different reality—a totally different apurva. The sages emphatically proclaimed that the creation of this new reality is not the work of God, but rather—assisted and empowered by fire—it is the work of humans. In fact, it is for this very reason that the scriptures say, "You are the creator of your destiny."

The manipulation of fire is the most potent action that human beings can ever perform. If it is performed wisely, it can lead to the acquisition of wisdom. If it is performed mindlessly, it can render us mindless. If we see the sacred in fire, life becomes sacred. If we see fire as just a form of matter and energy—an object to be possessed and exploited—then life and everything that comes with it becomes a commodity. Considering life a commodity is called being consumed by materialism. Breathing sanctity into life is called spirituality. This is the fundamental philosophy of agni vidya, the backbone of fire rituals.

Now let me explain how fire rituals work, how fire rituals can demolish a hell that we may have created deliberately or unknowingly, and how fire rituals can create a new reality that is celestial and auspicious. Due to our inherent nature, we cannot sit idle; we must perform actions. Some of our actions are propelled by love, kindness, compassion, and selflessness. Such actions bear auspicious fruits. Other actions are propelled by anger, hatred, greed, and possessiveness. They bear inauspicious and painful fruits. This is the law of karma: as you sow, so shall you reap.

Our present life is a result of our previous actions. Desirable and undesirable situations and circumstances that walk into our life uninvited are part of our destiny, which itself is a result of our cumulative *karmas,* actions of the past. We cannot travel into the past to fix such actions, yet we wish to avoid their undesirable consequences. This desire motivates us to discover ways of demolishing the hell that haunts our present and to create a heaven so that we can live joyfully in the days to come. Agni vidya is the solution to this desire.

As mentioned earlier, the actions performed in the form of fire rituals are the most potent ones. They bear fruit here and now. Fire rituals performed properly bear instant fruit. Since the fruit of the fire ritual is not a consequence of our old destiny, but rather is a newly created reality, apurva, it does not have a place in life's normal course of events. But it is so potent that it must find and claim its place in our life. The indomitable power emerging from a fire ritual forcefully breaks the feeble chains of our old destiny, adding a new dimension to our life here and hereafter.

Fire rituals should not be taken lightly, nor be performed in vain. Agni vidya is as evolved, if not more so, as today's highly prized nuclear science or bio- and nano-technologies. Only someone who is familiar with the spiritual dimension of quantum physics, the sacred nature of fire, the seven tongues of fire, the power of human intention, the power of mantra, and the power of the sequence in which mantrically charged ritual acts are led to precise destination points can qualify to officiate in the uniquely crafted fire rituals known as a *yaga*. Such a leader in the tradition is called Brahma, a person with the ability to create a new reality—apurva. Such a person is charged with the ability to displace and even erase the old reality that has been chasing us in the form of unwanted destiny.

Agni Vidya: The Science of Fire as Practiced by Yogis

The very same fire that pervades and permeates the whole universe is found in the human body, too. Due to its pervasive nature, the fire penetrates every cell of our body. The fire living in the body is known as *Vaishvanara.* The Vaishvanara fire is the miniature counterpart of *Virat,* the fire that pervades the whole universe. Both Vaishvanara and Virat refer to the general and all-pervading fire, one at the microcosmic and the other at the macrocosmic level. Just as the sun is the most concentrated discrete body of fire in our solar system, the concentrated energy field at our navel center is the most concentrated discrete body of fire within us. This fire within us is known as *Jatavedas Agni.* In other words, the fire that pervades every single cell in our body in a diffused manner is known as Vaishvanara, and the very same fire residing in its concentrated form at the navel center is called Jatavedas.

According to the scriptures, it is Jatavedas Agni, this uniquely concentrated fire residing in our body, that keeps us alive. This fire is intelligent. It exists before we are born. It continues to exist even after we die. It is there in our mother's womb before we are conceived. It is there even after the funeral fire has become cold. This is why this fire is said to be eternal—without a beginning and without an end. It is this fire that sustains the eternity of our soul. Because this fire is intelligent and pervades everything, not only spatially but also in terms of time, the sages call it Jatavedas, the One who knows *(vedas)* everything about anyone ever born *(jata)*. In other words, fire contains the knowledge of past, present, and future. Fire is the ground for all memories. Fire is the ground for all visions and revelations. In this respect, fire is the primordial pool of intelligence; it is omniscient. It is by discovering this fire and by gaining access to it that the mind is transformed and is blessed with the privilege to know that which lies beyond our normal ken.

Due to its intelligent nature, this fire guides and governs the arrangement of molecules of matter so that a fetus grows with qualities, capacities, and characteristics compatible with the karmic needs of the soul. In fact, it is the intrinsic intelligence of Jatavedas Agni that creates and maintains the unique ecology of the womb; it is the intrinsic intelligence of Jatavedas Agni that awakens and guides specific genetic characteristics while keeping the rest of the genetic pool in the background. It is the intrinsic intelligence of this fire that connects the link between the parents and the soul that must enter the world. It is this fire that decides how many of the memories of the past are to be kept awakened and how many of them are to be kept dormant. Thus it is this fire that determines the level of intelligence each individual possesses. Agni vidya, the science of sacred fire, aims at gaining a complete knowledge of this fire, thus acquiring a vast pool of knowledge and power that normally lies dormant at the core of our being. This is what the yogis of agni vidya call enlightenment.

There are many techniques to gain access to the sacred fire within. All of those techniques require that we first work with our body. The body is the gateway to the subtle dimensions of our life. An unkempt body can be a great barrier. Therefore, a prerequisite to recognizing the sacred fire and propitiating it is to understand how the body is a living temple. We must know exactly where in the body the altar is and how, on this altar of the body, nature has so beautifully built the fireplace. Similarly, we must know how to clean the altar, how to arrange the firewood inside the fireplace, how to light the fire, and how to systematically add an appropriate starter and fuel so that this fire intensifies and grows in strength and vigor in a contained fashion. We must also know how to capture the energy released from this fire practice, how to make that energy move upward toward the higher planes of consciousness, and ultimately, how to ensure that we'll not misuse and exploit the gifts emerging from this fire. Understanding this whole process is called the study of agni vidya, and actually committing ourselves to a methodical practice leading to direct experience of this fire within is called the practice of agni vidya.

According to agni vidya, there are seven centers in the body where fire resides in its most concentrated form. Such a center is called a kunda. In the tradition of kundalini yoga, these seven centers are called chakras, the wheels of consciousness. The first one is *muladhara,* the base center. Physiologically, it is located at the perineum. The fire residing at this center is called *kundalini,* the resident of the kunda. The fire here is normally covered with the ash of fear and doubt, sloth and inertia. Subdued fire at this center results in the formation of dullness, anxiety, and nervousness.

The second kunda is known as *svadhisthana.* It is located in the pelvis. Normally, this fire is buried deep within the ash of desires and attachments. Inner conflicts and confusion regarding wanting and not wanting put a heavy strain on this fire. Derangement of fire at this center drains the vitality of our senses and takes away our mental clarity. Dissipation of this fire makes us become confused regarding what we want and what we do not want. Damage to the fire at this center results in a complex personality. However, if we penetrate the mystery of this center and befriend the resident fire, then the very same center becomes the abode of creative intelligence. This is why this center is given the name, *svadhisthana,* "Her own abode."

The third chakra is *manipura,* the center "filled with life's all-shining gems." It is located at the navel. This is the center of vitality, vigor, inner strength, enthusiasm, and courage. This is the most prominent place of Jatavedas Agni, the fire that guides our destiny, the fire that guides our journey to this world. When deranged, the fire at this center becomes a source of our arrogance and egoism. Possessiveness becomes our trait. The hunger for power and prestige becomes limitless. We become confused in regard to our self-identity, and this confusion leads us to eliminate those who appear to be a threat to our identity. Thus, the fire at this center is the ground for our progress as well as our failure. Both success and defeat, which accompany us in the battlefield of life, find their full expression here at this center.

According to the yogis of agni vidya, the first center at the perineum (muladhara) represents our life on earth and all earthly concerns. The third chakra at the navel center (manipura) represents our heavenly life and heavenly concerns. And the second chakra at the pelvis (svadhisthana) lies in between. The other four chakras refer to much higher planes of consciousness. The domain of agni vidya, however, is limited to the first three chakras. Scriptures such as the *Saundaryalahari, Netra Tantra, Svacchanda Tantra,* and *Rudra Yamala* offer detailed instructions in regard to piercing all the chakras, including these three lower ones; igniting the fire; and making fire offerings in a purely yogic fashion—a subject that demands a thorough treatment in an independent treatise.

Living with Purpose: The Highest Blessing

ॐ

After imparting the knowledge of *agni vidya*, Yamaraja invited Nachiketa to select the third boon. Nachiketa answered with this request: "There is so much confusion regarding the continuity of life after death. Some say that the soul continues to exist; others say that it does not. Tell me, O Master, what is really true?"

At this his master responded, "In regard to this question, O Nachiketa, even the gods in heaven are doubtful. It is a very subtle matter; it cannot be known so easily. Ask for something else. You can ask for a long life filled with children, grandchildren, and great-grandchildren. You can have as much wealth, land, or anything you can imagine. You can even ask for objects of pleasure that normally do not exist on this earthly plane. You can have celestial nymphs and enjoy them as long as you wish. I offer you chariots that move at the speed of mind on land, water, and fire with equal ease. But please, spare me from teaching you about death and the essential nature of the soul."

Nachiketa responded, "I am very clear about the objects of the world and their relationship with our body, mind, and senses. Everything in this world is short-lived. The objects of the world are never satisfying. At each interaction, the objects of pleasure consume the vitality of our senses. How deep is our ignorance that we experience pleasure in this depletion of our vitality. Longevity is a highly sought objective, but that, too, is elusive, as the years fly by at the blink of an eye. People run after wealth, but so far I have not met anyone in the world who has gotten any satisfaction from wealth. A human being can never be satiated with what he has. The desire to have more takes away the joy of what he already has."

Finally, Nachiketa concluded: "Having found an immortal being like you, how can a mortal person living on this earthly plane afflicted by old age and death think of the pleasures derived from the senses or even have any interest in a long life? Share with me, O Master, the wisdom pertaining to the other shore of life that has so far been shrouded in mystery. I ask for nothing other than the revelation of the truth that penetrates every layer of our existence and remains hidden at the core of our being."

With this clear and straightforward response, Nachiketa won the heart of his master. Now there was nothing that the master could keep from his student. Words of truth flowed joyfully: "Bless you, Nachiketa. Having pondered the good and the pleasant, you turned away from those desires and objects of desires that are so dear to most people. Unlike many, you did not wear yourself down with worldly pleasures and possessions.

"Childish are those who are deluded by the charms and temptations of the world and consequently fail to comprehend the higher truth. To them, this world is the only reality; beyond this, nothing exists. One who is convinced of this false belief falls in the trap of birth and death again and again. You have seen from your direct experience how desires are the foundation of worldly endeavors, how trivial they are, how binding our attachment is to the objects of our desires, and how empty the relationships that we cherish so much. This has enabled you to reach the state of being that is ruled by fearlessness. You are a fully prepared student, and I am a fortunate teacher to have a student like you. Here is my final teaching.

"The knowledge of the Self cannot be achieved through lectures, through memory, or through book learning. The Self is attained by the one it chooses. To such a chosen one, the Self unveils its true essence. Furthermore, neither those engaged in unwholesome activities nor those who are undisciplined, nor those who are not composed, nor those who are not peaceful or content within, can experience it, even after knowing all about it. Remember, my son, the one who finds his social identity [self-image] as trivial as a fistful of rice, and the one to whom death is as significant as rinsing the mouth after meals—such a person has met the prerequisites for attaining the knowledge of the Self. And I am glad you are such a seeker."

With this, the master imparted *brahma vidya,* the knowledge of the highest truth, to his beloved student, Nachiketa. Brahma vidya is a recurring subject in all the scriptures of India. Brahma vidya literally means the science *(vidya)* pertaining to *Brahman.* Brahman is a technical term referring to the all-pervading, omnipresent, omniscient, and omnipotent reality. According to the scriptures, it is absolute and transcendental. This word *Brahman* refers to pure existence, pure consciousness, and pure bliss. In other words, it is the pure being, the essence of our soul, and the essence of everything that is there.

It is from this Brahman that the whole world, including ourselves, evolves. It is in this Brahman that we exist, and it is in this Brahman that we dissolve. From this highest peak of realization and understanding, there is nothing like coming and going, being born and dying. Thus, there is nothing like bondage and there is nothing like liberation. And yet, our day-to-day experience tells us that there is birth and there is death. There is something in us that perceives the notion of past, present, and future; here and there; life and death; pleasure and pain; bondage and liberation. Brahma vidya, from a practical standpoint, therefore, includes all those theories, doctrines, principles, and practices that help us understand ourselves at every level.

Brahma vidya proclaims that we are not body alone nor mind alone but we are a combination of both—and much more. This science divides our personal existence into five layers, all intertwined in perfect harmony. They are known as the *annamaya kosha* (physical sheath), *pranamaya kosha* (pranic sheath), *manomaya kosha* (sheath made of mind), *vijnanamaya kosha* (sheath made of intellect and decisive faculty), and *anandamaya kosha* (the sheath made of joy). The latter sheaths are more subtle, and yet more expansive, than the former ones. Pure consciousness, also known as *atman* or *Brahman,* pervades as well as permeates all these sheaths. How consciousness relates to all these sheaths, how it keeps all the sheaths awake and functional, and how one day consciousness disassociates itself from all these sheaths are all topics integral to the study of brahma vidya. This study also includes gaining direct experience of consciousness when it is no longer confined to these five sheaths.

The most immediate cause for gaining knowledge of the absolute truth, according to this scripture, is divine grace. Divine grace is unconditional. In the eyes of divine grace, no one is virtuous and no one is a sinner. It is like sunlight that shines forth equally to all. It touches a blossom and mud alike. Like sunlight, it breathes life into all, and yet it remains untouched by all. The question then arises, why are we not benefiting from the ever-flowing grace of the Divine? Why are some chosen and others not? This scripture offers a very practical and logically comprehensible answer.

Divine grace is always available to those who have time to receive it. From birth to death, we are busy doing one thing or another. We are constantly busy fulfilling the needs and demands of our body. Once our belly is full we relentlessly work to meet the cravings of our senses. The charms and temptations of the world have gotten a total grip over our body and mind. Despite the stress caused by sensory overload, we keep running after objects of pleasure. During each encounter, these pleasures add to our frustration and disappointment, for none of them linger long.

Desire to accumulate the objects of comfort and pleasure turns us into beggars. Greed turns us into thieves. Fear of losing what we have makes us become slaves to what we wish to protect. The beggar, the thief, and the slave within us often occupies every breath of our life. There is no time left to greet and embrace the grace of the Divine that contains the knowledge of higher reality. And thus, that knowledge never finds a place on the list of our priorities. How exhausting it sounds, and yet the reality of this fact is undeniable.

Unless we realize that life is a precious gift, we cannot and we will not make a decision to pause and discover what that gift is all about. It is important that we reflect on the simple and yet vivid facts that surround us: There are millions of species and each of them is great in number. Some are born and die in the deep darkness of the underworld. Billions live in the forests, and many more billions in the ocean. All of them feed, procreate, and die. If we do the same, then are we any different from them? If we do the same, do we deserve a different fate? If we do not do more than what other creatures can do, then do we deserve to have greater intelligence, greater freedom, and a greater range of choices? The *Srimad Bhagavatam* clearly proclaims, "*shishnodara-parayanah*—those committed only to serving the cravings of their belly and genitals definitely lose the gift of being human." It is a great loss. Brahma vidya, the subject matter of this scripture, tells us how not to end up with this great loss, but rather how to attain the liberating power of the knowledge that is exclusive to the domain of human birth.

Claiming the Highest Gift

According to the *Katha Upanishad,* brahma vidya is the highest of all knowledge. Brahma vidya includes the knowledge of oneself and one's relationship with one's body, breath, mind, and consciousness, on the one hand, and with the larger world on the other hand. Knowledge of the larger world includes understanding the dynamics of our society, culture, religion, and the day-to-day realities that give life to the world of commerce and politics. Brahma vidya refers to the broadest range of knowledge ever discovered by the human race. Yoga, meditation, spirituality, holistic health, and numberless fields of arts and sciences are part of brahma vidya. Brahma vidya, in other words, includes the study and experience of life in its fullness.

From a practical standpoint, the practice of brahma vidya begins with understanding the body. According to this Upanishad, the body is a living temple of God. It is a shrine. The health and well-being of the shrines in the external world are totally dependent on the health and well-being of this shrine. If you do not take care of this shrine, you will have neither the capacity nor the motivation to take care of the external shrines. Once the sanctity of the body is gone, the shrines in the outside world can no longer maintain their sanctity.

The reason is simple: a clear, calm, and tranquil mind requires that you have a healthy body. A body filled with toxins becomes an abode of disease. An unhealthy person is bound to brood on physical pain. Such a person becomes weak and frail. Physical weakness and the malfunctioning of the limbs and organs rob the peace and tranquility of the mind. Even the best of philosophers have a hard time maintaining a clear mind with an unhealthy body. Thus the sages say the body is the gateway to the inner dimensions of life. Physical health is dependent on how we eat, how we sleep, how we breathe, how we sit, how we walk, and how we conduct our daily life. These basic principles of good health are the foundation of any spiritual quest; but unfortunately, these principles have become the last priorities in our spiritual practice.

I was born and raised in India, the land where profound scriptures, including the *Katha Upanishad,* first found their expression. It is due to this great tradition of wisdom that India came to be known as the land of sages. It is in this India, however, that I found the greatest deficiency in spirituality. People visit temples, priests perform rituals, pandits recite scriptures, philosophers hold their debates, and the public celebrates time-honored customs and ceremonies. Yet the air in that society remains thick and stagnant.

Why? Because the majority of the people in that culture have forgotten the value of following a system. A system demands and common sense agrees that you start your journey from wherever you stand. The body is the first and foremost tool that we can use to start our quest. Condemn your body, and your body will condemn you. Don't care for your body, and your body will not care for you. An unhealthy body poses a great obstacle in your inner journey. A healthy body, on the other hand, can open the door to your inner quest.

The human body is the epitome of God's creation. Had it not been necessary, why would God create a body and then hide himself in it? In fact, to the enlightened ones, God does not hide in the body, but rather She resides in it. Only after piercing the different layers of our being do we reach the core and realize that the Lord of

Life is the true resident of this body, and we have been given the privilege to be its caretaker. The understanding of this truth is the beginning of the spiritual quest as described in this scripture.

The spiritual journey begins with the body. However, if you stay only at the level of your body, then you reach nowhere. A spiritual quest requires that you discover who resides in the body, how to embrace that indweller, and how to become one with it. This is called self-enlightenment and self-realization. To gain self-realization, we need to follow a systematic method to unveil one layer at a time and gain access to our inner being. This method is called yoga.

The practice of yoga described in this scripture is totally different from what is known by the term *yoga* in today's world. Today, yoga has become synonymous with asana, the postures and physical exercises. Asana is just a thin layer in the totality of yoga practice. The practice of yoga makes your body flexible and strong. It enhances your strength and stamina. It energizes your limbs and organs. Thus, with the practice of yoga, you become a healthier person. But only when you combine asana with pranayama, meditation, self-reflection, self-study, and other components of yoga *sadhana* (practice) does the practice of asana qualify as yoga asana. Without these components, asana is the same as any set of physical exercises. Its value is limited and it definitely cannot lead to spiritual enlightenment.

Yoga sadhana as described in this scripture requires that you first look at the nature of life: how wonderful it is to have a human body; how perfectly designed the nervous system is; how highly developed our brain is; and how powerful our mind is. Then pay attention to whether or not you are making the best use of this gift that you received as your birthright. Remind yourself there is no certainty that after death you'll be born as a human again. Therefore, make the best use of what you have and aspire to achieve that which is necessary to live a happier, healthier, and more peaceful, productive life.

As delineated in this scripture, the next step is to contemplate that life here on this plane is short-lived. A hundred years vanish with the blink of an eye. Just as, for example, forty years disappeared with the hope that you will start your quest tomorrow, the remaining years will slip away, too. Therefore, do not procrastinate. Do not postpone your happiness. Gather your courage, summon your willpower, and overcome your sloth, inertia, and habit of procrastination. Find a teacher; find a book; find anything that helps you create a plan for your progress. Your job also includes defining what progress is. Accomplishment that empowers you to come closer to yourself is called progress. Everything else is simply another burden.

Then, cultivate love for your practice. It is love that brings sustainability to your practice. Without love, you will start your practice, and then, under the spell of the charms and temptations of the world, you will drop it. And it is sustained practice that bears fruit. Love for practice comes when we know where this practice will lead us and how important the goal is.

In this respect, the *Katha Upanishad* makes a special point regarding our worldview and the role of money. It proclaims that to an inexperienced, childish person, the accumulation of wealth is life's greatest achievement. There may be some degree of truth to this, for with money you can gather the tools and means to have a comfortable life. But if you are not careful, you may forget that money is a means, not a goal in itself. In their ignorance, such people believe that money, and the world that can be bought and consumed by it, is the only reality. Therefore, they have no choice but to dwell in this reality. The result is that they keep falling into the tumultuous current of birth and death again and again. Contemplation of this phenomenon is an essential part of the yoga sadhana described in this scripture, for this contemplation empowers us to set our priorities and stick to them.

Then comes the actual, methodical practice of yoga. It begins with learning to sit quietly. In order to be quiet, you must adopt a meditative pose. A meditative pose refers to the position of the body in which you are most comfortable and steady. Comfort and steadiness come when your spine is straight, your shoulders are relaxed, the weight of your body is equally distributed on your buttocks, your lower and upper extremities are arranged in a comfortable manner, and your perineum has become your center of gravity. Yoga manuals describe many meditative poses, such as *sukhasana, svastikasana, padmasana, siddhasana,* and *maitryasana,* that can help you achieve steadiness and ease.

Sit in your meditative pose. Pay attention to your spine and make sure that it is straight. Relax your shoulders and place your hands either on your knees or in your lap. Withdraw your mind from all worldly concerns. Mentally draw a circle of light around you, separating yourself from the world around you. Then pay attention to your breathing. Breathe gently and naturally and diaphragmatically. With each breath, observe the gentle rise and fall of your abdominal muscles. This is called breath awareness. With breath awareness, you establish the most natural breathing pattern—you are breathing smoothly. There is no jerk, no noise, and no pause between your inhalation and exhalation. Once your breath has become calm and tranquil, the motion of the lungs is regulated, and the heartbeat has come back to normal, you begin to meditate.

As part of your meditation, first bring your attention to your forehead. Feel the presence of the Divine in the center of your forehead. Without putting any strain on your eyes, observe the presence of your pure being. Inhale and exhale as though you are trying to touch your very soul, in the center of your forehead, with your breath. This is called concentration. Make sure that your concentration is not accompanied by tension. Tension comes from making too much effort to be aware of the body at the point of concentration. True concentration simply means to become aware of your pure being at the point of your concentration.

Now bring your attention to the center between the eyebrows, become aware of the space between the eyebrows, and take one breath. One breath consists of one inhalation and one exhalation. Then bring your attention to your eyes, eyebrows, cheeks, facial muscles, neck, and shoulders. At each of these spots, take one breath and become aware of the presence of your pure being at those spots. Now bring your attention to your shoulders, upper arms, lower arms, wrists, palms, fingers, and fingertips, and again, take one breath at those parts of the body. And with the power of your mind, feel the presence of pure being wherever you breathe. Then, travel from your fingertips: bring your attention to your fingertips, fingers, palms, wrists, lower arms, upper arms, and shoulders, taking one breath at each part of the body. Finally, come to your heart center and take three complete breaths there.

Then bring your attention to your navel center. Take three complete breaths and feel the presence of your inner being while you inhale and exhale. Then bring your attention to your lower back, abdominal region, thighs, knees, calf muscles, ankles, feet, and toes, taking one breath at each part. Then reverse the process: bring your attention to your toes, feet, ankles, calf muscles, knees, thighs, abdominal region, lower back, and finally, back to the navel center. Here, take three deep breaths. Then, return to your heart center. Here, too, take three deep breaths. Then bring your attention to your shoulders, facial muscles, eyes, eyebrows, center between your eyebrows, and finally, come back to the center of your forehead. Here inhale and exhale deeply and smoothly. Feel the presence of your inner being with each breath.

This is how you restore and strengthen the links between the different limbs and organs of your body on the one hand, and between your body and pranic sheath, the energetic body, on the other hand. This scripture describes this process as *dharana,* concentration. Prolonged concentration eventually evolves into *dhyana,* meditation. To ensure that concentration matures into meditation, this scripture advises meditation on the lotus of the heart. Having completed your journey to the different regions of your body, you finally come to your forehead as described above. From there, as part of your meditation, draw your awareness down to your heart center.

The meditation at the heart center is methodical and profound. This form of meditation begins with formal initiation by a competent teacher. A competent teacher is he or she who has undergone the process of systematic study and practice and has emerged as a good student. Only a good student can be a good teacher. And only when taught by a good teacher can an aspirant reach his or her goal with fewer obstacles.

As the *Katha Upanishad* proclaims, fortunate is a student who is taught by a competent teacher, and even more fortunate is a teacher who has a competent student. The meeting of such a teacher and student is a sure sign of the descending grace of God. More than once, the grace of God walks into our life. It is only our burning desire that enables us to take advantage of this grace, letting this driving force shake off our inertia. It is during this auspicious moment that initiation takes place. Thereafter begins the true process of meditation, which in its due course of time loosens the knots of our ignorance, allowing the divine light to illuminate every aspect of our being—body, breath, mind, intellect, ego, unconscious mind. True meditation weakens the karmic bonds that keep us in this world, and strengthens the spiritual virtues that grant us freedom while living in this world.

KATHA UPANISHAD

ENGLISH TRANSLATION

part one - chapter one

Invocation

Om. May we protect and nurture each other.
May we rejoice together.
May our strength and vitality grow together.
May our knowledge shine.
May we not be jealous of each other.
Om. Peace, peace, peace.

Glowing with name and fame, there once lived a great philanthropist. His name was Vajashrava. In the course of time, he undertook a religious practice that required that he give away everything he owned. He had a son named Nachiketa.

Although he was still a young boy, Nachiketa was a person of conviction. Upon seeing his father's act of charity, Nachiketa began thinking:

"What is the use of giving away these cows? They have drunk their last drop of water, eaten their last mouthful of grass, been milked for the last time, and have nearly lost their limbs and organs. Definitely, the giver of such cows will go to the realm devoid of joy."

Nachiketa knew that his father was materialistic and thought that everything belonged to him, including his family. So, he asked bluntly, "Then to whom are you going to give me?" His father ignored him several times. Nachiketa asked once, twice, and three times. Finally, agitated, his father snapped, "I give you to Death!"

Nachiketa began to ponder: "Among many I stand first, or in some cases, maybe second. But I never stood last. Today my father said,

'I give you to Death.' I must discover the function of Yamaraja (the Lord of Death). What can I accomplish in the face of death?"

Seeing that his father regretted his words, Nachiketa said to him, "Look back, Father, at the ancients who honored their word, and look at the learned ones who honor their word today. If you are concerned about my life, then listen. Like a crop, life is harvested and then sown again."

Nachiketa arrived at the door of Death and waited for the Lord of Death for three nights. Finally, the Lord of Death appeared at the threshold, where his advisor counseled him: "O Lord of Death, the son of the Sun, please remember that it is the all-pervading fire, Vaishvanara, assuming a form, that comes to the door of the host. Greet your guest with water and make him peaceful and comfortable.

"Serious are the consequences when a guest, especially the one embodying the knowledge of higher truth, goes hungry at the home of his host. For such a host, all his expectations and hopes as well as the objects pertaining to them—sweetness of speech, as well as what is gained by speaking sweetly; the fruits of his philanthropic acts, even the ones that involve serving nature; his children; his cattle; and everything else—all are destroyed."

So Yamaraja said to Nachiketa: "My venerable guest, I am sorry that you waited three nights in my home without food. Please be kind to me. For those three nights, please ask for three boons."

Nachiketa asked: "May my father be filled with peaceful thoughts. May he be cheerful and free of grief and guilt. Upon my return, may he recognize me and speak with me. I ask this as the first of the three boons you have granted."

Yamaraja responded: "Your father will return to normal. After you are released by me, he will recognize you. Upon seeing you freed from the jaws of death, he will overcome his grief and guilt and will sleep peacefully at night."

Nachiketa continued: "I have heard that in heaven there is no fear of any kind. In heaven there is neither death nor old age. Crossing the realm of hunger and thirst, a person in heaven enjoys pleasures that transcend all worries.

"You, the Lord of Death, know all about the fire that leads to heaven. Those who reside in heaven enjoy immortality. Please give the knowledge of fire to me, for my heart is filled with faith in you. This is what I ask for my second boon."

Yamaraja replied: "I confess, Nachiketa, that I have full knowledge of this fire that leads to heaven. Learn it from me. Upon gaining this knowledge, you will become the master of endless spheres. This fire is the basis for the whole universe. It resides in the cave."

The Lord of Death, Yamaraja, went on explaining how this fire is the source of the universe, how the fireplace is built, how the bricks are arranged in building the fireplace, and describing the shapes, sizes, and number of bricks. At the end of the session, Nachiketa demonstrated his understanding. Pleased with his comprehension, Yamaraja spoke again.

Delighted with Nachiketa's understanding, Yamaraja exclaimed: "In addition to what I have promised you already, I grant you one more boon. From now on, the knowledge of fire that I have transmitted to you will be named after you. Please also accept this chain that assumes many forms.

"The knower of this fire arrives at the *sandhi* (the meeting ground) in a threefold manner. Performing actions in a threefold manner, he crosses over both birth and death. Upon gathering this venerable, brilliant fire, he comes to know the dynamics of this empirical world and consequently attains the highest peace.

"One who understands this science and gathers the fire within cuts asunder the snare of death, rises above the realm of worries, and rejoices in the heavenly planes.

"Leading to the celestial realm, this is the knowledge of fire that you chose as your second boon. This fire will be known by your name. Now, Nachiketa, ask for the third boon."

Nachiketa replied: "There is so much confusion regarding one who is departed (from the body). Some say he exists. Others say he does not. Taught by you, may I know this mystery. This is the third of my boons."

Yamaraja responded: "In regard to whether or not the soul exists after death, even the bright beings have their doubts. This is a subtle matter, which cannot be known so easily. Ask for some other boon. Do not insist. Release me from this promise."

Nachiketa insisted: "Even gods are full of doubt about this subject, and as you said, O Knower of Death, it cannot be easily known. There cannot be anyone better than you to speak on this subject. And there cannot be a better boon than this. Therefore, this is the boon that I really want."

Yamaraja replied: "Ask for children and grandchildren with lives of a hundred years. Or ask for cattle, elephants, horses, and as much wealth as you want. Have as much land as you want. Live as long as you want.

"Or, ask for any other boon that you think is equal to the one you just asked for. Have wealth and everlasting livelihood. On this earth, O Nachiketa, I will make you the enjoyer of any object that you desire.

"All those objects that are unattainable on this earthly plane, ask for them without any hesitation. Have beautiful celestial nymphs with their chariots and music. These kinds of pleasures cannot ordinarily be attained by mere mortals. Enjoy these pleasures, but a death-related question, O Nachiketa, do not ask."

Still Nachiketa insisted: "O Yamaraja, all these objects are short-lived. They drain the light of the senses. This whole life and all that exists in life is of little value. May all these chariots and this song and dance be yours.

"A human being cannot be satiated with wealth. Once I have found you, I will achieve them if I need them. As far as life goes, I will live as long as you wish. But that boon alone is the boon chosen by me.

"Having found an immortal being like you, how can a mortal person living on this mortal plane, afflicted with old age and death, think of the pleasures derived from the senses or even have any interest in having a long life?

"O Yamaraja, please share with me the wisdom pertaining to the other shore of life that has so far been shrouded in mystery. I, Nachiketa, ask for nothing other than the revelation of the truth that penetrates every layer of our existence and remains hidden at the core of our being."

part one - chapter two

[Yamaraja said:] The good *(shreya)* and the pleasant *(preya)* are two different things. They motivate a person to pursue two different goals. The one who embraces the good meets with auspiciousness. But the one who chooses the pleasant is lost.

The intermingled good and pleasant approach a human being. Understanding this clearly, a sincere seeker distinguishes one from the other. Separating the good from the pleasant, a sincere seeker chooses only that which is good, whereas under the influence of desire and fear *(yogakshema),* a slow person chooses that which is merely pleasant.

Having pondered the good and the pleasant, O Nachiketa, you turned away from those desires and objects of desire that are so dear to most people. Unlike many, you did not weigh yourself down with worldly possessions and pleasures.

There is a big difference between *avidya* (ignorance) and *vidya* (knowledge). And they lead to two entirely different ends. Also, there is a vast difference between the knower of truth and the ignorant. I consider you, O Nachiketa, a true seeker of knowledge because that which deludes others does not affect you.

Dwelling in the darkness of ignorance, the ignorant believe themselves to be wise and balanced. Like the blind led by the blind, they stagger round and round.

Childish are those who are deluded by the charms and temptations of the world, and consequently they fail to comprehend the higher truth. To them this world is the only reality: beyond this, nothing exists. One who is convinced of this false belief falls in my trap—the trap of birth and death—again and again.

Many people do not get a chance to hear this. Many of those who do hear don't understand. The one expounding this truth, an audience comprehending it, an adept with direct experience of this truth, and a disciple practicing under such an adept—all of these are wonders in themselves.

Regardless of how deeply and thoroughly one contemplates, this knowledge cannot be easily understood if taught by an inferior teacher. Unless taught by someone other than an inferior teacher there is no access to this knowledge, because it is subtler than subtle and beyond reasoning.

This knowledge cannot be attained through logic and reason. If taught by someone other than an intellectual teacher, that is, by an experienced master, only then is it well understood. Your resolution is firm, O Nachiketa. So far I have not had a student like you.

Yet to my knowledge, worldly wealth is transient. By the transient, no one can attain the eternal. Using transient objects, I gathered the fire that is named after you, Nachiketa. Thus, using non-eternal tools, I have attained the Eternal.

O Nachiketa, you have seen how desires are the foundation of worldly endeavors. You have seen that rituals are endless. You have reached the shore of fearlessness. You have seen the world that runs after name, fame, and prestige. Having found your place in inner wisdom, you have left that world behind.

The self-shining Divine Being is hard to see. Placed in the interior of the cave, it is hidden; it is most ancient and eternal. After knowing this Celestial Being through spiritual means, an aspirant is free from both pleasure and pain.

If someone listens, comprehends, practices accordingly, and as a result, gains the experience of this subtlemost truth, then he attains the joy of the highest delight. I consider you, O Nachiketa, an abode of learning, with a wide open door.

[Nachiketa said:] Please tell me about that which you see as different from *dharma,* different from *adharma;* different from this and that; different from the actions already performed and different from the actions not yet performed; and that which you see to be different from the past, present, and future.

[Yamaraja replied:] Briefly, I narrate the truth that all the Vedas proclaim, that which is the goal of all spiritual disciplines, that for which seekers follow the disciplines pertaining to *brahmacharya*—Om is That.

This eternal Om is Brahman. It is absolute. Upon knowing this Eternal One, the aspirant attains whatever he wishes.

This eternal Om is the best and highest resting point. Upon reaching this highest state of restfulness, the aspirant prospers in the realm of Brahman.

The Self is never born and never dies. It has neither come from anywhere nor does it go anywhere. The Self is unborn, eternal, most ancient, and is not destroyed with the destruction of the body.

If the slayer thinks that he slays and the slain thinks that he has been slain, then neither of them know the Self, for the Self neither slays nor is slain.

The Self is smaller than the smallest and bigger than the biggest. The Self dwells in the cave of the heart. With the help of the radiant energy within, an aspirant free of desire and grief comes to experience the glory of the Self.

While sitting still, the Self travels far; while resting, it goes everywhere. Who other than me can know that shining being, who is entirely different from pleasure and pain?

Though unembodied, the Self dwells in the body. Though dwelling in that which is unstable, the Self is stable. After realizing this great all-pervading Self, an adept does not grieve.

Knowledge of the Self cannot be achieved through lectures, through memory, or through book learning. The Self is attained by the one whom it chooses. To such a chosen one, the Self unveils its true essence.

Neither those engaged in unwholesome activities nor those who are undisciplined, nor those who are not composed, nor those who are not peaceful and content within can experience it, even after knowing all about it.

The one who finds caste identity as trivial as a fistful of rice, and the one to whom death is as significant as rinsing the mouth after meals—such a person has met the prerequisites for attaining knowledge of the Self.

part one - chapter three

[Yamaraja continued:] Living on the nectar of the divine will *(ritam),* both the higher and the lower self have entered the cave—the cave that exists in the highest realm of half of the Absolute. This realm is for those committed to self-endeavor. The knowers of Brahman, the fivefold fire, and the specific fire named after you say that the relationship between the higher and the lower self is that of the sun and the shade.

May we know the Nachiketa fire, which is like a bridge to the followers of the path of action. May we know the indestructible Brahman, which is transcendental. May we reach the other shore, where fear does not exist.

Know this Self to be the rider, the body to be the chariot, the intellect to be the charioteer, and the mind to be the reins.

The senses are the horses, and the sense objects are the path on which they run. One who is united with the Self, the senses, and the mind is called the enjoyer.

One who does not have right knowledge or who has an undisciplined mind suffers from the activities of his uncontrolled senses, just as a charioteer suffers from driving untrained horses.

One who has right understanding and has a disciplined mind enjoys having controlled senses, just as a charioteer enjoys driving trained horses.

One who does not have right understanding, who has a mind filled with thought constructs, and who lacks purity does not attain the highest realm, but rather remains caught in the cycle of birth and death.

One who has right understanding, a mind free of thought constructs, and is endowed with purity attains that state free of the snare of birth and death.

One who has right understanding as the chariot driver, and has a trained mind as reins, attains the other end of the path—that is the highest realm of Vishnu, the All-Pervading Truth.

Objects are more subtle than the senses, mind is subtler than the objects, intellect is subtler than the mind, and the Self is greater and more subtle than the intellect.

The unmanifest aspect of nature is higher than that which is manifest. Consciousness transcends even unmanifest nature. There is nothing beyond consciousness. Consciousness is the highest reality. Consciousness is the Self.

Hidden in all living beings, the Self remains unknown. Seers, however, see it through their subtle and penetrating intelligence.

The wise aspirant should merge speech into mind, mind into intellect, intellect into unmanifest nature, and unmanifest nature into the Self.

Awake, arise; find those who are wise and gain knowledge from them. This path is as sharp as the edge of a razor, as the knowers of truth say, and difficult to tread.

Upon gaining knowledge of the Self that is beyond articulation, touch, form, taste, and smell; that which is eternal, beginningless, and endless; that which is immutable; and that which is even beyond the purest form of nature, one attains freedom from the jaws of death.

By expounding and hearing the everlasting knowledge given by Yamaraja to Nachiketa, a person endowed with retentive power prospers in the highest realm of Brahman.

One who, in the assembly of Brahmins or during the ancestral rites, recites this great esoteric Upanishad with sincerity and purity is rewarded infinitely.

ॐ

part two - chapter one

[Yamaraja continued:] The self-born Divine Being designed the senses in a manner that they see only outside and not inside. Only a person blessed with patience and desiring immortality turns the senses inward and sees that which resides within.

Childish people seeking objects of their desire allow their senses to run in the external world, and as a result, remain caught in this ever-spread snare of death. However, the adepts blessed with patience realize the immortal truth, and thus they do not expect everlasting truth in this transitory world.

If someone knows this world only through taste, smell, touch, sight, hearing, and sexual pleasure, then what is there to be said? In that case, it's done.

The seer within us knows that which lies beyond the waking and dreaming states. Upon knowing that great and all-pervading inner Self, a person of patience no longer grieves.

The Self lives on honey. It is the lord of past, present, and future. Upon knowing that Self, an aspirant is no longer subject to confusion. This is the truth.

The Self was born before fire and water. It entered and began to reside in the cave. This is where it is to be seen. This is the truth.

Through the union with the life force *(prana),* the mother of all gods, Aditi, is born. Upon her birth, she entered and began to reside in the cave. This is where she is to be found. This is the truth.

Just as a fetus is hidden in the womb of the pregnant mother, so the omniscient fire is hidden in its source *(arani).* Only awakened aspirants propitiate this fire through oblations. This is the truth.

It is from the Self the sun rises, and it is where the sun sets. All celestial beings surrender to this Self. No one supersedes the Self. This is the truth.

That which is here, is there. That which is there, is here. One who sees a difference between here and there goes on wandering from death to death.

It is a matter of inner understanding that there is no difference between here and there. One who sees a difference goes on wandering from death to death.

Residing in all the limbs and organs, consciousness is seated in the center of the soul. It is the lord of the past, present, and future. Upon knowing that Self, an aspirant is no longer subject to confusion. This is the truth.

Residing in all the limbs and organs, consciousness is like a smokeless flame. It is the lord of the past, present, and future. It exists today, and it will continue existing tomorrow. This is the truth.

Just as rain at the summit runs downhill, similarly, the seer of differences chases what he sees.

Just as rainwater falling on pure ground remains pure and becomes impure on impure ground, similarly, O Nachiketa, the knowledge of the Self falling in a pure heart remains pure, and becomes distorted in an impure heart.

ॐ

part two - chapter two

The Self that in essence is never born resides in the eleven-gated city (the body) with its undistorted mind. There it does not worry about the results of its present endeavors or the results of its past deeds which are left behind anyway. This is the truth.

Having its seat in purity, the transcendental Self is the source of all inner and outer prosperity. It resides in the realm between heaven and earth; it is the one who offers oblations to the sacred fire; it resides at the altar; it is the unpredictable guest; it lives in humans, in the great ones, in the law that governs the forces of nature, and it resides in ever-expanding space. It is born of water, the senses, divine will, and the mountains. It is the Divine Will and the Highest One.

Seated at the center of everything, this little one *(Vamana)* exudes the boundless universe *(Virat)*. All the bright beings worship this mystery of mysteries—*Vamana.*

When the body falls apart and the Self residing in the body leaves it, what is left? This is the truth.

A human being subject to death is alive neither due to inhalation nor exhalation. Rather, he is alive due to something else that gives life to both inhalation and exhalation.

Blessed Nachiketa, I will impart to you the most secret knowledge of eternal truth. Being blessed with that knowledge, you will become eternal, even upon meeting death.

Others, devoid of this knowledge, go on migrating from one body to another. Depending on their actions, some devolve to the level of insentient beings.

Keeping track of every desire, this Self remains awake even during deep sleep. It is the self-effulgent, all-pervading, immortal Divine Being. All spheres rest in it. Nothing surpasses it. This is the truth.

Just as one fire, upon penetrating different spheres of existence, assumes different forms, similarly, the soul of all living beings, upon entering different bodies, assumes different forms.

Just as one air, upon penetrating different spheres of existence, assumes different forms, similarly, the soul of all living beings, upon entering different bodies, assumes different forms.

The sun is the eye of the whole world, and yet remains untainted by the impurities of the objects it perceives. Similarly, the soul of all living beings remains untainted by the pleasure and pain of the external world.

The soul of all living beings is one and autonomous. Through sheer will it becomes many. Everlasting joy is only for those blessed with patience who see it in the interior of their soul—and not for anyone else.

It is eternal among the eternal. It is the consciousness of consciousness. It is one among many. It is this highest being who fulfills all desires. Everlasting joy is only for those blessed with patience who see it in the interior of their soul—and not for anyone else.

This is known as the indescribable highest happiness. How can we really know it? How does it shine? How does it feel?

The sun doesn't shine there, nor does the moon, nor the stars, nor the lightning, not to mention this earthly fire. Only because This shines, all else shines through its effulgence.

part two - chapter three

This life is like a banyan tree with its roots up and the branches down. It is eternal. It is the self-effulgent, all-pervading, immortal Divine Being. All spheres rest in it. Nothing surpasses it. This is the truth.

It is the life force that animates everything in this world. To one who doesn't know this truth, life is full of fear. To such a person, life is just a series of calamities. But the knower of this truth is beyond death, decay, and destruction.

It is under the command of this truth that the fire burns and the sun shines. It is under the command of this truth that the Lord of the Heavens (Indra), the air, and death move.

If this truth is known here and now before the body falls apart, then the purpose of life is achieved. If not, then the individual goes on migrating from one body to another.

The relationship between the higher and the lower self is that of the sun and the shade. This relationship continues here in this world during both the waking and dreaming states. This relationship continues when we reside in the realm of the ancestors, in the world of imagination, and even in the highest realm known as Brahma Loka.

Sensory pleasure climaxes and then declines. Knowing this is a natural phenomenon, a person blessed with patience does not grieve.

The mind is superior to the senses. The intellect is superior to the mind. Unmanifest nature is superior to manifest nature, and the Self is superior to the finest aspect of nature *(sattva).*

The Self is all-pervading and beyond name, form, and gender. Upon knowing this Self, an aspirant is no longer subject to death, decay, or destruction.

KATHA UPANISHAD

SANSKRIT TEXT, TRANSLITERATION, AND TRANSLATION

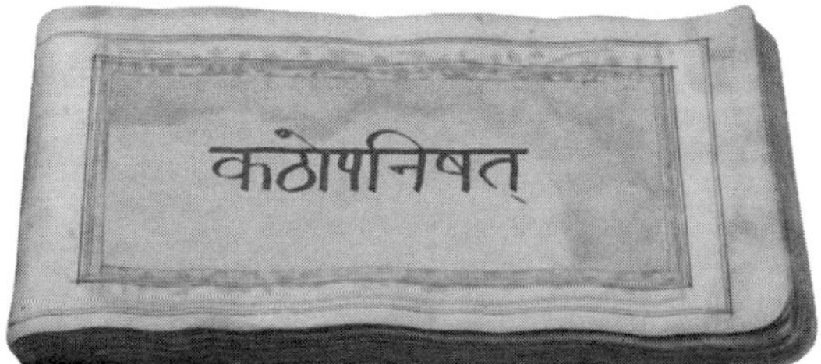

part one - chapter one

Invocation

ॐ
सह नाववतु ।
सह नौ भुनक्तु ।
सह वीर्यं करवावहै ॥
तेजस्वि नावधीतमस्तु मा विद्विषावहै ॥
ॐ शान्तिः शान्तिः शान्तिः ॥

om
saha nāvavatu |
saha nau bhunaktu |
saha vīryaṁ karavāvahai ||
tejasvi nāvadhītamastu mā vidviṣāvahai ||
om śāntiḥ śāntiḥ śāntiḥ ||

Om. May we protect and nurture each other.
May we rejoice together.
May our strength and vitality grow together.
May our knowledge shine.
May we not be jealous of each other.
Om. Peace, peace, peace.

ॐ

ॐ उशन् ह वै वाजश्रवसः सर्ववेदसं ददौ ।
तस्य ह नचिकेता नाम पुत्र आस ॥१ ॥

om uśan ha vai vājaśravasaḥ sarvavedasaṁ dadau |
tasya ha naciketā nāma putra āsa ||

1. Glowing with name and fame, there once lived a great philanthropist. His name was Vajashrava. In the course of time, he undertook a religious practice that required that he give away everything he owned. He had a son named Nachiketa.

तं ह कुमारं सन्तं दक्षिणासु नीयमानासु श्रद्धाविवेश सोऽमन्यत ॥२ ॥

taṁ ha kumāraṁ santaṁ dakṣiṇāsu nīyamānāsu śraddhāviveśa so'manyata ||

2. Although he was still a young boy, Nachiketa was a person of conviction. Upon seeing his father's act of charity, Nachiketa began thinking:

पीतोदका जग्धतृणा दुग्धदोहा निरिन्द्रियाः ।
अनन्दा नाम ते लोकास्तान् स गच्छति ता ददत् ॥३ ॥

pītodakā jagdhatṛṇā dugdhadohā nirindriyāḥ |
anandā nāma te lokāstān sa gacchati tā dadat ||

3. "What is the use of giving away these cows? They have drunk their last drop of water, eaten their last mouthful of grass, been milked for the last time, and have nearly lost their limbs and organs. Definitely, the giver of such cows will go to the realm devoid of joy."

स होवाच पितरं तत कस्मै मां दास्यसीति ।
द्वितीयं तृतीयं तं होवाच मृत्यवे त्वा ददामीति ॥४॥

sa hovāca pitaraṁ tata kasmai māṁ dāsyasīti |
dvitīyaṁ tṛtīyaṁ taṁ hovāca mṛtyave tvā dadāmīti ||

4. Nachiketa knew that his father was materialistic and thought that everything belonged to him, including his family. So, he asked bluntly, "Then to whom are you going to give me?" His father ignored him several times. Nachiketa asked once, twice, and three times. Finally, agitated, his father snapped, "I give you to Death!"

बहूनामेमि प्रथमो बहूनामेमि मध्यमः ।
किं स्विद्यमस्य कर्तव्यं यन्मयाद्य करिष्यति ॥५॥

bahūnāmemi prathamo bahūnāmemi madhyamaḥ |
kiṁ svidyamasya kartavyaṁ yanmayādya kariṣyati ||

5. Nachiketa began to ponder: "Among many I stand first, or in some cases, maybe second. But I never stood last. Today my father said, 'I give you to Death.' I must discover the function of Yamaraja (the Lord of Death). What can I accomplish in the face of death?"

अनुपश्य यथा पूर्वे प्रतिपश्य तथापरे ।
सस्यमिव मर्त्यः पच्यते सस्यमिवाजायते पुनः ॥६ ॥

anupaśya yathā pūrve pratipaśya tathāpare |
sasyamiva martyaḥ pacyate sasyamivājāyate punaḥ ||

6. Seeing that his father regretted his words, Nachiketa said to him, "Look back, Father, at the ancients who honored their word, and look at the learned ones who honor their word today. If you are concerned about my life, then listen. Like a crop, life is harvested and then sown again."

वैश्वानरः प्रविशत्यतिथिर्ब्राह्मणो गृहान् ।
तस्यैतां शान्तिं कुर्वन्ति हर वैवस्वतोदकम् ॥७ ॥

vaiśvānaraḥ praviśatyatithirbrāhmaṇo gṛhān |
tasyaitāṁ śāntiṁ kurvanti hara vaivasvatodakam ||

7. Nachiketa arrived at the door of Death and waited for the Lord of Death for three nights. Finally, the Lord of Death appeared at the threshold, where his advisor counseled him: "O Lord of Death, the son of the Sun, please remember that it is the all-pervading fire, Vaishvanara, assuming a form, that comes to the door of the host. Greet your guest with water and make him peaceful and comfortable.

आशाप्रतीक्षे संगतं सूनृतां चेष्टापूर्ते पुत्रपशूंश्च सर्वान्।
एतद् वृङ्क्ते पुरुषस्याल्पमेधसो यस्यानश्नन्वसति ब्राह्मणो गृहे ॥८॥

āśāpratīkṣe saṅgataṁ sūnṛtāṁ ceṣṭāpūrte
putrapaśūṁśca sarvān |
etad vṛṅkte puruṣasyālpamedhaso yasyānaśnanvasati
brāhmaṇo gṛhe ||

8. "Serious are the consequences when a guest, especially the one embodying the knowledge of higher truth, goes hungry at the home of his host. For such a host, all his expectations and hopes as well as the objects pertaining to them—sweetness of speech, as well as what is gained by speaking sweetly; the fruits of his philanthropic acts, even the ones that involve serving nature; his children; his cattle; and everything else—all are destroyed."

तिस्रो रात्रिर्यदवात्सीर्गृहे मेऽनश्नन्ब्रह्मन्नतिथिर्नमस्यः।
नमस्तेऽस्तु ब्रह्मन्स्वस्ति मेऽस्तु तस्मात्प्रति त्रीन्वरान्वृणीष्व ॥९॥

trisro rātriryadavātsīrgṛhe me'naśnan
brahmannatithirnamasyaḥ |
namaste'stu brahmansvasti me'stu tasmātprati
trīnvarānvṛṇīṣva ||

9. So Yamaraja said to Nachiketa: "My venerable guest, I am sorry that you waited three nights in my home without food. Please be kind to me. For those three nights, please ask for three boons."

शान्तसङ्कल्पः सुमना यथा स्याद्वीतमन्युर्गौतमो माभि मृत्यो ।
त्वत्प्रसृष्टं माभिवदेत्प्रतीत एतत् त्रयाणां प्रथमं वरं वृणे ॥१० ॥

śāntasaṅkalpaḥ sumanā yathā syādvītamanyurgautamo mābhi mṛtyo |
tvatprasṛṣṭaṁ mābhivadetpratīta etat trayāṇāṁ prathamaṁ varaṁ vṛṇe ||

10. Nachiketa asked: "May my father be filled with peaceful thoughts. May he be cheerful and free of grief and guilt. Upon my return, may he recognize me and speak with me. I ask this as the first of the three boons you have granted."

यथा प्रस्ताद् भविता प्रतीत औद्दालकिरारुणिर्मत्प्रसृष्टः ।
सुखं रात्रीः शयिता वीतमन्युस्त्वां ददृशिवान्मृत्युमुखात्प्रमुक्तम् ॥११ ॥

yathā prastād bhavitā pratīta auddālakirāruṇirmatprasṛṣṭaḥ |
sukhaṁ rātrīḥ śayitā vītamanyustvāṁ dadṛśivānmṛtyumukhātpramuktam ||

11. Yamaraja responded: "Your father will return to normal. After you are released by me, he will recognize you. Upon seeing you freed from the jaws of death, he will overcome his grief and guilt and will sleep peacefully at night."

स्वर्गे लोके न भयं किञ्चनास्ति न तत्र त्वं न जरया बिभेति ।
उभे तीर्त्वाशनायापिपासे शोकातिगो मोदते स्वर्गलोके ॥१२॥

svarge loke na bhayaṁ kiñcanāsti na tatra tvaṁ
na jarayā bibheti |
ubhe tīrtvāśanāyāpipāse śokātigo modate svargaloke ||

12. Nachiketa continued: "I have heard that in heaven there is no fear of any kind. In heaven there is neither death nor old age. Crossing the realm of hunger and thirst, a person in heaven enjoys pleasures that transcend all worries.

स त्वमग्निं स्वर्ग्यमध्येषि मृत्यो प्रब्रूहि तं श्रद्दधानाय मह्यम् ।
स्वर्गलोका अमृतत्वं भजन्त एतद् द्वितीयेन वृणे वरेण ॥१३॥

sa tvamagniṁ svargyamadhyeṣi mṛtyo prabrūhi taṁ
śraddadhānāya mahyam |
svargalokā amṛtatvaṁ bhajanta etad dvitīyena vṛṇe vareṇa ||

13. "You, the Lord of Death, know all about the fire that leads to heaven. Those who reside in heaven enjoy immortality. Please give the knowledge of fire to me, for my heart is filled with faith in you. This is what I ask for my second boon."

प्र ते ब्रवीमि तदु मे निबोध स्वर्ग्यमग्निं नचिकेतः प्रजानन्।
अनन्तलोकाप्तिमथो प्रतिष्ठां विद्धि त्वमेतं निहितं गुहायाम्॥१४॥

pra te bravīmi tadu me nibodha svargyamagniṁ
naciketaḥ prajānan |
anantalokāptimatho pratiṣṭhāṁ viddhi tvametaṁ
nihitaṁ guhāyām ||

14. Yamaraja replied: "I confess, Nachiketa, that I have full knowledge of this fire that leads to heaven. Learn it from me. Upon gaining this knowledge, you will become the master of endless spheres. This fire is the basis for the whole universe. It resides in the cave."

लोकादिमग्निं तमुवाच तस्मै या इष्टका यावतीर्वा यथा वा।
स चापि तत्प्रत्यवदद्यथोक्तमथास्य मृत्युः पुनरेवाह तुष्टः॥१५॥

lokādimagniṁ tamuvāca tasmai yā iṣṭakā
yāvatīrvā yathā vā |
sa cāpi tatpratyavadadyathoktamathāsya mṛtyuḥ
punarevāha tuṣṭaḥ ||

15. The Lord of Death, Yamaraja, went on explaining how this fire is the source of the universe, how the fireplace is built, how the bricks are arranged in building the fireplace, and describing the shapes, sizes, and number of bricks. At the end of the session, Nachiketa demonstrated his understanding. Pleased with his comprehension, Yamaraja spoke again.

तमब्रवीत् प्रीयमाणो महात्मा वरं तवेहाद्य ददामि भूयः ।
तवैव नाम्ना भवितायमग्निः सृङ्कां चेमामनेकरूपां गृहाण ॥१६ ॥

tamabravīt prīyamāṇo mahātmā varaṁ tavehādya dadāmi bhūyaḥ |
tavaiva nāmnā bhavitāyamagni? sṛṅkāṁ cemāmanekarūpāṁ gṛhāṇa ||

16. Delighted with Nachiketa's understanding, Yamaraja exclaimed: "In addition to what I have promised you already, I grant you one more boon. From now on, the knowledge of fire that I have transmitted to you will be named after you. Please also accept this chain that assumes many forms.

त्रिणाचिकेतस्त्रिभिरेत्य सन्धिं त्रिकर्मकृत्तरति जन्ममृत्यू ।
ब्रह्मजज्ञं देवमीड्यं विदित्वा निचाय्येमां शान्तिमत्यन्तमेति ॥१७ ॥

triṇāciketastribhiretya sandhiṁ trikarmakṛttarati janmamṛtyū |
brahmajajñaṁ devamīḍyaṁ viditvā nicāyyemāṁ śāntimatyantameti ||

17. "The knower of this fire arrives at the *sandhi* (the meeting ground) in a threefold manner. Performing actions in a threefold manner, he crosses over both birth and death. Upon gathering this venerable, brilliant fire, he comes to know the dynamics of this empirical world and consequently attains the highest peace.

त्रिणाचिकेतस्त्रयमेतद्विदित्वा य एवं विद्वांश्चिनुते नाचिकेतम् ।
स मृत्युपाशान्पुरतः प्रणोद्य शोकातिगो मोदते स्वर्गलोके ॥१८ ॥

triṇāciketastrayametadviditvā ya evaṁ
vidvāṁścinute nāciketam |
sa mṛtyupāśānpurataḥ praṇodya śokātigo
modate svargaloke ||

18. "One who understands this science and gathers the fire within cuts asunder the snare of death, rises above the realm of worries, and rejoices in the heavenly planes.

एष तेऽग्निर्नचिकेतः स्वर्ग्यो यमवृणीथा द्वितीयेन वरेण ।
एतमग्निं तवैव प्रवक्ष्यन्ति जनासस्तृतीयं वरं नचिकेतो वृणीष्व ॥१९ ॥

eṣa te'gnirnaciketaḥ svargyo yamavṛṇīthā dvitīyena vareṇa |
etamagniṁ tavaiva pravakṣyanti janāsastṛtīyaṁ varaṁ
naciketo vṛṇīṣva ||

19. "Leading to the celestial realm, this is the knowledge of fire that you chose as your second boon. This fire will be known by your name. Now, Nachiketa, ask for the third boon."

येयं प्रेते विचिकित्सा मनुष्येऽस्तीत्येके नायमस्तीति चैके ।
एतद्विद्यामनुशिष्टस्त्वयाहं वराणामेष वरस्तृतीयः ॥२० ॥

yeyaṁ prete vicikitsā manuṣye'stītyeke nāyamastīti caike |
etadvidyāmanuśiṣṭastvayāhaṁ varāṇāmeṣa varastṛtīyaḥ ||

20. Nachiketa replied: "There is so much confusion regarding one who is departed (from the body). Some say he exists. Others say he does not. Taught by you, may I know this mystery. This is the third of my boons."

देवैरत्रापि विचिकित्सितं पुरा न हि सुविज्ञेयमणुरेष धर्मः ।
अन्यं वरं नचिकेतो वृणीष्व मा मोपरोत्सीरति मा सृजैनम् ॥२१ ॥

devairatrāpi vicikitsitaṁ purā na hi
suvijñeyamaṇureṣa dharmaḥ |
anyaṁ varaṁ naciketo vṛṇīṣva mā
moparotsīrati mā sṛjainam ||

21. Yamaraja responded: "In regard to whether or not the soul exists after death, even the bright beings have their doubts. This is a subtle matter, which cannot be known so easily. Ask for some other boon. Do not insist. Release me from this promise."

देवैरत्रापि विचिकित्सितं किल त्वं च मृत्यो यन्न सुज्ञेयमात्थ ।
वक्ता चास्य त्वादृगन्यो न लभ्यो नान्यो वरस्तुल्य एतस्य कश्चित् ॥२२ ॥

devairatrāpi vicikitsitaṁ kila tvaṁ ca mṛtyo
yanna sujñeyamāttha |
vaktā cāsya tvādṛganyo na labhyo nānyo varastulya
etasya kaścit ||

22. Nachiketa insisted: "Even gods are full of doubt about this subject, and as you said, O Knower of Death, it cannot be easily known. There cannot be anyone better than you to speak on this subject. And there cannot be a better boon than this. Therefore, this is the boon that I really want."

शतायुषः पुत्रपौत्रान्वणीष्व बहून्पशून्हस्तिहिरण्यमश्वान् ।
भूमेर्महदायतनं वृणीष्व स्वयं च जीव शरदो यावदिच्छसि ॥२३ ॥

śatāyuṣaḥ putrapautrānvaṇīṣva
bahūnpaśūnhastihiraṇyamaśvān ǀ
bhūmermahadāyatanaṁ vṛṇīṣva
svayaṁ ca jīva śarado yāvadicchasi ǀǀ

23. Yamaraja replied: "Ask for children and grandchildren with lives of a hundred years. Or ask for cattle, elephants, horses, and as much wealth as you want. Have as much land as you want. Live as long as you want.

एतत्तुल्यं यदि मन्यसे वरं वृणीष्व वित्तं चिरजीविकां च ।
महाभूमौ नचिकेतस्त्वमेधि कामानां त्वा कामभाजं करोमि ॥२४ ॥

etattulyaṁ yadi manyase varaṁ vṛṇīṣva vittaṁ
cirajīvikāṁ ca ǀ
mahābhūmau naciketastvamedhi kāmānāṁ tvā
kāmabhājaṁ karomi ǀǀ

24. "Or, ask for any other boon that you think is equal to the one you just asked for. Have wealth and everlasting livelihood. On this earth, O Nachiketa, I will make you the enjoyer of any object that you desire.

ये ये कामा दुर्लभा मर्त्यलोके सर्वान् कामांश्छन्दतः प्रार्थयस्व ।
इमा रामाः सरथाः सतूर्या न हीदृशा लम्भनीया मनुष्यैः ।
आभिर्मत्प्रत्ताभिः परिचारयस्व नचिकेतो मरणं मानुप्राक्षीः ॥२५॥

ye ye kāmā durlabhā martyaloke sarvān
kāmāṁśchandataḥ prārthayasva |
imā rāmāḥ sarathāḥ satūryā na hīdṛśā
lambhanīyā manuṣyaiḥ |
ābhirmatprattābhiḥ paricārayasva naciketo
maraṇaṁ mānuprākṣīḥ ||

25. "All those objects that are unattainable on this earthly plane, ask for them without any hesitation. Have beautiful celestial nymphs with their chariots and music. These kinds of pleasures cannot ordinarily be attained by mere mortals. Enjoy these pleasures, but a death-related question, O Nachiketa, do not ask."

श्वोभावा मर्त्यस्य यदन्तकैतत् सर्वेन्द्रियाणां जरयन्ति तेजः ।
अपि सर्वं जीवितमल्पमेव तवैव वाहास्तव नृत्यगीते ॥२६॥

śvobhāvā martyasya yadantakaitat sarvendriyāṇāṁ
jarayanti tejaḥ |
api sarvaṁ jīvitamalpameva tavaiva vāhāstava nṛtyagīte ||

26. Still Nachiketa insisted: "O Yamaraja, all these objects are short-lived. They drain the light of the senses. This whole life and all that exists in life is of little value. May all these chariots and this song and dance be yours.

न वित्तेन तर्पणीयो मनुष्यो लप्स्यामहे वित्तमद्राक्ष्म चेत्त्वा ।
जीविष्यामो यावदीशिष्यसि त्वं वरस्तु मे वरणीयः स एव ॥२७ ॥

na vittena tarpaṇīyo manuṣyo lapsyāmahe
vittamadrākṣma cettvā |
jīviṣyāmo yāvadīśiṣyasi tvaṁ varastu me
varaṇīyaḥ sa eva ||

27. "A human being cannot be satiated with wealth. Once I have found you, I will achieve them if I need them. As far as life goes, I will live as long as you wish. But that boon alone is the boon chosen by me.

अजीर्यताममृतानामुपेत्य जीर्यन्मर्त्यः क्वधःस्थः प्रजानन् ।
अभिध्यायन् वर्णरतिप्रमोदानतिदीर्घे जीविते को रमेत ॥२८ ॥

ajīryatāmamṛtānāmupetya jīryanmartyaḥ
kvadhaḥsthaḥ prajānan |
abhidhyāyan varṇaratipramodānatidīrghe jīvite ko rameta ||

28. "Having found an immortal being like you, how can a mortal person living on this mortal plane, afflicted with old age and death, think of the pleasures derived from the senses or even have any interest in having a long life?

यस्मिन्निदं विचिकित्सन्ति मृत्यो यत्साम्पराये महति ब्रूहि नस्तत्।
योऽयं वरो गूढमनुप्रविष्ट नान्यं तस्मान्नचिकेता वृणीते ॥२९॥

yasminnidaṁ vicikitsanti mṛtyo yatsāmparāye
mahati brūhi nastat |
yo'yaṁ varo gūḍhamanupraviṣṭa nānyaṁ
tasmānnaciketā vṛṇīte ||

29. "O Yamaraja, please share with me the wisdom pertaining to the other shore of life that has so far been shrouded in mystery. I, Nachiketa, ask for nothing other than the revelation of the truth that penetrates every layer of our existence and remains hidden at the core of our being."

ॐ

part one - chapter two

अन्यच्छ्रेयोऽन्यदुतैव प्रेयस्ते उभे नानार्थे पुरुषं सिनीतः ।
तयोः श्रेय आददानस्य साधु भवति हीयतेऽर्थाद्य उ प्रेयो वृणीते ॥१ ॥

anyacchreyo'nyadutaiva preyaste ubhe nānārthe
puruṣaṁ sinītaḥ |
tayoḥ śreya ādadānasya sādhu bhavati hīyate'rthādya u
preyo vṛṇīte ||

1. [Yamaraja said:] The good *(shreya)* and the pleasant *(preya)* are two different things. They motivate a person to pursue two different goals. The one who embraces the good meets with auspiciousness. But the one who chooses the pleasant is lost.

श्रेयश्च प्रेयश्च मनुष्यमेतस्तौ सम्परीत्य विविनक्ति धीरः ।
श्रेयो हि धीरोऽभिप्रेयसो वृणीते प्रेयो मन्दो योगक्षेमाद् वृणीते ॥२ ॥

śreyaśca preyaśca manuṣyametastau samparītya
vivinakti dhīraḥ |
śreyo hi dhīro'bhipreyaso vṛṇīte preyo mando
yogakṣemād vṛṇīte ||

2. The intermingled good and pleasant approach a human being. Understanding this clearly, a sincere seeker distinguishes one from the other. Separating the good from the pleasant, a sincere seeker chooses only that which is good, whereas under the influence of desire and fear *(yogakshema)* a slow person chooses that which is merely pleasant.

स त्वं प्रियान्प्रियरूपांश्च कामानभिध्यायन् नचिकेतोऽत्यस्राक्षीः ।
नैतां सृङ्कां वित्तमयीमवाप्तो यस्यां मज्जन्ति बहवो मनुष्याः ॥३॥

sa tvaṁ priyānpriyarūpāṁśca kāmānabhidhyāyan naciketo'tyasrākṣīḥ |
naitāṁ sṛṅkāṁ vittamayīmavāpto yasyāṁ majjanti bahavo manuṣyāḥ ||

3. Having pondered the good and the pleasant, O Nachiketa, you turned away from those desires and objects of desire that are so dear to most people. Unlike many, you did not weigh yourself down with worldly possessions and pleasures.

दूरमेते विपरीते विषूची अविद्या या च विद्येति ज्ञाता ।
विद्याभीप्सिनं नचिकेतसं मन्ये न त्वा कामा बहवोऽलोलुपन्त ॥४॥

dūramete viparīte viṣūcī avidyā yā ca vidyeti jñātā |
vidyābhīpsinaṁ naciketasaṁ manye na tvā kāmā bahavo'lolupanta ||

4. There is a big difference between *avidya* (ignorance) and *vidya* (knowledge). And they lead to two entirely different ends. Also, there is a vast difference between the knower of truth and the ignorant. I consider you, O Nachiketa, a true seeker of knowledge because that which deludes others does not affect you.

अविद्यायामन्तरे वर्तमानाः स्वयं धीराः पण्डिमम्मन्यमानाः ।
दन्द्रम्यमाणाः परियन्ति मूढा अन्धेनैव नीयमाना यथान्धाः ॥५॥

avidyāyāmantare vartamānāḥ svayaṁ dhīrāḥ paṇḍitammanyamānāḥ |
dandramyamāṇāḥ pariyanti mūḍhā andhenaiva nīyamānā yathāndhāḥ ||

5. Dwelling in the darkness of ignorance, the ignorant believe themselves to be wise and balanced. Like the blind led by the blind, they stagger round and round.

न साम्परायः प्रतिभाति बालं प्रमाद्यन्तं वित्तमोहेन मूढम् ।
अयं लोको नास्ति पर इति मानी पुनः पुनर्वशमापद्यते मे ॥६॥

na sāmparāyaḥ pratibhāti bālaṁ pramādyantaṁ vittamohena mūḍham |
ayaṁ loko nāsti para iti mānī punaḥ punarvaśamāpadyate me ||

6. Childish are those who are deluded by the charms and temptations of the world, and consequently they fail to comprehend the higher truth. To them this world is the only reality: beyond this, nothing exists. One who is convinced of this false belief falls in my trap—the trap of birth and death—again and again.

श्रवणायापि बहुभिर्यो न लभ्यः शृण्वन्तोऽपि बहवो यं न विद्युः ।
आश्चर्यो वक्ता कुशलोऽस्य लब्धाश्चर्यो ज्ञाता कुशलानुशिष्टः ॥७॥

śravaṇāyāpi bahubhiryo na labhyaḥ śṛṇvanto'pi
bahavo yaṁ na vidyuḥ |
āścaryo vaktā kuśalo'sya labdhāścaryo jñātā kuśalānuśiṣṭaḥ ||

7. Many people do not get a chance to hear this. Many of those who do hear don't understand. The one expounding this truth, an audience comprehending it, an adept with direct experience of this truth, and a disciple practicing under such an adept—all of these are wonders in themselves.

न नरेणावरेण प्रोक्त एष सुविज्ञेयो बहुधा चिन्त्यमानः ।
अनन्यप्रोक्ते गतिरत्र नास्त्यणीयान् हि अतर्क्यमणुप्रमाणात् ॥८॥

na nareṇāvareṇa prokta eṣa suvijñeyo bahudhā
cintyamānaḥ |
ananyaprokte gatiratra nāstyaṇīyān hi
atarkyamaṇupramāṇāt ||

8. Regardless of how deeply and thoroughly one contemplates, this knowledge cannot be easily understood if taught by an inferior teacher. Unless taught by someone other than an inferior teacher there is no access to this knowledge, because it is subtler than subtle and beyond reasoning.

नैषा तर्केण मतिरापनेया प्रोक्तान्येनैव सुज्ञानाय प्रेष्ठ ।
यां त्वमापः सत्यधृतिर्बतासि त्वादृग् नो भूयान्नचिकेतः प्रष्टा ॥९॥

naiṣā tarkeṇa matirāpaneyā proktānyenaiva
sujñānāya preṣṭha |
yāṁ tvamāpaḥ satyadhṛtirbatāsi tvādṛg no
bhūyānnaciketaḥ praṣṭā ||

9. This knowledge cannot be attained through logic and reason. If taught by someone other than an intellectual teacher, that is, by an experienced master, only then is it well understood. Your resolution is firm, O Nachiketa. So far I have not had a student like you.

जानाम्यहं शेवधिरित्यनित्यं न हि अध्रुवैः प्राप्यते हि ध्रुवं तत् ।
ततो मया नाचिकेतश्चितोऽग्निरनित्यैर्द्रव्यैः प्राप्तवानस्मि नित्यम् ॥१०॥

jānāmyahaṁ śevadhirityanityaṁ na hi adhruvaiḥ
prāpyate hi dhruvaṁ tat |
tato mayā nāciketaścito'gniranityairdravyaiḥ
prāptavānasmi nityam ||

10. Yet to my knowledge, worldly wealth is transient. By the transient, no one can attain the eternal. Using transient objects, I gathered the fire that is named after you, Nachiketa. Thus, using non-eternal tools, I have attained the Eternal.

कामस्याप्तिं जगतः प्रतिष्ठां क्रतोरानन्त्यमभयस्य पारम्।
स्तोमं महदुरुगायं प्रतिष्ठां दृष्ट्वा धृत्या धीरो नचिकेतोऽत्यस्राक्षीः ॥११॥

kāmasyāptiṁ jagataḥ pratiṣṭhāṁ
kratorānantyamabhayasya pāram |
stomaṁ mahadurugāyaṁ pratiṣṭhāṁ dṛṣṭvā dhṛtyā
dhīro naciketo'tyasrākṣīḥ ||

11. O Nachiketa, you have seen how desires are the foundation of worldly endeavors. You have seen that rituals are endless. You have reached the shore of fearlessness. You have seen the world that runs after name, fame, and prestige. Having found your place in inner wisdom, you have left that world behind.

तं दुर्दर्शं गूढमनुप्रविष्टं गुहाहितं गह्वरेष्ठं पुराणम्।
अध्यात्मयोगाधिगमेन देवं मत्वा धीरो हर्षशोकौ जहाति ॥१२॥

taṁ durdarśaṁ gūḍhamanupraviṣṭhaṁ guhāhitaṁ
gahvareṣṭhaṁ purāṇam |
adhyātmayogādhigamena devaṁ matvā dhīro
harṣaśokau jahāti ||

12. The self-shining Divine Being is hard to see. Placed in the interior of the cave, it is hidden; it is most ancient and eternal. After knowing this Celestial Being through spiritual means, an aspirant is free from both pleasure and pain.

एतच्छ्रुत्वा सम्परिगृह्य मर्त्यः प्रवृह्य धर्म्यमणुमेतमाप्य ।
स मोदते मोदनीयं हि लब्ध्वा विवृतं सद्म नचिकेतसं मन्ये ॥१३॥

etacchrutvā samparigṛhya martyaḥ pravṛhya dharmya maṇumetamāpya |
sa modate modanīyaṁ hi labdhvā vivṛtaṁ sadma naciketasaṁ manye ||

13. If someone listens, comprehends, practices accordingly, and as a result, gains the experience of this subtlemost truth, then he attains the joy of the highest delight. I consider you, O Nachiketa, an abode of learning, with a wide open door.

अन्यत्र धर्मादन्यत्राधर्मादन्यत्रास्मात्कृताकृतात् ।
अन्यत्र भूताच्च भव्याच्च यत्तत्पश्यसि तद्वद ॥१४॥

anyatra dharmādanyatrādharmādanyatrāsmātkṛtākṛtāt |
anyatra bhūtācca bhavyācca yattatpaśyasi tadvada ||

14. [Nachiketa said:] Please tell me about that which you see as different from *dharma,* different from *adharma;* different from this and that; different from the actions already performed and different from the actions not yet performed; and that which you see to be different from the past, present, and future.

सर्वे वेदा यत्पदमामनन्ति तपांसि सर्वाणि च यद्वदन्ति ।
यदिच्छन्तो ब्रह्मचर्यं चरन्ति तत् ते पदं संग्रहेण ब्रवीम्योमित्येतत् ॥१५ ॥

sarve vedā yatpadamāmananti tapāṁsi sarvāṇi
ca yadvadanti |
yadicchanto brahmacaryaṁ caranti tat te padaṁ
saṅgraheṇa bravīmyomityetat ||

15. [Yamaraja replied:] Briefly, I narrate the truth that all the Vedas proclaim, that which is the goal of all spiritual disciplines, that for which seekers follow the disciplines pertaining to *brahmacharya*—Om is That.

एतद्ध्येवाक्षरं ब्रह्म एतद्ध्येवाक्षरं परम् ।
एतद्ध्येवाक्षरं ज्ञात्वा यो यदिच्छति तस्य तत् ॥१६ ॥

etaddhyevākṣaraṁ brahma etaddhyevākṣaraṁ param |
etaddhyevākṣaraṁ jñātvā yo yadicchati tasya tat ||

16. This eternal Om is Brahman. It is absolute. Upon knowing this Eternal One, the aspirant attains whatever he wishes.

एतदालम्बनं श्रेष्ठमेतदालम्बनं परम् ।
एतदालम्बनं ज्ञात्वा ब्रह्मलोके महीयते ॥१७ ॥

etadālambanaṁ śreṣṭhametadālambanaṁ param |
etadālambanaṁ jñātvā brahmaloke mahīyate ||

17. This eternal Om is the best and highest resting point. Upon reaching this highest state of restfulness, the aspirant prospers in the realm of Brahman.

न जायते म्रियते वा विपश्चिन्नायं कुतश्चिन्न बभूव कश्चित् ।
अजो नित्यः शाश्वतोऽयं पुराणो न हन्यते हन्यमाने शरीरे ॥१८ ॥

na jāyate mriyate vā vipaścinnāyaṁ kutaścinna
babhūva kaścit |
ajo nityaḥ śāśvato'yaṁ purāṇo na hanyate
hanyamāne śarīre ||

18. The Self is never born and never dies. It has neither come from anywhere nor does it go anywhere. The Self is unborn, eternal, most ancient, and is not destroyed with the destruction of the body.

हन्ता चेन्मन्यते हन्तुं हन्तश्चेन्मन्यते हतम् ।
उभौ तौ न विजानीतो नायं हन्ति न हन्यते ॥१९ ॥

hantā cenmanyate hantuṁ hantaścenmanyate hatam |
ubhau tau na vijānīto nāyaṁ hanti na hanyate ||

19. If the slayer thinks that he slays and the slain thinks that he has been slain, then neither of them know the Self, for the Self neither slays nor is slain.

अणोरणीयान् महतो महीयानात्मास्य जन्तोर्निहितो गुहायाम् ।
तमक्रतुः पश्यति वीतशोको धातुप्रसादान्महिमानमात्मनः ॥२० ॥

aṇoraṇīyān mahato mahīyānātmāsya jantornihito guhāyām |
tamakratuḥ paśyati vītaśoko
dhātuprasādānmahimānamātmanaḥ ||

20. The Self is smaller than the smallest and bigger than the biggest. The Self dwells in the cave of the heart. With the help of the radiant energy within, an aspirant free of desire and grief comes to experience the glory of the Self.

आसीनो दूरं व्रजति शयानो याति सर्वतः ।
कस्तं मदामदं देवं मदन्यो ज्ञातुमर्हति ॥२१ ॥

āsīno dūraṁ vrajati śayāno yāti sarvataḥ |
kastaṁ madāmadaṁ devaṁ madanyo jñātumarhati ||

21. While sitting still, the Self travels far; while resting, it goes everywhere. Who other than me can know that shining being, who is entirely different from pleasure and pain?

अशरीरं शरीरेष्वनवस्थेष्ववस्थितम् ।
महान्तं विभुमात्मानं मत्वा धीरो न शोचति ॥२२ ॥

aśarīraṁ śarīreṣvanavastheṣvavasthitam |
mahāntaṁ vibhumātmānaṁ matvā dhīro na śocati ||

22. Though unembodied, the Self dwells in the body. Though dwelling in that which is unstable, the Self is stable. After realizing this great all-pervading Self, an adept does not grieve.

नायमात्मा प्रवचनेन लभ्यो न मेधया न बहुना श्रुतेन ।
यमेवैष वृणुते तेन लभ्यस्तस्यैष आत्मा विवृणुते तनूं स्वाम् ॥२३ ॥

nāyamātmā pravacanena labhyo na medhayā
na bahunā śrutena |
yamevaiṣa vṛṇute tena labhyastasyaiṣa ātmā vivṛṇute
tanūṁ svām ||

23. Knowledge of the Self cannot be achieved through lectures, through memory, or through book learning. The Self is attained by the one whom it chooses. To such a chosen one, the Self unveils its true essence.

नाविरतो दुश्चरितान्नाशान्तो नासमाहितः ।
नाशान्तमानसो वापि प्रज्ञानेनैनमाप्नुयात् ॥२४ ॥

nāvirato duścaritānnāśānto nāsamāhitaḥ |
nāśāntamānaso vāpi prajñānenainamāpnuyāt ||

24. Neither those engaged in unwholesome activities nor those who are undisciplined, nor those who are not composed, nor those who are not peaceful and content within can experience it, even after knowing all about it.

यस्य ब्रह्म च क्षत्रं च उभे भवत ओदनः ।
मृत्युर्यस्योपसेचनं क इत्था वेद यत्र सः ॥२५ ॥

yasya brahma ca kṣatraṁ ca ubhe bhavata odanaḥ |
mṛtyuryasyopasecanaṁ ka itthā veda yatra saḥ ||

25. The one who finds caste identity as trivial as a fistful of rice, and the one to whom death is as significant as rinsing the mouth after meals—such a person has met the prerequisites for attaining knowledge of the Self.

part one - chapter three

ऋतं पिबन्तौ सुकृतस्य लोके गुहां प्रविष्टौ परमे परार्धे ।
छायातपौ ब्रह्मविदो वदन्ति पञ्चाग्नयो ये च त्रिणाचिकेताः ॥१॥

ṛtaṁ pibantau sukṛtasya loke guhāṁ praviṣṭau parame parārdhe |
chāyātapau brahmavido vadanti pañcāgnayo ye ca triṇāciketāḥ ||

1. [Yamaraja continued:] Living on the nectar of the divine will *(ritam)*, both the higher and the lower self have entered the cave—the cave that exists in the highest realm of half of the Absolute. This realm is for those committed to self-endeavor. The knowers of Brahman, the fivefold fire, and the specific fire named after you say that the relationship between the higher and the lower self is that of the sun and the shade.

यः सेतुरीजानानामक्षरं ब्रह्म यत् परम् ।
अभयं तितीर्षतां पारं नाचिकेतं शकेमहि ॥२॥

yaḥ seturījānānāmakṣaraṁ brahma yat param |
abhayaṁ titīrṣatāṁ pāraṁ nāciketaṁ śakemahi ||

2. May we know the Nachiketa fire, which is like a bridge to the followers of the path of action. May we know the indestructible Brahman, which is transcendental. May we reach the other shore, where fear does not exist.

आत्मानं रथिनं विद्धि शरीरं रथमेव तु ।
बुद्धिं तु सारथिं विद्धि मनः प्रग्रहमेव च ॥३॥

ātmānaṁ rathinaṁ viddhi śarīraṁ rathameva tu |
buddhiṁ tu sārathiṁ viddhi manaḥ pragrahameva ca ||

3. Know this Self to be the rider, the body to be the chariot, the intellect to be the charioteer, and the mind to be the reins.

इन्द्रियाणि हयानाहुर्विषयांस्तेषु गोचरान् ।
आत्मेन्द्रियमनोयुक्तं भोक्तेत्याहुर्मनीषिणः ॥४॥

indriyāṇi hayānāhurviṣayāṁsteṣu gocarān |
ātmendriyamanoyuktaṁ bhoktetyāhurmanīṣiṇaḥ ||

4. The senses are the horses, and the sense objects are the path on which they run. One who is united with the Self, the senses, and the mind is called the enjoyer.

यस्त्वविज्ञानवान् भवत्ययुक्तेन मनसा सदा ।
तस्येन्द्रियाण्यवश्यानि दुष्टाश्वा इव सारथेः ॥५॥

yastvavijñānavān bhavatyayuktena manasā sadā |
tasyendriyāṇyavaśyāni duṣṭāśvā iva sāratheḥ ||

5. One who does not have right knowledge or who has an undisciplined mind suffers from the activities of his uncontrolled senses, just as a charioteer suffers from driving untrained horses.

यस्तु विज्ञानवान्भवति युक्तेन मनसा सदा ।
तस्यैन्द्रियाणि वश्यानि सदश्वा इव सारथेः ॥६ ॥

yastu vijñānavānbhavati yuktena manasā sadā |
tasyaindriyāṇi vaśyāni sadaśvā iva sāratheḥ ||

6. One who has right understanding and has a disciplined mind enjoys having controlled senses, just as a charioteer enjoys driving trained horses.

यस्त्वविज्ञानवान्भवत्यमनस्कः सदाशुचिः ।
न स तत्पदमाप्नोति संसारं चाधिगच्छति ॥७ ॥

yastvavijñānavānbhavatyamanaskaḥ sadāśuciḥ |
na sa tatpadamāpnoti saṁsāraṁ cādhigacchati ||

7. One who does not have right understanding, who has a mind filled with thought constructs, and who lacks purity does not attain the highest realm, but rather remains caught in the cycle of birth and death.

यस्तु विज्ञानवान्भवति समनस्कः सदा शुचिः ।
स तु तत् पदमाप्नोति यस्माद्भूयो न जायते ॥८ ॥

yastu vijñānavānbhavati samanaskaḥ sadā śuciḥ |
sa tu tat padamāpnoti yasmādbhūyo na jāyate ||

8. One who has right understanding, a mind free of thought constructs, and is endowed with purity attains that state free of the snare of birth and death.

विज्ञानसारथिर्यस्तु मनःप्रग्रहवान्नरः ।
सोऽध्वनः पारमाप्नोति तद्विष्णोः परमं पदम् ॥९॥

vijñānasārathiryastu manaḥpragrahavānnaraḥ |
so'dhvanaḥ pāramāpnoti tadviṣṇoḥ paramaṁ padam ||

9. One who has right understanding as the chariot driver, and has a trained mind as reins, attains the other end of the path—that is the highest realm of Vishnu, the All-Pervading Truth.

इन्द्रियेभ्यः परा ह्यर्था अर्थेभ्यश्च परं मनः ।
मनसस्तु परा बुद्धिर्बुद्धेरात्मा महान्परः ॥१०॥

indriyebhyaḥ parā hyarthā arthebhyaśca paraṁ manaḥ |
manasastu parā buddhirbuddherātmā mahānparaḥ ||

10. Objects are more subtle than the senses, mind is subtler than the objects, intellect is subtler than the mind, and the Self is greater and more subtle than the intellect.

महतः परमव्यक्तमव्यक्तात्पुरुषः परः ।
पुरुषान्न परं किञ्चित् सा काष्ठा सा परा गतिः ॥११॥

mahataḥ paramavyaktamavyaktātpuruṣaḥ paraḥ |
puruṣānna paraṁ kiñcit sā kāṣṭhā sā parā gatiḥ ||

11. The unmanifest aspect of nature is higher than that which is manifest. Consciousness transcends even unmanifest nature. There is nothing beyond consciousness. Consciousness is the highest reality. Consciousness is the Self.

एष सर्वेषु भूतेषु गूढोऽऽत्मा न प्रकाशते ।
दृश्यते त्वग्र्यया बुद्ध्या सूक्ष्मया सूक्ष्मदर्शिभिः ॥१२ ॥

eṣa sarveṣu bhūteṣu gūḍho'tmā na prakāśate |
dṛśyate tvagryayā buddhyā sūkṣmayā sūkṣmadarśibhiḥ ||

12. Hidden in all living beings, the Self remains unknown. Seers, however, see it through their subtle and penetrating intelligence.

यच्छेद्वांमनसी प्राज्ञस्तद्यच्छेज्ज्ञान आत्मनि ।
ज्ञानमात्मनि महति नियच्छेत्तद्यच्छेच्छान्त आत्मनि ॥१३ ॥

yacchedvāṅmanasī prājñastadyacchejjñāna ātmani |
jñānamātmani mahati niyacchettadyacchecchānta ātmani ||

13. The wise aspirant should merge speech into mind, mind into intellect, intellect into unmanifest nature, and unmanifest nature into the Self.

उत्तिष्ठत जाग्रत प्राप्य वरान्निबोधत ।
क्षुरस्य धारा निशिता दुरत्यया दुर्गम्पथस्तत्कवयो वदन्ति ॥१४ ॥

uttiṣṭhata jāgrata prāpya varānnibodhata |
kṣurasya dhārā niśitā duratyayā
durgampathastatkavayo vadanti ||

14. Awake, arise; find those who are wise and gain knowledge from them. This path is as sharp as the edge of a razor, as the knowers of truth say, and difficult to tread.

अशब्दमस्पर्शमरूपमव्ययं तथारसं नित्यमगन्धवच्च यत् ।
अनाद्यनन्तं महतः परं ध्रुवं निचाय्य तन्मृत्युमुखात् प्रमुच्यते ॥१५॥

aśabdamasparśamarūpamavyayaṁ tathārasaṁ
nityama gandhavacca yat |
anādyanantaṁ mahataḥ paraṁ dhruvaṁ nicāyya
tanmṛtyumukhāt pramucyate ||

15. Upon gaining knowledge of the Self that is beyond articulation, touch, form, taste, and smell; that which is eternal, beginningless, and endless; that which is immutable; and that which is even beyond the purest form of nature, one attains freedom from the jaws of death.

नाचिकेतमुपाख्यानं मृत्युप्रोक्तं सनातनम् ।
उक्त्वा श्रुत्वा च मेधावी ब्रह्मलोके महीयते ॥१६॥

nāciketamupākhyānaṁ mṛtyuproktaṁ sanātanam |
uktvā śrutvā ca medhāvī brahmaloke mahīyate ||

16. By expounding and hearing the everlasting knowledge given by Yamaraja to Nachiketa, a person endowed with retentive power prospers in the highest realm of Brahman.

य इमं परमं गुह्यं श्रावयेत् ब्रह्मसंसदि ।
प्रयतः श्राद्धकाले वा तदानन्त्याय कल्पते तदानन्त्याय कल्पत इति ॥१७॥

ya imaṁ paramaṁ guhyaṁ śrāvayet brahmasaṁsadi |
prayataḥ śrāddhakāle vā tadānantyāya kalpate
tadānantyāya kalpata iti ||

17. One who, in the assembly of Brahmins or during the ancestral rites, recites this great esoteric Upanishad with sincerity and purity is rewarded infinitely.

ॐ

part two - chapter one

पराञ्चि खानि व्यतृणत्स्वयम्भूस्तस्मात्पराङ् पश्यति नान्तरात्मन्।
कश्चिद्धीरः प्रत्यगात्मानमैक्षदावृत्तचक्षुरमृतत्वमिच्छन्॥१॥

parāñci khāni vyatṛṇatsvayambhūstasmātparāṅ
paśyati nāntarātman |
kaściddhīraḥ pratyagātmānamaikṣadāvṛttacakṣur-
amṛtatvamicchan ||

1. [Yamaraja continued:] The self-born Divine Being designed the senses in a manner that they see only outside and not inside. Only a person blessed with patience and desiring immortality turns the senses inward and sees that which resides within.

पराचः कामाननुयन्ति बालास्ते मृत्योर्यन्ति विततस्य पाशम्।
अथ धीरा अमृतत्वं विदित्वा ध्रुवमध्रुवेष्विह न प्रार्थयन्ते॥२॥

parācaḥ kāmānanuyanti bālāste mṛtyoryanti
vitatasya pāśam |
atha dhīrā amṛtatvaṁ viditvā dhruvamadhruveṣviha
na prārthayante ||

2. Childish people seeking objects of their desire allow their senses to run in the external world, and as a result, remain caught in this ever-spread snare of death. However, the adepts blessed with patience realize the immortal truth, and thus they do not expect everlasting truth in this transitory world.

येन रूपं रसं गन्धं शब्दान्स्पर्शांश्च मैथुनान्।
एतेनैव विजानाति किमत्र परिशिष्यते॥ एतद्वै तत्॥३॥

yena rūpaṁ rasaṁ gandhaṁ śabdānsparśāṁśca maithunān |
etenaiva vijānāti kimatra pariśiṣyate || etadvai tat ||

3. If someone knows this world only through taste, smell, touch, sight, hearing, and sexual pleasure, then what is there to be said? In that case, it's done.

स्वप्नान्तं जागरितान्तं चोभौ येनानुपश्यति।
महान्तं विभुमात्मानं मत्वा धीरो न शोचति॥४॥

svapnāntaṁ jāgaritāntaṁ cobhau yenānupaśyati |
mahāntaṁ vibhumātmānaṁ matvā dhīro na śocati ||

4. The seer within us knows that which lies beyond the waking and dreaming states. Upon knowing that great and all-pervading inner Self, a person of patience no longer grieves.

य इमं मध्वदं वेद आत्मानं जीवमन्तिकात्।
ईशानं भूतभव्यस्य न ततो विजुगुप्सते॥ एतद्वै तत्॥५॥

ya imaṁ madhvadaṁ veda ātmānaṁ jīvamantikāt |
īśānaṁ bhūtabhavyasya na tato vijugupsate || etadvai tat ||

5. The Self lives on honey. It is the lord of past, present, and future. Upon knowing that Self, an aspirant is no longer subject to confusion. This is the truth.

यः पूर्वं तपसो जातमद्भ्यः पूर्वमजायत ।
गुहां प्रविश्य तिष्ठन्तं यो भूतेभिर्व्यपश्यत ॥ एतद्वै तत् ॥६ ॥

yaḥ pūrvaṁ tapaso jātamadbhyaḥ pūrvamajāyata |
guhāṁ praviśya tiṣṭhantaṁ yo bhūtebhirvyapaśyata ||
etadvai tat ||

6. The Self was born before fire and water. It entered and began to reside in the cave. This is where it is to be seen. This is the truth.

या प्राणेन सम्भवत्यदितिर्देवतामयी ।
गुहां प्रविश्य तिष्ठन्तीं या भूतेभिर्व्यजायत ॥ एतद्वै तत् ॥७ ॥

yā prāṇena sambhavatyaditirdevatāmayī |
guhāṁ praviśya tiṣṭhantīṁ yā bhūtebhirvyajāyata ||
etadvai tat ||

7. Through the union with the life force *(prana),* the mother of all gods, Aditi, is born. Upon her birth, she entered and began to reside in the cave. This is where she is to be found. This is the truth.

अरण्योर्निहितो जातवेदा गर्भ इव सुभृतो गर्भिणीभिः ।
दिवे दिव ईड्यो जागृवद्भिर्हविष्मद्भिर्मनुष्येभिरग्निः ॥ एतद्वै तत् ॥८ ॥

araṇyornihito jātavedā garbha iva subhṛto garbhiṇībhiḥ |
dive diva īḍyo jāgṛvadbhirhaviṣmadbhirmanuṣyebhiragniḥ ||
etadvai tat ||

8. Just as a fetus is hidden in the womb of the pregnant mother, so the omniscient fire is hidden in its source *(arani).* Only awakened aspirants propitiate this fire through oblations. This is the truth.

यतश्चोदेति सूर्योऽस्तं यत्र च गच्छति ।
तं देवाः सर्वेऽर्पितास्तदु नात्येति कश्चन ॥ एतद्वै तत् ॥९॥

yataścodeti sūryo'staṁ yatra ca gacchati |
taṁ devāḥ sarve'rpitāstadu nātyeti kaścana || etadvai tat ||

9. It is from the Self the sun rises, and it is where the sun sets. All celestial beings surrender to this Self. No one supersedes the Self. This is the truth.

यदेवेह तदमुत्र यदमुत्र तदन्विह ।
मृत्योः स मृत्युमाप्नोति य इह नानेव पश्यति ॥१० ॥

yadeveha tadamutra yadamutra tadanviha |
mṛtyoḥ sa mṛtyumāpnoti ya iha nāneva paśyati ||

10. That which is here, is there. That which is there, is here. One who sees a difference between here and there goes on wandering from death to death.

मनसैवेदमाप्तव्यं नेह नानास्ति किञ्चन ।
मृत्योः स मृत्युं गच्छति य इह नानेव पश्यति ॥११ ॥

manasaivedamāptavyaṁ neha nānāsti kiñcana |
mṛtyoḥ sa mṛtyuṁ gacchati ya iha nāneva paśyati ||

11. It is a matter of inner understanding that there is no difference between here and there. One who sees a difference goes on wandering from death to death.

अंगुष्ठमात्रः पुरुषो मध्य आत्मनि तिष्ठति ।
ईशानं भूतभव्यस्य न ततो विजुगुप्सते ॥ एतद्वै तत् ॥१२ ॥

aṅguṣṭhamātraḥ puruṣo madhya ātmani tiṣṭhati |
īśānaṁ bhūtabhavyasya na tato vijugupsate || etadvai tat ||

12. Residing in all the limbs and organs, consciousness is seated in the center of the soul. It is the lord of the past, present, and future. Upon knowing that Self, an aspirant is no longer subject to confusion. This is the truth.

अंगुष्ठमात्रः पुरुषो ज्योतिरिवाधूमकः ।
ईशानो भूतभव्यस्य स एवाद्य स उ श्वः ॥ एतद्वै तत् ॥१३ ॥

aṅguṣṭhamātraḥ puruṣo jyotirivādhūmakaḥ |
īśāno bhūtabhavyasya sa evādya sa u śvaḥ || etadvai tat ||

13. Residing in all the limbs and organs, consciousness is like a smokeless flame. It is the lord of the past, present, and future. It exists today, and it will continue existing tomorrow. This is the truth.

यथोदकं दुर्गे वृष्टं पर्वतेषु विधावति ।
एवं धर्मान्पृथक्पश्यंस्तानेवानुविधावति ॥१४ ॥

yathodakaṁ durge vṛṣṭaṁ parvateṣu vidhāvati |
evaṁ dharmānpṛthakpaśyaṁstānevānuvidhāvati ||

14. Just as rain at the summit runs downhill, similarly, the seer of differences chases what he sees.

यथोदकं शुद्धे शुद्धमासिक्तं तादृगेव भवति ।
एवं मुनेर्विजानत आत्मा भवति गौतम ॥१५॥

yathodakaṁ śuddhe śuddhamāsiktaṁ tādṛgeva bhavati |
evaṁ munervijānata ātmā bhavati gautama ||

15. Just as rainwater falling on pure ground remains pure and becomes impure on impure ground, similarly, O Nachiketa, the knowledge of the Self falling in a pure heart remains pure, and becomes distorted in an impure heart.

ॐ

part two - chapter two

पुरमेकादशद्वारमजस्यावक्रचेतसः ।
अनुष्ठाय न शोचति विमुक्तश्च विमुच्यते ॥ एतद्वै तत् ॥१॥

puramekādaśadvāramajasyāvakracetasaḥ |
anuṣṭhāya na śocati vimuktaśca vimucyate || etadvai tat ||

1. The Self that in essence is never born resides in the eleven-gated city (the body) with its undistorted mind. There it does not worry about the results of its present endeavors or the results of its past deeds which are left behind anyway. This is the truth.

हंसः शुचिषद्वसुरन्तरिक्षसद्धोता वेदिषदतिथिर्दुरोणसत् ।
नृषद्वरसदृतसद्व्योमसदब्जा गोजा ऋतजा अद्रिजा ऋतं बृहत् ॥२॥

haṁsaḥ śuciṣadvasurantarikṣasaddhotā
vediṣadatithirduroṇasat |
nṛṣadvarasadṛtasadvyomasadabjā gojā ṛtajā
adrijā ṛtaṁ bṛhat ||

2. Having its seat in purity, the transcendental Self is the source of all inner and outer prosperity. It resides in the realm between heaven and earth; it is the one who offers oblations to the sacred fire; it resides at the altar; it is the unpredictable guest; it lives in humans, in the great ones, in the law that governs the forces of nature, and it resides in ever-expanding space. It is born of water, the senses, divine will, and the mountains. It is the Divine Will and the Highest One.

ऊर्ध्वं प्राणमुन्नयत्यपानं प्रत्यगस्यति ।
मध्ये वामनमासीनं विश्वे देवा उपासते ॥३॥

ūrdhvaṁ prāṇamunnayatyapānaṁ pratyagasyati |
madhye vāmanamāsīnaṁ viśve devā upāsate ||

3. Seated at the center of everything, this little one *(Vamana)* exudes the boundless universe *(Virat)*. All the bright beings worship this mystery of mysteries—*Vamana.*

अस्य विस्रंसमानस्य शरीरस्थस्य देहिनः ।
देहाद्विमुच्यमानस्य किमत्र परिशिष्यते ॥ एतद्वै तत् ॥४॥

asya visraṁsamānasya śarīrasthasya dehinaḥ |
dehādvimucyamānasya kimatra pariśiṣyate || etadvai tat ||

4. When the body falls apart and the Self residing in the body leaves it, what is left? This is the truth.

न प्राणेन नापानेन मर्त्यो जीवति कश्चन ।
इतरेण तु जीवन्ति यस्मिन्नेतावुपाश्रितौ ॥५॥

na prāṇena nāpānena martyo jīvati kaścana |
itareṇa tu jīvanti yasminnetāvupāśritau ||

5. A human being subject to death is alive neither due to inhalation nor exhalation. Rather, he is alive due to something else that gives life to both inhalation and exhalation.

हन्त त इदं प्रवक्ष्यामि गुह्यं ब्रह्म सनातनम् ।
यथा च मरणं प्राप्य आत्मा भवति गौतम ॥६ ॥

hanta ta idaṁ pravakṣyāmi guhyaṁ brahma sanātanam |
yathā ca maraṇaṁ prāpya ātmā bhavati gautama ||

6. Blessed Nachiketa, I will impart to you the most secret knowledge of eternal truth. Being blessed with that knowledge, you will become eternal, even upon meeting death.

योनिमन्ये प्रपद्यन्ते शरीरत्वाय देहिनः ।
स्थाणुमन्येऽनुसंयन्ति यथाकर्म यथाश्रुतम् ॥७ ॥

yonimanye prapadyante śarīratvāya dehinaḥ |
sthāṇumanye'nusaṁyanti yathākarma yathāśrutam ||

7. Others, devoid of this knowledge, go on migrating from one body to another. Depending on their actions, some devolve to the level of insentient beings.

य एष सुप्तेषु जागर्ति कामं कामं पुरुषो निर्मिमाणः ।
तदेव शुक्रं तद्ब्रह्म तदेवामृतमुच्यते ।
तस्मिँल्लोकाः श्रिताः सर्वे तदु नात्येति कश्चन ॥ एतद्वै तत् ॥८ ॥

ya eṣa supteṣu jāgarti kāmaṁ kāmaṁ puruṣo nirmimāṇaḥ |
tadeva śukraṁ tadbrahma tadevāmṛtamucyate |
tasmiṁllokāḥ śritāḥ sarve tadu nātyeti kaścana ||
etadvai tat ||

8. Keeping track of every desire, this Self remains awake even during deep sleep. It is the self-effulgent, all-pervading, immortal Divine Being. All spheres rest in it. Nothing surpasses it. This is the truth.

अग्निर्यथैको भुवनं प्रविष्टो रूपं रूपं प्रतिरूपो बभूव ।
एकस्तथा सर्वभूतान्तरात्मा रूपं रूपं प्रतिरूपो बहिश्च ॥९॥

agniryathaiko bhuvanaṁ praviṣṭo
rūpaṁ rūpaṁ pratirūpo babhūva |
ekastathā sarvabhūtāntarātmā
rūpaṁ rūpaṁ pratirūpo bahiśca ||

9. Just as one fire, upon penetrating different spheres of existence, assumes different forms, similarly, the soul of all living beings, upon entering different bodies, assumes different forms.

वायुर्यथैको भुवनं प्रविष्टो रूपं रूपं प्रतिरूपो बभूव ।
एकस्तथा सर्वभूतान्तरात्मा रूपं रूपं प्रतिरूपो बहिश्च ॥१०॥

vāyuryathaiko bhuvanaṁ praviṣṭo
rūpaṁ rūpaṁ pratirūpo babhūva |
ekastathā sarvabhūtāntarātmā
rūpaṁ rūpaṁ pratirūpo bahiśca ||

10. Just as one air, upon penetrating different spheres of existence, assumes different forms, similarly, the soul of all living beings, upon entering different bodies, assumes different forms.

सूर्यो यथा सर्वलोकस्य चक्षुर्न लिप्यते चाक्षुषैर्बाह्यदोषैः ।
एकस्तथा सर्वभूतान्तरात्मा न लिप्यते लोकदुःखेन बाह्यः ॥११ ॥

sūryo yathā sarvalokasya cakṣurna lipyate
cākṣuṣairbāhyadoṣaiḥ |
ekastathā sarvabhūtāntarātmā na lipyate
lokaduḥkhena bāhyaḥ ||

11. The sun is the eye of the whole world, and yet remains untainted by the impurities of the objects it perceives. Similarly, the soul of all living beings remains untainted by the pleasure and pain of the external world.

एको वशी सर्वभूतान्तरात्मा एकं रूपं बहुधा यः करोति ।
तमात्मस्थं येऽनुपश्यन्ति धीरास्तेषां सुखं शाश्वतं नेतरेषाम् ॥१२ ॥

eko vaśī sarvabhūtāntarātmā ekaṁ rūpaṁ
bahudhā yaḥ karoti |
tamātmasthaṁ ye'nupaśyanti dhīrāsteṣāṁ sukhaṁ
śāśvataṁ netareṣām ||

12. The soul of all living beings is one and autonomous. Through sheer will it becomes many. Everlasting joy is only for those blessed with patience who see it in the interior of their soul—and not for anyone else.

नित्योऽनित्यानां चेतनश्चेतनानामेको बहूनां यो विदधाति कामान्।
तमात्मस्थं येऽनुपश्यन्ति धीरास्तेषां शान्तिः शाश्वती नेतरेषाम् ॥१३॥

nityo'nityānāṁ cetanaścetanānāmeko bahūnāṁ
yo vidadhāti kāmān |
tamātmasthaṁ ye'nupaśyanti dhīrāsteṣāṁ śāntiḥ
śāśvatī netareṣām ||

13. It is eternal among the eternal. It is the consciousness of consciousness. It is one among many. It is this highest being who fulfills all desires. Everlasting joy is only for those blessed with patience who see it in the interior of their soul—and not for anyone else.

तदेतदिति मन्यन्तेऽनिर्देश्यं परमं सुखम्।
कथं नु तद्विजानीयां किमु भाति विभाति वा ॥१४॥

tadetaditi manyante'nirdeśyaṁ paramaṁ sukham |
kathaṁ nu tadvijānīyāṁ kimu bhāti vibhāti vā ||

14. This is known as the indescribable highest happiness. How can we really know it? How does it shine? How does it feel?

न तत्र सूर्यो भाति न चन्द्रतारकं नेमा विद्युतो भान्ति कुतोऽयमग्निः।
तमेव भान्तमनुभाति सर्वं तस्य भासा सर्वमिदं विभाति ॥१५॥

na tatra sūryo bhāti na candratārakaṁ nemā vidyuto bhānti kuto'yamagniḥ |
tameva bhāntamanubhāti sarvaṁ tasya bhāsā sarvamidaṁ vibhāti ||

15. The sun doesn't shine there, nor does the moon, nor the stars, nor the lightning, not to mention this earthly fire. Only because This shines, all else shines through its effulgence.

ॐ

part two - chapter three

ऊर्ध्वमूलोऽवाक्शाख एषोऽश्वत्थः सनातनः ।
तदेव शुक्रं तद्ब्रह्म तदेवामृतमुच्यते ।
तस्मिँल्लोकाः श्रिताः सर्वे तदु नात्येति कश्चन ॥ एतद्वै तत् ॥१ ॥

ūrdhvamūlo'vākśākha eṣo'śvatthaḥ sanātanaḥ |
tadeva śukraṁ tadbrahma tadevāmṛtamucyate |
tasmiṁllokāḥ śritāḥ sarve tadu nātyeti kaścana ||
etadvai tat ||

1. This life is like a banyan tree with its roots up and the branches down. It is eternal. It is the self-effulgent, all-pervading, immortal Divine Being. All spheres rest in it. Nothing surpasses it. This is the truth.

यदिदं किञ्च जगत्सर्वं प्राण एजति निःसृतम् ।
महद्भयं वज्रमुद्यतं य एतद्विदुरमृतास्ते भवन्ति ॥२ ॥

yadidaṁ kiñca jagatsarvaṁ prāṇa ejati niḥsṛtam |
mahadbhayaṁ vajramudyataṁ ya etadviduramṛtāste bhavanti ||

2. It is the life force that animates everything in this world. To one who doesn't know this truth, life is full of fear. To such a person, life is just a series of calamities. But the knower of this truth is beyond death, decay, and destruction.

भयादस्याग्निस्तपति भयात्तपति सूर्यः ।
भयादिन्द्रश्च वायुश्च मृत्युर्धावति पञ्चमः ॥३॥

bhayādasyāgnistapati bhayāttapati sūryaḥ ।
bhayādindraśca vāyuśca mṛtyurdhāvati pañcamaḥ ॥

3. It is under the command of this truth that the fire burns and the sun shines. It is under the command of this truth that the Lord of the Heavens (Indra), the air, and death move.

इह चेदशकद्बोद्धुं प्राक्शरीरस्य विस्रसः ।
ततः सर्गेषु लोकेषु शरीरत्वाय कल्पते ॥४॥

iha cedaśakadboddhuṁ prākśarīrasya visrasaḥ ।
tataḥ sargeṣu lokeṣu śarīratvāya kalpate ॥

4. If this truth is known here and now before the body falls apart, then the purpose of life is achieved. If not, then the individual goes on migrating from one body to another.

यथादर्शे तथात्मनि यथा स्वप्ने तथा पितृलोके ।
यथाप्सु परीव ददृशे तथा गन्धर्वलोके छायातपयोरिव ब्रह्मलोके ॥५॥

yathādarśe tathātmani yathā svapne tathā pitṛloke ।
yathāpsu parśva dadṛśe tathā gandharvaloke
chāyātapayoriva brahmaloke ॥

5. The relationship between the higher and the lower self is that of the sun and the shade. This relationship continues here in this world during both the waking and dreaming states. This relationship continues when we reside in the realm of the ancestors, in the world of imagination, and even in the highest realm known as Brahma Loka.

इन्द्रियाणां पृथग्भावमुदयास्तमयौ च यत् ।
पृथगुत्पद्यमानानां मत्वा धीरो न शोचति ॥६ ॥

indriyāṇāṁ pṛthagbhāvamudayāstamayau ca yat |
pṛthagutpadyamānānāṁ matvā dhīro na śocati ||

6. Sensory pleasure climaxes and then declines. Knowing this is a natural phenomenon, a person blessed with patience does not grieve.

इन्द्रियेभ्यः परं मनो मनसः सत्त्वमुत्तमम् ।
सत्त्वादधि महानात्मा महतोऽव्यक्तमुत्तमम् ॥७ ॥

indriyebhyaḥ paraṁ mano manasaḥ sattvamuttamam |
sattvādadhi mahānātmā mahato'vyaktamuttamam ||

7. The mind is superior to the senses. The intellect is superior to the mind. Unmanifest nature is superior to manifest nature, and the Self is superior to the finest aspect of nature *(sattva).*

अव्यक्तात्तु परः पुरुषो व्यापकोऽलिंग एव च ।
यं ज्ञात्वा मुच्यते जन्तुरमृतत्वं च गच्छति ॥८ ॥

avyaktāttu paraḥ puruṣo vyāpako'liṅga eva ca |
yaṁ jñātvā mucyate janturamṛtatvaṁ ca gacchati ||

8. The Self is all-pervading and beyond name, form, and gender. Upon knowing this Self, an aspirant is no longer subject to death, decay, or destruction.

न सन्दृशे तिष्ठति रूपमस्य न चक्षुषा पश्यति कश्चनैनम् ।
हृदा मनीषा मनसाभिक्लृप्तो य एतद्विदुरमृतास्ते भवन्ति ॥९॥

na sandṛśe tiṣṭhati rūpamasya
  na cakṣuṣā paśyati kaścanainam |
hṛdā manīṣā manasābhiklṛpto
  ya etadviduramṛtāste bhavanti ||

9. There is nothing in this world similar to the Self. No one can see it through their eyes. With both mind and heart in place, a person with right thinking can experience this truth, and upon experiencing it, is no longer subject to death, decay, and destruction.

यदा पञ्चावतिष्ठन्ते ज्ञानानि मनसा सह ।
बुद्धिश्च न विचेष्टति तामाहुः परमां गतिम् ॥१०॥

yadā pañcāvatiṣṭhante jñānāni manasā saha |
buddhiśca na viceṣṭati tāmāhuḥ paramāṁ gatim ||

10. The state in which the five senses, along with the mind, rests within, and where the intellect (the conduit for intelligence) also does not waver, is called the highest state.

तां योगमिति मन्यन्ते स्थिरामिन्द्रियधारणाम् ।
अप्रमत्तस्तदा भवति योगो हि प्रभवाप्ययौ ॥११ ॥

tāṁ yogamiti manyante sthirāmindriyadhāraṇām |
apramattastadā bhavati yogo hi prabhavāpyayau ||

11. The state in which the senses are stable is called yoga. It is only by practicing that kind of yoga that an aspirant remains free from carelessness, and only such yoga is the source of creation and destruction.

नैव वाचा न मनसा प्राप्तुं शक्यो न चक्षुषा ।
अस्तीति ब्रुवतोऽन्यत्र कथं तदुपलभ्यते ॥१२ ॥

naiva vācā na manasā prāptuṁ śakyo na cakṣuṣā |
astīti bruvato'nyatra kathaṁ tadupalabhyate ||

12. This truth cannot be achieved through speech and mind, nor can it be seen through the eyes. How can it be achieved by someone who just goes on saying, "It exists, it exists"?

अस्तीत्येवोपलब्धव्यस्तत्त्वभावेन चोभयोः ।
अस्तीत्येवोपलब्धस्य तत्त्वभावः प्रसीदति ॥१३ ॥

astītyevopalabdhavyastattvabhāvena cobhayoḥ |
astītyevopalabdhasya tattvabhāvaḥ prasīdati ||

13. The one who has truly gained direct experience of this self-existent reality rejoices in his experience.

यदा सर्वे प्रमुच्यन्ते कामा येऽस्य हृदि श्रिताः ।
अथ मर्त्योऽमृतो भवत्यत्र ब्रह्म समश्नुते ॥१४ ॥

yadā sarve pramucyante kāmā ye'sya hṛdi śritāḥ |
atha martyo'mṛto bhavatyatra brahma samaśnute ||

14. Upon attaining freedom from all desires previously stored in one's heart, a mortal becomes immortal and experiences his oneness with the Absolute Reality here and now.

यदा सर्वे प्रभिद्यन्ते हृदयस्येह ग्रन्थयः ।
अथ मर्त्योऽमृतो भवत्येतावद्ध्यनुशासनम् ॥१५ ॥

yadā sarve prabhidyante hṛdayasyeha granthayaḥ |
atha martyo'mṛto bhavatyetāvaddhyanuśāsanam ||

15. Upon cutting asunder all the knots in the heart, a mortal becomes immortal here and now. That is the discipline.

शतं चैका च हृदयस्य नाड्यस्तासां मूर्धानमभिनिःसृतैका ।
तयोर्ध्वमायन्नमृतत्वमेति विष्वङ्ङन्या उत्क्रमणे भवन्ति ॥१६ ॥

śataṁ caikā ca hṛdayasya nāḍyastāsāṁ
mūrdhānamabhiniḥsṛtaikā |
tayordhvamāyannamṛtatvameti viṣvaṅṅanyā
utkramaṇe bhavanti ||

16. Originating from the heart, there are hundreds of energy channels *(nadis)*. One of these energy channels goes toward the head. By making that channel move upward, one is no longer subject to death, decay, and destruction. The rest of the energy channels by nature flow in every direction.

अंगुष्ठमात्रः पुरुषोऽन्तरात्मा सदा जनानां हृदये सन्निविष्टः ।
तं स्वाच्छरीरात्प्रवृहेन्मुञ्जादिवेषीकां धैर्येण ।
तं विद्याच्छुक्रममृतं तं विद्याच्छुक्रममृतमिति ॥१७ ॥

aṅguṣṭhamātraḥ puruṣo'ntarātmā sadā janānāṁ
hṛdaye sanniviṣṭaḥ |
taṁ svāccharīrātpravṛhenmuñjādiveṣīkāṁ dhairyeṇa |
taṁ vidyācchukramamṛtaṁ taṁ vidyācchukramamṛtamiti ||

17. Residing in every limb and organ, the inner Self has entered the heart of all living beings. An aspirant accompanied by patience should attempt to free this inner Self from the confines of his body to experience its glorious and boundless expanse. Remember this Self is self-effulgent and immortal, and upon knowing it, you are no longer subject to death, decay, and destruction.

मृत्युप्रोक्तां नचिकेतोऽथ लब्ध्वा विद्यामेतां योगविधिं च कृत्स्नम् ।
ब्रह्म प्राप्तो विरजोऽभूद्विमृत्युरन्योऽप्येवं यो विदध्यात्ममेव ॥१८ ॥

mṛtyuproktāṁ naciketo'tha labdhvā vidyāmetāṁ
yogavidhiṁ ca kṛtsnam |
brahma prāpto virajo'bhūdvimṛtyuranyo'pyevaṁ
yo vidadhyātmameva ||

18. Upon receiving this knowledge as well as the entire method of systematic practice from the Lord of Death, Nachiketa realized the Absolute Truth, obtained freedom from even the most subtle of all impurities—ignorance—and rose above the sphere of death. Others, too, who embrace this knowledge and commit themselves to this methodical practice will be blessed with the same gift of Self-realization and immortality.

Invocation

ॐ
सह नाववतु ।
सह नौ भुनक्तु ।
सह वीर्यं करवावहै ॥
तेजस्वि नावधीतमस्तु मा विद्विषावहै ॥
ॐ शान्तिः शान्तिः शान्तिः ॥

om
saha nāvavatu ǀ
saha nau bhunaktu ǀ
saha vīryaṁ karavāvahai ǀǀ
tejasvi nāvadhītamastu mā vidviṣāvahai ǀǀ
om śāntiḥ śāntiḥ śāntiḥ ǀǀ

Om. May we protect and nurture each other.
May we rejoice together.
May our strength and vitality grow together.
May our knowledge shine.
May we not be jealous of each other.
Om. Peace, peace, peace.

ॐ

ABOUT THE AUTHOR

Pandit Rajmani Tigunait, PhD, the spiritual head of the Himalayan Institute, is the successor to Swami Rama of the Himalayas. Lecturing and teaching worldwide for more than a quarter of a century, he is a regular contributor to *Yoga + Joyful Living* magazine (formerly *Yoga International*), and the author of thirteen books, including the best-selling *At the Eleventh Hour: The Biography of Swami Rama of the Himalayas*.

Pandit Tigunait lives in Honesdale, Pennsylvania. He holds two doctorates: one in Sanskrit from the University of Allahabad in India, and another in Oriental Studies from the University of Pennsylvania. Family tradition gave Pandit Tigunait access to a vast range of spiritual wisdom preserved in both the written and oral traditions. Before meeting his master, Pandit Tigunait studied Sanskrit, the language of the ancient scriptures of India, as well as the languages of the Buddhist, Jaina, and Zoroastrian traditions. In 1976, Swami Rama ordained Pandit Tigunait into the 5,000-year-old lineage of the Himalayan masters.

The Himalayan Institute

The main building of the Institute headquarters near Honesdale, Pennsylvania

FOUNDED IN 1971 BY SWAMI RAMA, the Himalayan Institute has been dedicated to helping people grow physically, mentally, and spiritually by combining the best knowledge of both the East and the West.

Our international headquarters is located on a beautiful 400-acre campus in the rolling hills of the Pocono Mountains of northeastern Pennsylvania. The atmosphere here is one to foster growth, increase inner awareness, and promote calm. Our grounds provide a wonderfully peaceful and healthy setting for our seminars and extended programs. Students from all over the world join us here to attend programs in such diverse areas as hatha yoga, meditation, stress reduction, ayurveda, nutrition, Eastern philosophy, psychology, and other subjects. Whether the programs are for weekend meditation retreats, week-long seminars on spirituality, month-long residential programs, or holistic health services, the attempt here is to provide an environment of gentle inner progress. We invite you to join with us in the ongoing process of personal growth and development.

The Institute is a nonprofit organization. Your membership in the Institute helps to support its programs. Please call or write for information on becoming a member.

Programs and Services include:

- Weekend or extended seminars and workshops
- Meditation retreats and advanced meditation instruction
- Hatha yoga teachers training
- Residential programs for self-development
- Holistic health services and pancha karma at the Institute's Center for Health and Healing
- Spiritual excursions
- Varcho Veda® herbal products
- Himalayan Institute Press
- *Yoga + Joyful Living* magazine
- Sanskrit Home Study Course

A guide to programs and other offerings is free within the USA. To request a copy, or for further information, call 800-822-4547 or 570-253-5551, write to the Himalayan Institute, 952 Bethany Turnpike, Honesdale, PA 18431, USA, or visit our website at www.HimalayanInstitute.org.

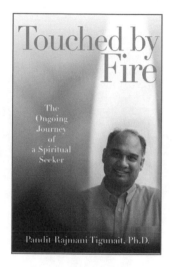

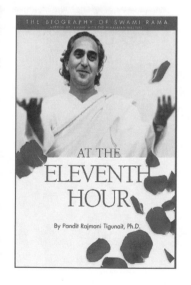